George Douglas Campbell Duke of Argyll

Irish Nationalism

An Appeal to History

George Douglas Campbell Duke of Argyll

Irish Nationalism
An Appeal to History

ISBN/EAN: 9783744730563

Printed in Europe, USA, Canada, Australia, Japan

Cover: Foto ©ninafisch / pixelio.de

More available books at **www.hansebooks.com**

IRISH NATIONALISM.

IRISH NATIONALISM:

AN APPEAL TO HISTORY.

BY THE

DUKE OF ARGYLL, K.G., K.T.

LONDON:
JOHN MURRAY, ALBEMARLE STREET.
1893.

LONDON:
PRINTED BY WILLIAM CLOWES AND SONS, LIMITED,
STAMFORD STREET AND CHARING CROSS.

CONTENTS.

CHAPTER I.

IRISH HISTORY BEFORE THE EXPEDITION OF HENRY II., IN A.D. 1172.

An example—The accusation against England—Alleged conquest of Ireland—Suzerainty not government—Evidence of Irish writers—The English invited—An erroneous assertion—Early Irish culture—A momentary monarchy—Who destroyed it—Early Irish annals—Deepening barbarism—The Irish Celtic Church—Irish authorities—English barbarism compared—Ireland's golden age—Cause of Irish anarchy—Irish apologies for Ireland—The Irish made themselves 1

CHAPTER II.

EFFECTS OF SUZERAINTY OF ENGLAND OVER IRELAND.

English Colonists degraded—Contrast with Scotland—Same danger in Scotland—Anglo-Normans in Scotland—Irish dread of government—English government powerless—Daniel O'Connell's speech—O'Connell's erroneous assertion—Irish hatred of law—The English barons Ersefied—Adoption of Irish customs—Irish intertribal wars—Ireland made the Anglo-Irish—The Latin Church 41

CHAPTER III.

EFFECT OF NATIVE IRISH LAWS AND USAGES.

PAGE

Contradictory charges—Irish tribalism—Septs intensely aristocratic—Clans were not tribes—Intensified inequalities—Irish feudalism—Evidence of Professor Sullivan—Irish gradations of rank—Irish form of wealth—Irish property in land—Evidence of ancient books—Alleged communal ownership—Dr. Sullivan on ownership—Irremovability was bondage—Bondage to the soil—Removability was personal freedom—Laws of succession—Interest of poorer classes—Evils of native customs—Irish inconsistency 70

CHAPTER IV.

HISTORY CONTINUED FROM A.D. 1172 TO THE END OF THE FIFTEENTH CENTURY.

Right of England—Irish analogy in Scotland—Scots' invasion of Ireland—Devastation of Ireland—Lasting ruin—English law in Ireland—Statutes of Kilkenny—English action diverted—Expedition of Richard II.—Supremacy of the Irish—Irish support House of York—Poyning's law—Necessity of Poyning's law—Condition of Ireland ... 110

CHAPTER V.

IRELAND UNDER THE TUDORS DOWN TO THE DEATH OF HENRY VIII.

The Geraldine rebellion—Results of Irish Home Rule—Testimony of native annals—Dr. Richey's confessions—Results of native institutions—Ersefied Englishmen—Irish intrigues with foreigners—Policy of Henry VIII.—Some law a necessity—Military weakness of England—A demand for England—Religion not yet concerned—Irish not Papal—Barbarism of native clergy 139

CHAPTER VI.

THE EPOCH OF CONQUEST AND COLONISATION.

Irish land rents—Condition of tenants—Irish confiscations—The Catholic queen—Queen Mary's plantations—Queen Elizabeth—Shane O'Neill's rebellion—The Catholic conspiracy—Tyrone's rebellion—England's case stated 168

CHAPTER VII.

THE SEVENTEENTH CENTURY.

Inevitable antagonisms—Philosophy in history—Ireland not governed by England—Comparative intolerance—Short period of English rule—Physical condition of Ireland—Instincts of dominion wholesome—England in permanent danger—The penal laws—Reality of danger—Two motives balanced 189

CHAPTER VIII.

THE EIGHTEENTH CENTURY—ECONOMIC CAUSES.

Economic effects of penal laws—The commercial system—Irish protectionism—An Irish folly—Ruinous effects—Those effects traced—Continuity of vicious policy—Irish inconsistency—An Irishman's evidence—Hereditary survivals—Penal effects of an Irish custom—Survival not degradation—The potato—Irish famines—Combination of causes ... 213

CHAPTER IX.

CONCLUSIONS.

Geographical position—Barbarous agriculture—Irish subletting—Irish education—Rebels of 1798—Position of government—Dates in the rebellion—Catholic emancipation—Abstract principle not admitted—Irish history re-read—Sentence of Edmund Burke 245

IRISH NATIONALISM:

AN APPEAL TO HISTORY.

CHAPTER I.

IRISH HISTORY BEFORE THE EXPEDITION OF HENRY II., IN A.D. 1172.

HISTORY has fared ill in many hands. But in no hands has she ever fared worse than in those of party-leaders. When they engage her as their maid-of-all-work, she sinks to the level of a very slattern. Truth in the hands of a casuist;—morals in the hands of the proverbial Jesuit;—facts in the hands of a special pleader,—all these combined are but a feeble image of the fate of history when it is put to use by professional politicians. And when this position is held by any man who is, or finds it convenient to assume the character of an Ethnogogue, then the corrupting influence is aggravated to an intense degree. No element, or influence, that can vitiate knowledge or pervert judgment is left unemployed. The merely dull and unobservant eye that sees nothing on either side of one narrow line of vision—this is the commonest influence of all. But passions of all kinds come in to play their part, and to convert mere misconception into the most violent misrepresentation. The least disparaging image to which a party politician can be compared, who uses history as one of the tools in his trade, is that of a legal Advocate pushing to its utmost extremes, in favour of his client, the acknowledged licence of the Bar. How far that licence may legitimately go has never been settled, and is perhaps incapable of definition. Certain it is that both the *suppressio veri* and the *suggestio falsi* are among the legitimate and ordinary weapons of the calling. Lord Brougham once said that an Advocate has nothing whatever to think of except the interests of his client. That there are some vague limits assigned to this doctrine, by professional opinion, may be true. I recollect a famous case in which the Counsel for a murderer went so far as to indicate another person than his client, who, so far as the evidence went, might possibly be the criminal. In this he was held to have gone too far, and his conduct met with general condemnation. On the whole, however, the licence of the Bar is thoroughly understood; and it is so understood just because it is reasonably held to be an absolute necessity in the interests of society. But though a jury may be occasionally misled, nobody is really deceived. Nobody is expected to believe that a

Counsel is really presenting either facts or arguments in their true relation. No such understanding however exists, or ought to exist, in the case of statesmen and politicians. They have no professional duty or right to be unscrupulous, or passionate, or even careless and one-sided in dealing with history. The interests of society do not demand from them any sacrifice of the strictest regard for truth in any of its forms, and especially for historical truth. On the contrary, the public interest, as regards political questions, is bound up with the most faithful truthfulness in using the records of the past. That there is a very large element of opinion in the presentation and interpretation of historical facts is undeniable. But this only renders it all the more incumbent on Statesmen to deal as completely and fairly as they can, at least with the facts to be quoted, or referred to, in support of political contentions. Moreover, this duty rises in the scale of obligation in proportion as those contentions may affect the vital interests of any political society with which we may have to do.

I make these observations with express reference to the use which Mr. Gladstone, since 1885, has made of history, on the Irish Question. I hold that use to have been little better than one long tissue of passionate misrepresentation. Having expressed this opinion strongly on a late occasion—in referring to his language as "inflated fable"—when addressing an

American audience,* I have been most properly challenged by Mr. Gladstone in his reply to make it good by definite evidence and quotation. My object in these pages is to take up that challenge.† In doing so I will follow Mr. Gladstone's own reference to the materials which he specifies as legitimate for the purpose of testing his contentions. These materials are, first, " A series of utterances which fill a moderate volume," meaning, I presume, the whole body of his speeches and writings since 1885; and second, these utterances as specially represented in a particular volume, lately published under the truly descriptive and significant title of "Special Aspects of the Irish Question." ‡ "Special" they are—in a very high degree. This volume, extending over three hundred and seventy pages, contains ten separate papers, all of them interlarded more or less extensively with arguments and assertions purporting to be historical, and one of the ten (No. III.) is expressly entitled "Lessons of Irish History in the Eighteenth Century." Its "special aspect" is that which represents all the ills that Ireland has suffered as being due entirely to the conduct and government of England.

Now, there are two different and almost opposite senses in which this accusation may be made. It may mean that England is responsible for all the ills of

* *North American Review*, August 1892.
† Ibid., October, 1892.
‡ J. Murray. 1892.

Ireland because she never put forth her full strength to complete the conquest of the island, and to impose, effectually and universally, her own more civilised system of law upon its people:—that she tolerated, as she ought not to have done, the long continuance and the desolating effect of native customs which oppressed and impoverished the people:—and that she was even tempted by dangers arising from time to time, to enter into partial alliances with some one or more of the savage factions which were always tearing at each other's vitals in that country. In this sense the accusation against England does, at least, represent a real, although a very partial "aspect" of the truth. It ascribes the ills of Ireland primarily to causes of native origin, and only secondarily to England as having by negligence failed to apply a remedy which, it is assumed, was easily within her power; and as having indirectly aggravated those causes by occasional complicity.

The other sense in which the accusation against England may be made, rests upon assumptions directly opposite:—upon the assumption, namely, that "seven centuries" ago, in 1172, she did conquer Ireland effectually;—that she did establish a foreign law alien to the happier customs of its native people;—that before this conquest Ireland had been comparatively a happy and prosperous nation;—that English rule was so effectively established as to be the one great cause and fountain of all their subsequent distress; and that the native laws and usages of Ireland cannot be charged with any part, or at least any serious share, in her long centuries of pain.

This last is the sense—the "special aspect"—in which the accusation is made by Mr. Gladstone. It is in this sense that he presses it with all the vehemence of Counsel holding a brief for the prosecution—and, as I hope to show, with an audacity both in the statement and in the suppression of facts, which exhibit, in their very highest development, at once the utmost dexterity, and the utmost licence, of the Bar.

The first step he takes is to lay down the fundamental assumption needed for his purpose by a bold and confident assertion implying that there was an effectual conquest of Ireland in the twelfth century by Henry II. Without this assumption the accusation against England, in the second of the two senses above defined, cannot, of course, for a moment be sustained. But upon that assumption the accusation may be at least plausible. Accordingly, Mr. Gladstone makes the assertion in perhaps the extremest form in which it has ever been expressed. "Ireland," he says, "for more than seven hundred years has been part of the British territory, and has been, with slight exceptions, held by English arms, or governed, in the last resort, from this side of the water." * Notwithstanding the characteristic dexterity of the qualifying words, "in

* "Aspects," p. 109.

the last resort"—which may mean anything or nothing,—and are obviously intended as a bolt-hole of escape,—there need be no hesitation in at once pronouncing this sentence to be a broad and palpable perversion of historical facts. Looking at it both in the natural meaning of its words, and in its place in the general context of the whole paper, there can be no doubt that it is intended to assert that Ireland was conquered by Henry II. in 1172, very much as England had been conquered by the Duke of Normandy a little more than a hundred years before. The whole aim and effect of the sentence is to assert the full responsibility of England for all the domestic government and condition of Ireland from that time forward.

My very first contention here is that there is no excuse whatever for this fundamental assertion,— unless it be the very superficial fact that in many histories the transactions of 1172 are often, for shortness, called, or referred to as, the "Conquest of Ireland." But there is no real dispute whatever about the true nature of those transactions in themselves. Henry II. did not conquer Ireland. He did not even pretend to do so. He did not fight a single battle on its shores. Any little fighting that took place at all had been accomplished a year and a half before his expedition by a few adventurous knights, who were invited by a native Irish chief or kinglet, to assist him in domestic war. In one single fray those knights, themselves half Celts from Wales, had "clashed with their fiery few and won." Henry II. had nothing whatever of this kind to do. He came, indeed, with great military pomp. But he came simply to receive, as a Feudal Sovereign, the homage of a great number of Irish Tribes and Chiefs, all of whom, with one solitary exception, were willing to become his feudal vassals.* The Irish did not dispute his title. It came from an acknowledged authority. The universal consent of Christian Europe,—however absurd it may seem to us now,—had then assigned to the Popes or Bishops of Rome, a large and indefinite power and right to confer the dignity and the prerogatives of Sovereignty or Feudal suzerainty at their will. For four hundred years at least—ever since the greatest man of the Middle Ages, Charlemagne, had been crowned by the Pope with the Imperial crown,— this power and right of the Roman Pontiffs had grown up as an acknowledged doctrine. Henry II. did not even take the title of King at all. He took the title of Lord of Ireland, which continued to be the legal title of the Kings of England till the reign of Henry VIII.† And this distinction was by no means in those days a distinction of form only. It is an ignorant notion, indeed, that in the twelfth century the Feudal Sovereigns of any territory made themselves necessarily, or even usually, responsible for the domestic

---

* Professor Stokes' "Ireland and the Anglo-Norman Church," p. 134.   † Ibid., p. 136.

government administered within it. That government was, of necessity, left to those by whose hands its powers had been acquired, and with whom it was an essential part of the Feudal system, that it should remain. Founded entirely upon usages and customs varying more or less in every country—those usages being themselves again absolutely controlled by the universal conditions of a state of society which was from top to bottom military—the domestic rule exercised over the mass of the people by vassal and local chiefs, rested everywhere in Europe on the paramount necessity of obedience on one side and of protection on the other. The interference of mere Suzerainty in the affairs of ordinary life, was simply impracticable. It could not possibly arise until, in the course of centuries, the idea of a strong central government and of an Imperial jurisprudence had been developed. To talk of Ireland being "governed," even "in the last resort," by the King of England in the twelfth century, or in several succeeding centuries, is a grotesque anachronism indeed.

Fortunately, there is no dispute about the facts which Mr. Gladstone thus perverts. The very spirit of Irish national feeling itself, even when expressed in the most temperate and legitimate forms, has always led Irishmen to emphasise those facts which distinguish between the Conquest of England by the Duke of Normandy in the eleventh century, and the claim of Sovereignty over Ireland which was established by Henry II. in the twelfth. When it suits their purpose Irish orators have always denied a conquest. Mr. Gladstone has had many opportunities of knowing this; and one of the most remarkable of these was in 1834, some two years after he entered the House of Commons. On the 22nd of April of that year Daniel O'Connell,—of whom he now speaks effusively in this volume as equal in greatness, as an Irishman, to Burke or Wellington,—made a memorable speech in that House in favour of a repeal of the Union. Its very first passages were devoted to an emphatic argument that Ireland had never been conquered by England, and that the title to dominion over Ireland had never been acquired by the sword. "No title by conquest or subjugation:"—"No title of subjection was acquired by battle:" nothing had happened that "jurists would consider as giving any claim to England to say that there had been submission on the part of the Irish people as subjects," or, "above all, recognition of them as being subjects" on the part of England herself,—such were the repeated declarations of O'Connell in that elaborate address.* The same language is still almost unanimously held by all Irishmen who treat the question historically, whether they belong to the Repeal party, or to the number of those who desire to maintain the Legislative Union. Thus, the late Professor Richey, of Dublin, in his excellent work, "A Short History of the Irish People,"†

* "Mirror of Parliament," vol. ii. p. 1188.   † Dublin, 1887.

—full as it is of Irish patriotic feeling—says of the common phrase, "Conquest of Ireland by England," that it is "an expression in every way incorrect."* Still more emphatic testimony is given to this view by a yet living writer, whose spirit is so intensely Irish as to border on what must be considered as extravagance. For Mr. Prendergast, in his chapter † on the earlier Plantations of Ireland, speaks of the native Celts of Ireland as "a people of original sentiments and institutions, the native vigour of whose mind had not been weakened by another mind;" ‡ and he goes so far in his patriotic enthusiasm as to exclaim, "Had the Irish only remained honest pagans, holding, no matter who might tell them to the contrary, that true religion was to hate one's enemies, and to fight for one's country, Ireland perhaps had been unconquered still." Yet this is the Irish writer who—in condemning a later phrase, "the Irish enemy," as applied to the native Irish—gives us the following true and striking account of the reputed "Conquest" of 1172:—" Now the 'Irish enemy' was no nation in the modern sense of the word, but a race divided into many nations or tribes, separately defending their lands from the English barons in their immediate neighbourhood. There had been no ancient national government displaced, no national dynasty overthrown. The Irish

---

* P. 128.
† Cromwellian Settlement of Ireland " (1870), pp. 1–48.
‡ Ibid., p. 11.

had no national flag, nor any capital city as the metropolis of their common country, nor any common administration of the law; nor did they ever give a combined opposition to the English. The English coming in the name of the Pope, with the aid of the Irish bishops, and with a superior national organisation, which the Irish easily recognised, <u>were accepted by the Irish</u>. Neither King Henry II., nor King John, ever fought a battle in Ireland."*

This short and pregnant passage is taken from the work of an enthusiastic Irishman, published twenty-seven years ago, before the smoke of our present controversy had arisen to obscure the view. It is, perhaps, the purest bit of truth that is to be found in all the angry literature of Irish history. It shines like a gem " of purest ray serene." With one slight qualification, which the author himself would probably admit, it is not only accurately true in all that it directly says, but in every line and almost in every word, it is full of further suggestions of truths as important as those which it expressly affirms. The English were " accepted " by the Irish:—so it says. Let us ask—in what capacity were they accepted? And the answer must be that they were accepted in two special capacities. First, the English King was " accepted " as Feudal Sovereign of Ireland according to the ideas and usages of that time; and secondly, English knights and barons were " accepted " as settlers

* "Cromwellian Settlement of Ireland" (1870), p. 28.

domesticated and naturalized in Ireland, also according to the ideas and usages of that age. It was an age of roving adventurers all over Europe. In accordance with one of the commonest of all its habits, the English knights were invited as allies, came, and were accepted as settlers in the country, taking by bargain, by feats of arms, and by marriage, their natural place and rank in the pre-existing system of Irish Chiefry. And this last kind of acceptance was chronologically the first. The plantation of Norman soldier-colonists had begun before the coming of Henry II. And it began not only with acquiescence on the part of the Irish, but with active solicitation on the part of some of them. The Chief of one of the many septs, or "nations," into which Ireland was then divided— divided with a depth of cleavage which it is difficult for us now even to conceive,—had invited the entrance and the aid of the Norman element. Intermarriage had taken place. And with intermarriage had come also the holding and the guaranteed inheritance of territory as the inducement and reward of military service and of military alliance. Thus the Anglo-Normans and Gallo-Normans from Wales, had been firmly planted in Ireland, and had been accepted as husbands and as sons, and as holders and as inheritors of all the power that belonged to Irish Chiefs, before the expedition of Henry II. Hence we see that Mr. Prendergast's phrase—"accepted by the Irish"—is not only accurate, but is true with a fullness of meaning which it needs much explanation to exhaust. The Norman element had been already not only accepted, but had been specially invited, and that amalgamation and "Ersefication" of the Norman colonists had begun which was one of the most determining features in all that followed.

But this is not all. The truthful and significant sentence above quoted from an intensely Irish historian, not only thus gives us a true account of the transactions of 1172, and a true indication of all that they involved for the future, but it takes us back into a still older history, and lets in a flood of light on what had gone before. Why was it that the Norman King was so easily "accepted" as Feudal Sovereign over Ireland? Why had it been that Norman knights were invited, accepted, and adopted as sons and brothers in Ireland? Because, says Mr. Prendergast, their "superior national organisation" was "easily recognised by the Irish." But in what did the comparative inferiority of the Irish consist? In what degree, and to what extent did it exist? How great and how evident must it have been to admit of such a frank confession—such a ready submission to a manifest superiority? How was it that this alleged "conquest" of Ireland came about so noiselessly—so naturally—with so little sound of arms,—with only one short clash of battle? What was the previous condition of things which made such events possible?

It is when we ask these questions that Mr. Gladstone's perversion of history comes out in all its breadth and depth. In the same year in which he wrote the "Lessons of Irish History," *—on May 12, 1887,—he addressed a Nonconformist party in London at a luncheon, and in pursuance of the argument now before us, he declaimed as follows:—"But who made the Irishman? The Irish, in very old times indeed, if you go back to the earlier stages of Christianity, were among the leaders of Christendom. But WE went in among them: WE sent among them numbers of our own race. These were mixed with the Irish, and ever since our blood has been mixed with theirs there has been this endless trouble and difficulty." † Here we have the key-note of the "Special Aspects" struck at once. And the special methods are as remarkable. There is, in the first place, a complete oblivion, or a clever omission, of the many centuries which intervened between the really creditable age of the Irish Church, and the coming of the Normans. There is, in the second place, a complete misconception, and consequent misrepresentation, of the nature of that "leadership in Christendom" which in one sense, and in one great work, had really at one time belonged to Irish Celts; there is, in the third place, a dexterous confounding of later events which were separated by many hundred years; there is, in the fourth place, an absolute suppression of all the relevant and notorious facts respecting the condition

* "Aspects," p. 109.   † *Times*, May 12, 1887.

into which Ireland had fallen between the "leadership of Christendom" and the advent of the Norman colonists. Let us see how some of these matters stand.

So far as Ireland was concerned, the "earlier stages of Christianity" must be reckoned as having begun about A.D. 450. It is not true that at any much earlier date than this the Irish Celts were Christian at all. The British Celtic Church began long before the Irish. British bishops were members of some of the great Councils of the middle of the fourth century.* Whatever infiltration of Christianity had percolated into Ireland before the fifth century seems to have come directly from contact with Roman Christians. The claim for Ireland as regards the "earlier stages of Christianity" is at best a loose oratorical exaggeration in keeping with all its context. But from the middle of the fifth century a well-established Celtic Christian Church did exist in Ireland, which took a memorable share in spreading the faith of Christ among heathen races, not only in their own island, but especially in Scotland and elsewhere in Western Europe. This is true, and in itself alone it is an imperishable glory. But unfortunately it does stand quite alone. The Celtic Church carried in its hands, indeed, the precious seed of Christian belief. But it carried that seed in the most earthy of all earthen vessels. It had about three hundred and fifty

* "Ireland and the Celtic Church," by Professor Stokes (1885), p. 11.

years of at least external peace for the development of all its powers (450–795). It developed a rude art in painting, illumination, and metal work. It had also a peculiar literature of its own. Even as to these there has been much absurd exaggeration. They were remarkable not for the time, but for the locality. They pale a feeble and ineffectual light beside the splendid literature and art of the contemporary Roman people, and even of the Romanised natives of Britain. But as compared with other tribes, whom the Romans justly considered as barbarians, the Irish Celts had a truly native and a very curious culture. There was a genuine literature of its kind in the native language. But this literature is chiefly valuable for the light it casts upon the utter sterility of the Celtic Church as regards any good influence on the economic condition, or on the social state, or on the political organisation of the people. This is all that we have to do with here. We are not discussing gold filagree work, or the copying and rude illumination of manuscripts. We are discussing the state of Ireland in those social and political conditions which determine the comfort and real welfare of a people.

It is literally true that the heathen Danes, who began their invasions of Ireland in the year A.D. 795, and were finally defeated in 1014, did more, during these two hundred and nineteen years, to establish the beginnings of commerce, of wealth, and of the civilisation which depends on these, than the Celtic Church or people did during all the centuries of their previous, or of their subsequent and separate existence. Even when they first came as heathen rovers they were far in advance of the Celts in the matter of house-building, one of the surest tests of comparative civilisation. There is not, at the present day, one single town of any importance in Ireland which does not owe its origin to the Danes. "The cities," says Professor Richey, "built by the Danes, altogether differed from the temporary constructions of the Celtic tribes: they were at once garrisons and emporia, well fortified, and capable of defence." Trade and commerce began with them, and the Danes continued in possession of the towns which they had created even after they had been driven from possible reclamation of the bogs and woods of the rest of Ireland. Dublin, Wexford, Waterford, Limerick, etc., were all originally, and always continued to be, Danish cities.* During all this time—nearly two hundred years of the domination of a race which was still largely pagan, over, at least, a great part of Ireland—the native Irish hardly ever,—even for a moment—intermitted their own internecine tribal feuds, and never scrupled to ally themselves with the heathen Norsemen whenever it was in the slightest degree convenient to do so. This is the account of a thoroughly

* Richey's "Short History," p. 110.

Irish historian, but of one who is faithful to historic truth. "The chiefs," says Professor Stokes, "were murdering and plundering one another, and every one of them ready to sell his country to the northern invader, if only he himself could be thus secure of a temporary triumph." * And not only is this true, but it is also a memorable fact that when one tribal chief, more fortunate than others, did really win an important victory over the common enemy in A.D. 968, he was, within six years, treacherously slain by a conspiracy of his rival compatriot chiefs.† It is a further fact that when his brother, the celebrated Brian, did prosecute, very nearly to success, the same great enterprise of founding a united and a native Irish kingdom, he was again encountered in his last battle near Dublin, in 1014, by a factious and unpatriotic alliance between Danes and native Irish. Nor is it, again, a less characteristic fact that his death, even in victory, was followed by an immediate outburst of native inter-tribal and internecine strife. Within three days of the death of King Brian, his only surviving son was assailed by the remnant of his father's army, and every hope, or prospect, or even the very idea of a united Irish nation under one government, was dissipated for ever in continuous storms of internal war. Of no other people in Christendom could it be said in those days, that a triumph and a victory over heathen invaders was a misfortune to themselves,

* "Celtic Church," p. 268.   † "Short History," p. 114.

because of the very fact that it left them face to face with their own vices. Yet this is the verdict of one of the very best of modern Irish historians. "Such," says Professor Richey, "was the end of the battle of Clontarf, in which, if the foreigners were defeated, a far greater disaster fell upon the Irish people, and the real victory was won by anarchy over order." *

It was the truly indigenous constitution of Irish society—unchecked and even stimulated by the similar constitution of the Celtic Church,—that alone seems to have been the curse of Ireland at this memorable epoch. There may be some hyperbole in the language of the Irish Chronicler who describes the great things done, or undertaken, by the native Celtic King, Brian, in the brief period—some fifteen years—during which he held "the chief sovereignty of Erinn" —the churches and sanctuaries he built,—the teachers and professors he engaged,—the books he brought from beyond the seas,—the bridges and roads he made, —the fortresses he built or strengthened. Monks were easily pleased by any ruler who conferred favours on what was called the Church. But, in spite of possible exaggeration, there seems to be good historical evidence that Ireland really had then a fair opportunity of starting on a new path—such as had been entered upon, and followed to glorious results, by many other European nations. And what hindered her? It certainly was not the "we" of whom Mr.

* "Short History," p. 124.

Gladstone spoke with such effusive, but also such cheap, and vicarious, humility. For be it noted that this great opportunity was opened to Ireland more than half a century before the Normans had landed even in England, and more than a whole century and a half before the "we" had crossed the farther channel into Ireland.

The question, therefore, may well be asked—What had the Irish been doing all that time? And what was the cause of their not taking that great "occasion by the hand"? What again says the Irish historian? He says that it was the very excellence of King Brian's government that made it hateful to his countrymen. "A truly national government of this description found its bitterest enemies among the provincial chiefs, who longed to restore anarchy, and were willing to league with the foreigner for that purpose."* And now, when Danish power was broken down, what the Irish Tribes and Chiefs did was to fight with each other in perpetual and ferocious wars. "Upon the Celtic nation fell ruin and disorder." And so, from the date of Brian's death in 1014 to "our" arrival in the person of Strongbow, in 1170—or for a period of one hundred and fifty-six years—"Ireland was a chaos in which the chiefs of the great separate tribes struggled to secure a temporary supremacy." † "The Irish Nation was in the condition of social and political dissolution." Few of the kinglets ever

* "Short History," p. 116.   † Ibid., p. 125.

reached their thrones except by crime. Few died a bloodless death. If such a state of things could continue, "the world would relapse into worse than ancient barbarism." *

Now, let it be observed that there is, and can be no dispute about these facts. They are authenticated by a cloud of witnesses—not only by many honest Irish historians of our own day, like Dr. Richey and Mr. Prendergast, but by a kind of testimony which—in anything like the same authenticity and detail—exists nowhere else in Europe. In the Irish Annals we have evidence which is said to rest on written documents probably as old as the second century of our era, and to embody, at least, good oral traditions of a much earlier date.† One old Irish Annalist, who seems to have been a critic in his own time, very modestly sets aside all records later than B.C. 305, but seems to regard true contemporary history as beginning at that date.‡ From the year A.D. 664, at all events, the records are verified by minute accuracy in the narrative of solar eclipses; and there seems to be no reasonable doubt of the perfect genuineness and authority of these remarkable Annals for several hundred years earlier. We have therefore in the Irish Annals a photographic picture taken in the

---

* "Short History," p. 127.
† "Annals of Ireland," "The Four Masters," vol. I. Introduction, p. liii.
‡ Ibid., p. xlvi.

light of Irish self-consciousness—giving us an excellent idea of what Irish society was for nearly a thousand years before the Norman invasion.

Now it is, to say the least, remarkable that Mr. Gladstone, in his search after an answer to the question, "Who made the Irishman?" never quotes those very Irishmen who tell us most about their own early national, or rather tribal, education. I do not recollect ever seeing in any of Mr. Gladstone's many speeches or writings, one single quotation from, or even allusion to, the most authentic and detailed account that is possessed by any European people, of their own early life. I am not surprised. The Irish Annals are ugly reading for him, and for all who try to make out that England has "made the Irish." For what is the picture which those Annals present? Let us take the second entry. "The age of Christ 10. The first year of Carbre the Cat-headed, after he had killed the nobility, except a few who escaped from the massacre in which the nobles were murdered by the Attacotti." Three nobles had escaped from that massacre, and as to these it is added with a genuine touch of true Irish humour, "it was in their mothers' wombs that they escaped." All the nobles were killed except three who escaped, and these were babes unborn! And who were the Attacotti? The explanation reveals, here too, a much forgotten fact. The native Irish "Scoti" had been themselves invaders, and held Ireland by no other title than conquest.

The "Attacotti" are believed to have been the remnant of the older and conquered race—also Celtic—and we are told in a note that they "were treated as a servile and helot class by the dominant Scoti." * Thus all the elements that "made the Irishman" were even then in full play from the beginning of the Christian era at least, or about twelve centuries before Mr. Gladstone's "we" had anything to do with Ireland.

But let us pass on to a later date—after a contemporary literature had certainly begun,—and take another entry in this sad journal:—"The age of Christ 227. The massacre of the girls at Cleonfearta (in Munster) by Dunlang, King of Leinster. Thirty royal girls was the number, and a hundred maids with each of them." † The progress here indicated is singular. From the earlier entry we should gather that women at least were spared in Irish broils. Two centuries later we find that they were massacred without mercy. Much later we find again that they were regularly summoned to serve in war, and were seen tearing each other's breasts with reaping-hooks. And so on—and on—and on—for eight centuries. These Annals contradict absolutely Mr. Gladstone's monstrous misrepresentation that from the "earlier stages of Christianity" the Irish were among the leaders of Christendom, "till WE went in among them." In any sense which has the most distant bearing upon the

---

* "Annals," vol. i. p. 96.   † Ibid., p. 115.

social condition, the peace, welfare, prosperity,—or any shadow of a hope from the political institutions—of the Irish people, the assertion is not only "inflated fable" destitute of any historical foundation, but it is the direct opposite of the truth. Even after the establishment of Christianity about A.D. 450, for six hundred years, at least, this barbarous condition had been going from bad to worse. Nor must we forget that this steady and continuous decline had gone on notwithstanding long contact, and perfect familiarity with, the high civilisation of Roman Britain. Hundreds and even in some cases, thousands of Roman coins, have been found in Ireland,—coins of the first and second centuries. For some centuries the Irish were continually attempting to conquer Britain. For ten years in the middle of the fourth century they are said to have at least partially succeeded, till beaten and expelled by Theodosius in 369.* It cannot be said, therefore, that isolation alone, so far as mere knowledge is concerned, was the cause of the long continuance of Irish barbarism. They had seen what civilisation was, and what government meant. And having seen both, the Irish chiefs returned to their own country as chaotic as before, and as incapable of laying even the rudest foundations of civilised condition among their own people.

But even these facts, striking though they be, are an inadequate exposure of Mr. Gladstone's "inflated fable"

* Stokes, "Celtic Church," p. 17.

that the introduction of a foreign element into Ireland in the twelfth century, was the ending of her time of peace, and the beginning of her time of troubles. Not only is this absolutely contradicted by the evidence of history, but the converse proposition can be clearly established—that the only elements of civilisation which did exist in Ireland when the Normans came to settle, were foreign elements which had already secured an earlier footing in the country. And one of those elements was no less important than that superior organisation of the Christian Church which elsewhere had grown up in Christendom out of the necessities of its position in contact with the heathen world. The Irish Danes were the cousins of the French and English Normans; and they had been settled in Ireland for some three hundred and fifty years before the coming of Strongbow. Not only were they the founders of all the commercial cities of Ireland, but they were the main instruments in the reconstitution of her Church. Whatever may have been the achievements of the Missionaries of that Church when removed from the local influences of their own race and country, as at Iona and at Lindisfarne, nothing can be clearer than that, in its own country, it can hardly be said to have had any civilising influence at all. Its organisation was unlike anything that existed elsewhere in any part of the Christian world. It had no parochial clergy; it had no territorial bishops. Its so-called monastic bodies had none of the characteristics we are accustomed to associate with the name. They were tribes like the other purely secular tribes around them—hereditary castes animated with all the passions which raged throughout the land; and actually taking part in the cruel and ferocious wars to which these passions led.

It may well seem incredible, but it stands on the firmest historical evidence that, more than two hundred years after St. Patrick had established the Celtic Church in Ireland, its so-called clergy were regularly bound by the customs of the country to take part in all the wars of the chief or tribe under which they lived. And when we consider what those wars were—that there was not one single aim or object which could be dignified by the name "political,"— that they were wars of mere plunder, slaughter, and devastation,—we may conceive what the degradation of Christianity must have been, and how completely, in this form, it was divorced from all the influences which, elsewhere in Europe, made it the precious seed-bed of civilisation. Accordingly, when the Danes of Ireland became largely converted to Christianity in the tenth century, they did not owe their conversion to the native Celtic Church. They hated that Church and despised it as not less barbarous than its laity. They were converted by agencies which came not from Ireland but from England, and they established their connection at once, not with the old Irish ecclesiastical centre of Armagh, but with the sees of Canterbury and Rome. It was they who established the first Bishopric of Dublin. And they did this no less than one hundred and thirty years before the invasion of Henry II., and even twenty-two years before the Norman Conquest of England. In like manner it was the Danes again who established the sees of Waterford and Limerick; and through the ecclesiastical influences which were thus firmly established in Ireland, a conquest was won over her native Church far more real and effective than that which Henry II. even tried to accomplish in her political condition.

We must not allow any modern prejudice to hide from us the real significance and true interpretation of the great triumph which had been thus won in Ireland long before the invasion of the Fitzgeralds, by the earlier invasion of the English and Latin Church. Two very different currents of feeling have combined to misrepresent and misconceive this far more real and earlier conquest. One of these currents has been the feeling of Irish patriotism, which has clung to the supposed glories of an indigenous Church. The other has been the desire of some Protestants to see in that Celtic Church an anti-papal, and even a non-episcopal stage of ecclesiastical organisation. Between these two influences and a widespread ignorance of what Irish life really had been under that native Church, the part played by inflated fiction has been riotous indeed. There are, however, plenty of honest Irish historians who give us all the facts. Besides the irrefragable evidence of the contemporary Annals we have such excellent modern historians as Professor Richey, Professor Stokes, Professor Sullivan, Professor O'Curry, and Mr. Prendergast. Every one of these writers is animated by the purest spirit of Irish patriotism, and in detail they not only give us the facts, but occasionally express themselves strongly on the frightfulness of the picture which they themselves present. But they shrink most sensitively from any similar language when used by writers who are not Irish, and they enter pleas of mitigation which are generally quite irrelevant. Thus Professor Stokes reminds us quite truly that at least as regards some of the centuries when Irishmen were always fighting with each other, Englishmen were fighting with each other too. He reminds us, further, that Chroniclers and Annalists in early times did not think of recording much else than wars; and that the omission of other subjects may thus convey an erroneous general impression. There is some truth in this plea as regards the general character of early Chroniclers, but it is very little true as regards the Irish Annalists. It is one of their peculiarities that they are full of specimens of poetry and song, which give us very vivid glimpses indeed of the sentiments, pursuits, and opinions of the time. Moreover, even if the Annalists were defective in their account owing to their mere omission of other aspects of Irish life, we have other sources of information against which no such supposed deficiency can be charged. Among the treasures of ancient Celtic literature in Ireland there are some,—and one especially, known as The "Book of Leinster," which is a collection of narratives, tales, and traditions of Irish life,—which go back to its supposed heroic age.*

The picture of life and manners which they all present is precisely the same as the picture presented by the later Annalists of the Middle Ages. The longest and most elaborate of the tales is called the "Cattle-Spoil of Cuailuge," a place now called Collon in Louth. It narrates wars of the second century, and by its very title proclaims the immemorial sameness of those wars with all its desolating successors. But even if it were true that war and war alone is prominent in all those ancient documents, merely because it attracted most prominent attention in a rude age, this consideration has nothing to do with the peculiarities of the Irish case. It is not the fact of wars—even the most savage wars—being waged by Irishmen that is singular. Neither is it the mere fact of the long persistent continuance of those wars —that alone distinguishes her history. It is the utterly useless and worse than useless character of those wars, in which they stand alone. Out of war all modern nations have been made. Out of the Irish wars no nation did, or ever could, emerge. They

* "National Manuscripts of Ireland," vol. ii. pp. xxvi.–xxx.

were purely destructive. There was not one organic or reconstructive element in them. Englishmen who are enlightened have no objection to being told by others, or to confessing for themselves the fact, that their ancestors passed through a stage of barbarism. The late Professor Freeman was an intense Englishman. He was proud of the very name. Speaking of the Angles and Saxons when they landed in Britain in the middle of the fifth century (449), he says, "We may now be thankful for the barbarism and ferocity of our forefathers."*

Here we have the statement of a fact, and the expression of a sentiment. The fact is stated because it is the duty and the pleasure of an historian to speak the truth. The sentiment is justified by this —that the savagery and barbarism of the tribes who made the English people was a barbarism full of noble elements. Their wars were ferocious, but they fought for things worth fighting for. They were re-constructive, not purely destructive. In all their contests, whether with the Celts whom they almost exterminated, or whether among themselves, they contended for true conquest—dominion—settlement—not for mere plunder, devastation, and ravage. This is the fundamental difference between their barbarism and savagery, and the corresponding barbarism of the Celts in Ireland. We have only to look at the practical results to see all that this

* "Norman Conquest," vol. i. p. 20.

contrast involved. Within a hundred and fifty years of their landing in Britain the Anglo-Saxons had conquered the whole country from the Solent to the Forth, and from the Channel to the Severn. They had founded kingdoms in the full sense of that word—political communities with well-established principles of government, of industry, and of law. Within another period of three centuries and a half they had consolidated these kingdoms into one central monarchy, highly civilised, Christian, and to some degree even Imperial. During all these centuries the Celtic tribes in Ireland had not made one single step towards any such results. On the contrary, they had sunk continually from bad to worse, and their interminable wars were mere savage raids on each other's territory, destructive alike of peaceful industry and of the very beginnings of political organisation.

As to the Celtic Church nothing can be more thoughtless than to allow our Protestant feelings against the Roman See, or our interest in an ancient organisation which was independent of it, to blind us to the real condition of the early Irish Church. Professor Stokes speaks of the "ecclesiastical chaos which reigned in the Celtic Church"* in the early part of the eleventh century before the Anglo-Norman Bishoprics were established. It never had exercised, even in its golden age, the smallest influence in civilising the habits or institutions of

* "Celtic Church," p. 324.

the Irish people. That golden age lay in the sixth and seventh centuries. But the annals of those centuries show no pause in the revolting repetition of bloody feuds, with plunder, murder, and devastation. It is indeed recorded, far on in the seventh century, that the Clergy of Ireland procured for themselves an exemption from the obligation of "hosting," that is, of taking a personal part in those interminable and ferocious tribal wars. But as to any influence in preventing them, we hear nothing of it, and we have good reason to know that even personal participation in them, though not compulsory, continued to be frequent if not habitual. The truth is, that the Celtic Church was in all social and political matters identified with the Celtic people. They were continually identified even in actual offices and functions. In the ninth century Phelim, King of Munster, was at once Abbot, Bishop, and King. He ravaged Ulster and murdered its monks and clergy.* The same authority tells us that the Bishops of Armagh were just as bad.†

It is most curious to observe how even the most honest Irish historians are swayed either by a local patriotism, or by Protestant feeling on the supremacy of the Roman See, in their language about the native Celtic Church. Thus, even Professor Stokes, liberal and enlightened as he is, in his history of that Church goes out of his way to censure St.

* "Celtic Church," p. 199.   † Ibid., p. 200.

D

Patrick for having in the fifth century accepted the authority of the Pope; an act which the Professor stigmatises as a "betrayal of the liberties of his country." Yet, in his capacity of historian of the Anglo-Norman Church in Ireland, when he has occasion to tell us in what those liberties consisted, and in what they resulted, he is far too honest to suppress the truth. Then indeed—when thus facing another way—he does not mince his words in describing what the Celtic Church had come to be "when," as Mr. Gladstone expresses it, "we went in." He points out that so far as dogma or ritual, or even the nominal supremacy of the Pope, were concerned, there was nothing whatever to distinguish between the two Churches, or to justify any special sympathy with the Celtic rather than with the Anglo-Norman. Yet he tells us that they hated each other with as perfect a hatred as that which has ever divided Protestant from Catholic, or Orangeman from Nationalist. Nor does he leave us in any doubt as to the comparative merits, religious, social, and political, of the indigenous Irish, as compared with the foreign or Anglo-Norman element. He represents the Celtic Church as having become utterly corrupt. "Celtic monasticism," he says, "was played out. It had done its work and was now corrupt." The so-called "Culdees," or God's servants, had "only the name and nothing of the reality;" and then, summing up, he says, "The work of the Church of Rome in the twelfth century was that of a real reformation; and in no department was that reforming work more needed than in sweeping away, in Scotland and in Ireland alike, that Culdee system which had lost its primitive power, and was good for nothing save for the purposes of ecclesiastical plunder and degradation." *

But this is not all. Professor Stokes is far too honest as an historian to conceal the cause and nature of this corruption any more than he conceals the extent and existence of it as a fact. He identifies it with that one great feature in their character which was purely and characteristically Irish: namely, the close and inseparable connection with the septs, clans, and tribes into which Celtic society had been always divided in Ireland. Bad as the Celtic ecclesiastical communities had become in morals—"useless, corrupt, lax and easy-going in discipline" †—this was not altogether peculiar to them. But in one matter they stood alone—their full participation in the fierce passions and deeds of violence of the septs against each other. It was they who carried on this spirit from generation to generation, even after the higher organisation of the Anglo-Norman and Catholic Church had extended itself over all the more civilised parts of Ireland. They lived on with a pestilent survival in the north and west, almost down to

* "Anglo-Norman Church," p. 355.
† Ibid., p. 357.

the period of the Reformation. Speaking of the thirteenth century, Professor Stokes says, "The monasteries were as completely tribal institutions, bound up with certain septs, and hated by other hostile septs, as they were in the seventh and eighth centuries. There was not the slightest reverence for a monastery as such. The tribes venerated—sometimes, but not always—the monasteries belonging to their own patron Saint, or their own tribe. But the monasteries of a hostile tribe, or of a different Saint, were regarded as fair game for murder, plunder, and arson."* The dues which the Celtic Abbots most delighted to gather from the people were arms, battle-dresses, war-horses, and gold. "A fierce, passionate, bloodthirsty spirit was universal." The most sacred places in Ireland, connected with the early Christianity of Ireland, such as Clonmacnoise, Inescleraun, and Derry, were plundered and burnt over and over again, and always by native Irishmen, such as the O'Currys, the O'Donnells, the O'Neills, and the O'Briens. Nor does Professor Stokes fail to note the weird and fateful continuity of this Irish savagery. He relates an example of a bloody fight between Celtic Abbots and Bishops, so late as the middle of the fifteenth century. One Bishop, with his son, two brothers, and two sons of his Archdeacon, were all slain. On this, Professor Stokes exclaims, "How thoroughly Celtic the whole thing!' How it reminds

* "Anglo-Norman Church," pp. 363, 364.

us of what we read, seven or eight hundred years earlier, when the monasteries of Durrow and Clonmacnoise, with their retainers, tenantry, and slaves, used to join in deadly battle! Yet this episcopal warrior died sixty years after Wickcliffe, and but forty years before Luther was born." *

This is a retrospect—eight hundred years from 1450—which takes us back to the so-called "golden age" of the Irish Celtic Church; and Professor Stokes, in another passage, pursues this clue of continuity in the opposite direction down to our own time. Casting his eye—not backward, from the fifteenth century for eight hundred years, but—forward from the ninth century, for a thousand years, he traces this continuity of character as having had its roots in ages when no foreigner, not even the naughty Danes, had any influence upon it. Referring to the charge, which he does not deny, against the Irish, that they are even in our own time comparatively indifferent to human life—to "their agrarian murders—to their fierce faction fights"—he does not hesitate to ascribe all these to an hereditary survival of the taint which was conspicuous in all the centuries of which he wrote.† It is not necessary for any of us to adopt this view either as a full explanation, or as any adequate excuse. Other causes may have added their contribution, just as most assuredly other pleas must be used in mitigation of censure, if

---

* "Anglo-Norman Church," p. 369.
† "Celtic Church," pp. 200, 201.

Ethics are to hold their ground at all in our judgments of human conduct. It is enough for my purpose here to point out that it is the explanation offered by an Irishman writing in his character as an historian, and yet writing in a spirit of the warmest sympathy with early Celtic institutions.

Whatever may be the value of the doctrine of an hereditary taint, either as explanation or as an excuse, it is quite certain that the essential property of matter which physicists call "Inertia," is likewise a property of mind as we know it in ourselves. It is that property in virtue of which any motion or movement imparted, tends to run on unchanged for ever—unless, and until, it is changed—checked, accelerated, or diverted — by the intervention of some external force. It is in virtue of this property that early customs and habits of life in any people become so ingrained as to be almost indelible—only to be reformed by new and compelling causes being brought to bear upon them. It is thus that streams of water, in some countries, cut their own channels so deep that nothing can divert them except a complete break up of the physical geography of the land through which they run. And so it is that, in the case of Ireland, we have the fact proved by the most unquestionable evidence of history, that her exemption from foreign conquest, at least up to the twelfth century, had left her people to have their character and habits determined by purely indigenous institutions. Up to that date, at all events, therefore, Mr. Gladstone's passionate question, "Who made the Irishman?" can be answered in no faltering voice. Celtic customs, Celtic ideas, Celtic Institutions, operating unchecked through more than a thousand years, in Mr. Prendergast's words, "uncontaminated with another mind"—these made the Irishman what the Anglo-Normans found him. And on the evidence of the same historic facts, frankly acknowledged by the same author, we can affirm farther that when the Anglo-Normans did "go in," they effected an easy entrance, because of that "superior national organisation" which the Irish themselves could not fail to recognise. Nor is this all. On the accumulated evidence of Irish Annalists and modern historians, we know that this acknowledged superiority of organisation extended to everything that makes the difference between barbarism and civilisation, as distinguished from mere learning or an aptitude for some of the decorative Arts. It was an immense superiority in arms, in all the useful arts, in laws, and in religion. To conceal, or to slur over these facts, still more to deny and to contradict them, is a betrayal of historic truth. And when such denial is made in the spirit of mere political passion, it deserves some much severer name than "inflated fiction." At all events, we now see that Mr. Gladstone starts with all he has to say on the famous "seven centuries" so often thrown in the teeth of England, with a thoroughly perverted view of the pre-established forces and conditions with which England has had to deal, and it will not be difficult to show that the same tone of vicious misrepresentation characterises all he says on later times.

CHAPTER II.

EFFECTS OF SUZERAINTY OF ENGLAND OVER IRELAND.

So far, then, we have a clear answer to give to the inflated fiction implied in Mr. Gladstone's question, "Who made the Irishman?" Not for seven hundred years—which is the stereotyped phrase for the supposed period of English Government—but for the immense period of 1170 years, from the Christian era to the landing of Henry II., we have a tolerably clear account of the native Irish Celts. During that long lapse of time,—unlike almost all the other nations of modern Europe,—they were never conquered. The Romans did not conquer Ireland, as they conquered England and Scotland up to the line of the Forth and Clyde. The Danes did not conquer it, as they did a large part of England and finally the whole. The Danes conquered bits of it—and in return they only did for the Irish Celt what he had never done for himself,—they founded all his important cities. They founded all his commerce. They refounded, also, and effectively reformed his Church.

Neither were the Irish conquered by the tardy and transitory Norman invasion of the twelfth century. For another long period of time they were left to their own devices,—in all domestic matters practically uncontrolled.

"More than four centuries" is the time specified by Professor Richey as the interval which elapsed before anything like a real conquest was effected. Four hundred and thirty-three years—from 1170 to 1603—is the time he means. In the last year of Queen Elizabeth's reign the last of the Old Irish Chiefs were subdued, and fled. "The flight of the Earls" is a well-known epoch in Irish history. During all this time we have the light of the native Annals. The continuity is perfect. It is a continuity of horrors—sometimes a little better, sometimes a little worse, but always in its essential character, and in its immediate causes, absolutely unchanged. England had far less power of reforming the domestic laws, usages, and ideas of the people than she now has of changing the habits and manners of Central Africa. The same writer, Professor Richey, has well explained the impossibility of any effective conquest of Ireland during any of those centuries. The country was covered with impassable bogs and impenetrable forests. English Sovereigns had no standing armies. They had their own troubles to attend to—their wars with France—their own disputed successions. The cost of feudal levies was enormous, and practically prohibitory. Where there is no effective power there is no real responsibility. But more than this: such indirect responsibility as could alone exist in those centuries was discharged in vain when the action it took, and which alone it could take, was met by insuperable causes of resistance and reaction. And this is precisely what took place. The English Colonists assumed, like fish, the colour of the ground on which they had come to live. The typical boast of the first and most powerful among them—the Geraldines—came to be that they were "more Irish than the Irish." Under such conditions the beneficent influences of conquest, or even of colonisation, by a stronger race, and of that "higher organisation" which Mr. Prendergast tells us was "easily recognised" by the Irish, had no chance of working out the effects which they produced all over the rest of Europe. All the weapons of England, even those of the highest kind, were thus broken in her hands. The fine and the famous saying of Rome, that she "took captive her barbarian captors," may be literally applied with a terrible inversion of meaning to the pretended conquest of Ireland in the twelfth century. She took captive with her barbaric customs the rising civilisation of her invaders. That rising civilisation not only ceased to be developed, but became blighted on her soil. It may even be said, perhaps, that it made her own old savagery worse than it had been before. It added an element of persistence and of strength which threw off with fierce disdain, as foreign and intrusive, every attempt on the part of England to teach her "purer manners, nobler laws." Those nobler elements in the Celtic character itself, which had always existed, and which we all recognise, did indeed survive as germs—but they were never developed. They were shut up, as before, in the cells of ecclesiastics, and absolutely divorced from all civilising power, or even influence on the social habits or political institutions of the people. Some lingering love of learning, a strong natural vein of poetry, and a genuine turn for curious forms of art, apparently indigenous—all these lived on—with no other effect than, perhaps, lending some additional charm to a national sentiment which had no central rallying-point, and no definite political ambition to give it any constructive power. We have only to compare the results of the Anglo-Norman colonisation of Ireland with the contemporaneous Anglo-Norman colonisation of Scotland, to see the true causes of amazing difference. In Scotland—at least in the lowlands of Scotland—the Norman settlers found an ancient Teutonic civilisation well established—one which had been founded, first on Roman conquest, and then on Anglo-Saxon occupation. Professor Freeman insists upon it with emphasis that the suzerainty of the Anglo-Saxon Kings of England over Teutonic Scotland up to the Forth had been long established. There is much debate on this point. But it does not concern us here. What is certain is that Teutonic—or, as we now call it, Lowland—Scotland before the Norman Conquest of England had been at one time simply part of one of the Kingdoms of the Anglo-Saxon Heptarchy—the Kingdom of Northumbria. Freeman's contention that in the succeeding century—the tenth—it had accepted the suzerainty of the consolidated English "Empire" is—to say the least of it—open to much dispute. It is said that for the first time in 828, King Ecgbehrt, who had begun as King of "Mercia" alone, appears in the title of a charter as *Rex* Anglorum, King of all the Angles in Great Britain.* In 924 King Edward, son of the great Alfred, is alleged to have become King and Over-Lord of the whole of Britain, and the enthusiasm of this intensely English writer, Professor Freeman, asserts that "from this time to the fourteenth century the Vassalage of Scotland was an essential part of the public law of the Isle of Britain." † Scottish historians, quite as learned and much less excitable, have shown clearly enough that this is an assertion which cannot be sustained. And it is well to be thus reminded that the spirit of exaggeration, due to what may be called a provincial patriotism, is to be found in an English, as well as in Irish, historians. The late Mr. Robertson, in his standard work, the "History of the Early Kings of Scotland," ‡ has

* Freeman's "Norman Conquest," vol. i. p. 40.
† Ibid., p. 61.
‡ Vol. i. p. 69; and vol. ii. Appendix.

effectually disposed of the pretensions put forward by the later Kings of England to a feudal sovereignty over Scotland. But Robertson does not deny—on the contrary, he carefully states—that, so far back as the seventh century, both Pictish and Scottish Kings were, for a time at least, tributary to the Anglo-Saxon Kingdom of Northumberland. Province after province in Scotland was subdued by the Angles, until in 670 the Anglian King took the step of appointing a Pictish Bishopric of the Picts with the seat of the See on the Forth. But a tremendous defeat by the Picts and Scots in 684 showed the unbroken vitality of the incipient Scottish Kingdom, and not less the rapid advance which the Angles had made in founding a still more powerful monarchy, as well as in spreading their own Teutonic race and civilisation. All these facts establish the contention here maintained, that mere suzerainty, in the early Middle Ages, was not necessarily, or even usually such a condition of dependence as to prevent the free development of separate and independent political institutions.

But political institutions, in order to be developed, must first exist, at least in germ. In Scotland they had long existed not in germ only, but in well-planted growths. In Ireland they did not exist at all. Hence a perfect explanation of the different results in the two countries upon the chameleon nature of the Norman settlers. In Scotland the divided tribes and races, long before the Norman Conquest of England, had begun to aggregate. The nucleus of a central monarchy had been formed, and formed, too, by a wonderful and still mysterious revolution round the axis, and in the name, of the Scoti—an Irish Celtic tribe. The peculiar receptivity of the Normans was, therefore, in Scotland, brought into immediate contact with something which was really worthy of being so received,—something which, by assimilation with their own strong and manly nature, could strike its roots downwards, and spread its branches upwards in the light of a glorious day. Yet even in Scotland, we did not altogether escape the Irish danger. Those colonists of Norman blood—and they were many—who pushed forward beyond the central and eastern area in which all the civilisation of Scotland has begun, and from which alone it spread—those Normans who wandered far into the predominantly Celtic area, and who married and settled there—were often tempted to fall, and did sometimes actually fall, under the same influences by which the Anglo-Irish were so fatally seduced. The Scottish Kingdom had a long and a hard fight to maintain in the West Highlands and in the Hebrides against that same Celtic element of tribal faction, and intertribal anarchy. In that fight some men of Teutonic blood took what may justly be called a rebellious part. But, on the whole, the Anglo-Norman element in Scotland not only accepted the Saxon and Roman civilisation which they found, but carried it onwards and upwards as they did in England. Out of their number arose all the most powerful champions of Scottish independence, when Edward I. tried to convert the mere antiquarian claim of an ancient and dubious "commendation" into the direct rule of a complete dominion. Sir William Wallace and Robert Bruce were both Normans, and although Bruce rallied round him powerful contingents of the Scoto-Celtic element from Argyllshire, of the old Gallo-Celtic element from Galloway, and of the ancient Britons from Strathclyde, he was able through a powerful personal character to organise this great work of united action only because the idea of a central monarchy, and the constructive ambitions connected with it, had been long established in Scotland.

Professor Richey, in referring to the different fate and effects of Anglo-Normans in Scotland and in Ireland, has been led, by a natural feeling of patriotic exculpation, to dwell upon the mere geographical explanation that in Scotland the Teutonic population had the advantage of a good natural frontier, easily defensible against the Celtic population of the Highlands. But this is no adequate explanation of one of the most curious facts in history—the growth and establishment of the Scottish Nation and Kingdom. The Clyde in those days was no barrier at all. Down almost to our own time it was a shallow and wandering stream, fordable here and there at low tide as far down as below Dumbarton. The Romans had not trusted to it as a military barrier, for they built a wall and garrisoned it with legions. North of the Clyde and Forth, on the long line between the eastern lowlands and the highlands of Scotland, there was no geographical frontier which could be easily defended. The line of the Grampians opened upon the richer country, and upon its early Teutonic settlers, by the ready access of a hundred glens. Through these, if Irish habits had prevailed, raids could always be made, and through these some very serious Celtic invasions did actually take place down to times comparatively late. The causes were far more deeply seated, which can alone explain the early growth of Scotland as a nation under the final leadership of King Robert the Bruce. Those causes may be all traced in the fact that he was a Norman Knight, a born leader of men, inheriting the traditions of an ancient civilisation, and sharing also in the blood of a Celtic family which had already founded a real monarchy. In Scotland the Norman element was Scottified. In Ireland the Norman element was Ersefied. In Scotland the Norman element became assimilated by a germ of political civilisation which had been growing through stages of much obscurity for at least three hundred years before the Norman Conquest. In Ireland it was still more assimilated with a barbarism which had been getting steadily worse and worse through the history of a whole millennium. In Scotland the three centuries of this building-up—amidst much obscurity of detail—can in outline be clearly traced through several long steps of constructive work, which are full of historical and political interest. They were emphatically centuries of union—effected partly by conquest, partly by marriage, partly by alliance with, and even tribute paid to, English kings, partly by social, partly by ecclesiastical amalgamation. At least three great men and three great events mark corresponding stages through which the Scottish Kingdom rose. So early as 730 the Pictish King, Angus MacFergus, laid its foundation-stone in establishing one rule over Picts and Scots. A little more than one hundred years later, in 843, Kenneth MacAlpine still farther cemented the union of those two Celtic bloods in one dynasty. For two hundred years all Scotland acknowledged the Sovereignty of this Celtic House. In 1068 Malcolm Canmore crowned the edifice with an Anglo-Saxon Queen, who gave birth to a family whose descendants still reign in England. In Scotland, therefore, one central monarchy had been consolidated, of which all its subjects were every year more and more learning to be proud. In Ireland, on the contrary, during the same epoch, there was no such progress towards union—nothing, indeed, but increasing and deepening disintegration. And when at last—not till early in the eleventh century—one gallant Irishman of purely native race did very nearly accomplish a like work, the monarchy which he for a moment did actually attain, was instantly torn to pieces by his compatriot chiefs and tribes. And Professor Richey himself tells us that those chiefs and tribes did so tear it to pieces for the very reason that a central and civilised government was, of all other things, that which they dreaded most. We may all render honour to King "Brian Boru" personally. He might have been another Angus MacFergus, or like another Kenneth MacAlpine—his Scottish kinsman by blood. They and he alike proved by their life that it is not because of anything indelible in their race that the Irish Celt failed so miserably to found a nation. They proved that it was something in the habits and institutions of Ireland that we have to look to for the cause. It was indeed the Danes who actually killed Brian Boru, for he fell in battle with them. But he fell in victory. And who was it that killed not him alone, but also the fruits of that victory, and obliterated from the annals of Ireland everything but the record of a barren triumph? It was not the "we" of Mr. Gladstone's inflated fiction. For "we" did not enter Ireland for a hundred and sixty years later. It was the native Irish tribes themselves, and they did this with feelings and intentions thoroughly indigenous, which have never received more vigorous condemnation than in the words of Professor Richey—one of the very best of their own historians.

But here we come upon an extraordinary discrepancy between the facts which these historians relate, and —at least—the occasional language which they hold concerning them. About the facts themselves there is practically no dispute. But as to the light in which they are represented—as to the use made of them— there is the widest difference between the interpretation which is obvious to others, and that which even the best of Irish historians are tempted to enforce. There is no dispute, for example, about the perfect continuity of intertribal feuds, fightings, and devastations, before and after the invasion of Norman settlers in the twelfth century. The contemporary Annals are sufficient to confute any attempt to deny that perfect continuity. Again, there is no dispute about the fact that this continuity depended on, and in itself consisted in, the more or less complete adoption by the Anglo-Norman barons and chiefs, of the habits, and manners, and sentiments of the Celtic chiefs and people amongst whom they settled. With them they established the most intimate relations by marriage, by "fosterage," by complete participation in common enmities, and by common methods of exercising the rudest forms of military power over all below them, and towards all around them. Further, there is no dispute that for centuries the English Sovereign and Government had not the physical power to counteract this condition of things. Daniel O'Connell, in his great speech of 1834, reiterated emphatically that not until 1614, in the reign of James I., did Ireland come under one Government with England.*

Professor Richey not only enforces the same view, but gives an excellent and detailed explanation of the fact. He points out that in an age when there were no standing armies, the cost of feudal levies was so enormous that it far exceeded the cost even of modern troops regularly paid. Moreover, feudal levies could not be long kept together. They were thus incapable from many causes of really conquering a country covered with enormous bogs and forests, into which the native population could always retreat, and where they could not be followed. Neither could feudal levies be used as permanent garrisons. There was but one way, in the Middle Ages, of representing Sovereignty—the way universally adopted —that of the delegation and devolution of government into the hands of strong feudatory vassals. These were armed with all the powers of petty kings and rulers in all things that pertained to domestic government and administration. But this was no novelty in Ireland. This had been the old condition of things for a thousand years at least; and, practically, during some centuries, a like condition of things obtained over the whole of Europe. The great difference of result which arose in Ireland was due entirely to the fact that the new chiefs sank down to the level of

* "Mirror of Parliament," vol. ii. (1834), p. 1189.

the old, and did not, as elsewhere, introduce or maintain more developed institutions. Here, again, there is no dispute as to the facts. Irish historians and even Irish declaimers do not deny that the system of English law, even as it existed in those rude military ages, was immeasurably superior to the old Celtic usages. At least, when it serves the purpose of their charges against England, they blame her vehemently, as O'Connell did, for not having at once established her own higher principles of jurisprudence over the whole of Ireland. It is true that the very same historians and declaimers, when their accusations are best served by an opposite contention, do continually face round the other way, and utter the contradictory complaint that England did cruelly or stupidly force upon Ireland English laws which were entirely unsuited to the people, and subversive of their ancient rights. I shall return to this alternative directly. Meantime, let us get what historic truth we can out of the first of these accusations, as urged on a great occasion by the very best Counsel for the prosecution.

With a glaring inconsistency between his vehement denial of any conquest, and consequently of any corresponding power, O'Connell, in the same speech, bitterly inveighed against England because she had not extended to the Irish the protection of her own laws. He admits the fact that "a number of the Irish did in 1246—only seventy-six years after the so-called conquest—apply for the benefit of British law, and to be considered as British subjects." He admits and records the farther fact that Henry III. did accordingly "issue a mandate, under the Great Seal, commanding the English barons, who possessed a portion of Ireland, that for the peace and tranquillity of the land they should permit the Irish to be governed by the law of England." And on whom does O'Connell throw the whole blame of the failure of a consummation which he admits was devoutly to be wished? Not upon the English Sovereign, but entirely on the new Anglo-Norman barons who had taken—and because of their taking—the position of Irish chiefs. And he explains the motives of their conduct precisely as Professor Richey explains the parallel conduct of the native Celtic chiefs two hundred and forty years before, when they fiercely tore to pieces the work of King Brian, because they hated above all things the prospect of a well-ordered central government, and of a more civilised monarchy. Just as they had clung to the old Irish usages as the stronghold of their barbarous power, and the great instrument of their arbitrary exactions, so did those Norman barons, who were now associated with them in the same life, dread above all things the introduction of English law, and for exactly the same reasons. Nothing can be more emphatic than O'Connell's language in identifying the motives which animated the Ersefied Normans in clinging to the Irish customs. It was because those customs lent themselves to a life of constant war and constant plunder.* He goes on to narrate how the same petition came again "from many of the Irish" in the reign of Edward I., in 1278, and again in the reign of Richard II. He narrates how in all those cases the petition was well received in England, and how in the case of Edward I. he expressly made the grant of it dependent on the "general consent of his people in Ireland," or at least of the prelates and nobles who were loyal to their Liege Lord. Now, in all this story there are but three clear and admitted truths— namely, first, the bare historical fact of such applications or petitions coming from Ireland; secondly, the farther fact that they were well and favourably entertained in England; and, thirdly, that English law and institutions would have been the salvation of Ireland, and that the survival and persistence of the old Irish usages were the real source of its continued miseries. These three things are true, and it is well to have them, not only admitted, but dwelt upon, by such a man as Daniel O'Connell. But the moment we come to the link by which he connects these three truths with his charges against the English Sovereign and the English nation in their whole relation to Ireland, we find that it is a link forged by his own imagination, or by his cunning and sleight of hand. That link consists in the designation given to those from whom came those beggings and petitions for

* "Mirror of Parliament," p. 1189.

English law. His dexterity in handling this cardinal point is admirable. He begins gently. He first says the petition came from "a number of the Irish." He next advances one step farther, and calls the petitioners "many of the Irish." Next he speaks of "the Irish as a whole." From this he passes insensibly, insidiously, and at last audaciously, to language which identifies the petitioners with the whole Irish people. "Thus," he says, "up to the period of the reign of James I. we find repeated endeavours *on the part of Ireland* to be governed by British laws instead of its own." *

Here we have the genuine element, not only of inflated fable, but of gross, yet cunning, misrepresentation. In Professor Richey's conscientious pages and in numerous other authorities more original and authoritative, we may see the object of the fraud. It was the English settlers of the lower ranks in power and wealth who speedily discovered the intolerable evils of native Irish customs. The feudal dependence on their lords under whom they had lived in England, was a dependence regulated, restrained, and limited, by the precepts and principles of a rising jurisprudence, which tended more and more to define the rights and consequently to limit obligations of men. They now found that the feudal dependence under which they had to live in Ireland according to the long-established and native customs of that

* "Mirror of Parliament," vol. ii. p. 1189.

country, was a dependence, absolute, servile, exhausting, and often ruinous. Nothing they had could be called their own. Under Celtic customs unlimited exactions were levied from them, against which they had no redress. The very idea of law did not exist—at least for the subordinate and the poor. Professor Richey mentions especially—as indeed all Irish historians do—one desperate Celtic custom which, even if it stood alone, was enough to make life unbearable to civilised men—the custom, namely, by which the chief had always the acknowledged right to quarter himself and his followers upon all those below him who had anything to be devoured or used. Antiquarian historians do, indeed, tell us that this evil custom was, in primitive times, not confined to Celts, but can be traced also in the early tribal usages of the Teutonic races. This may be true, and it may be true also that in certain rude conditions of a fighting society, this custom, and many others of a like kind, had their origin in some real necessity of those conditions. But this has nothing to do with the question now in hand. It cannot be too often repeated that what was peculiar to the Celts of Ireland was the continued survival and even the aggravation of this custom and other equally barbarous customs for long centuries, during which all other races had grown out of them and had cast them off. To the poorer English settlers even of the twelfth and thirteenth centuries, they were intolerable. It was from these unfortunate poorer English settlers, and from some native chiefs of the weaker class who felt the need of some protection from Over-Lords, that the petitions came which O'Connell and many other Irish speakers and writers have twisted into a general desire on the part of the Irish people to live under the blessings of the English law, and into a special accusation against the English Chiefs and barons as compared with the rest of the population among whom they came to settle. O'Connell forgot to tell the House of Commons that in any resistance which the English barons and Chiefs may have made to the introduction of English law, they were acting in thorough sympathy with at least all the more powerful native Celtic Chiefs, and with all that great body of the Celtic people in the very soil of whose mind these ancient customs were indelibly rooted, and to which they passionately clung. No doubt those of them who were beaten in their interminable wars, were sometimes ready enough to claim the protection of English laws against their stronger rivals, or against their native over-lords. But they never thought of submitting to the restraint of those laws in their dealings with their own people. Those opportunities for plunder which O'Connell said the English barons desired to keep, were precisely the same opportunities of plunder which the Irish Chiefs had enjoyed for centuries,—of which they were continuing at that very time to take full advantage, and which they never ceased to cultivate to their own ruin, and the ruin of their country, until, four hundred years later, it was at last really conquered.

Professor Richey has given a striking and graphic account of the complete Ersefication of the Anglo-Norman Barons in the centuries immediately succeeding the pretended Conquest of 1172. In the first place he tells us that the moment Henry II. turned his back on Ireland, and the native chiefs saw that all his imposing array meant nothing but a temporary occupation, "they returned to their former independence." Practically they were remitted to their original position.* We know what this means—what that position was. In the second place he tells us that the Norman Sub-Feudatories were scattered more or less over large portions of the country still largely occupied by, or in contact with, native populations against whom they could not organise any combined defence. They did, indeed, build castles,—and this was really new,—for no Irish chief seems ever to have built one stone upon another. But with whom did the Ersefied Normans garrison their castles? With the native Celts. They gathered bands of Irishmen at arms, called "Gallowglasses." These Irish Gallowglasses exhibited towards their new lords, we are told, a more absolute personal devotion than English vassals or tenants have ever shown—just because under the old native system they were

* "Short History," p. 166.

more absolutely dependent on the lord for all upon which alone they lived. The Norman barons did also bring with them some English dependants and tenants. But how did they treat them? They treated them with the adoption of the most obnoxious and destructive of all Irish customs—that of "coigne and livery,"—that is to say, by free quartering of the Celtic bands upon their unfortunate countrymen. And when those poorer English settlers, in despair of getting the protection of the more civilised laws to which they had been accustomed at home, abandoned their holdings under their Ersefied lords, and fled back to England, how did those barons repeople their estates? They stocked them with the native Irish, who, if they had long been accustomed to be plundered in the same way, were at least equally accustomed to be repaid out of the plunder of the neighbouring tribes. The capture of cattle by the hundred and sometimes by the thousand—at that time and country the only form of wealth, and almost the only sustenance of life—was the habitual aim and practice in all Irish predatory wars. "Great Distributor of Cows" is one of the epithets of glory which we find applied by the contemporary Irish bards in the verses celebrating the dead heroes of their race. But cows did not fall down from heaven, and the cattle so generously "distributed" in one place had been always rudely abstracted from another. There was therefore always every inducement for the native Irish to settle under any chief who could best defend such cattle as they had, and could best add to their store by the robbery of others. Thus there came about in many cases, an almost complete amalgamation between the two races. The English settlers married Irish wives. They fostered their children with Irish mothers—and this, under native usages, constituted one of the very nearest ties of human life. A number of the English went farther. We are told that in their new delight in a life of lawless freedom from all restraint, which was the great charm of native usages, they sometimes threw off even the clothing of their race and country. They " donned the saffron "—that is to say, they habited themselves in the rude native stuffs that were dyed in the browns and yellows which were obtainable from certain lichens encrusting Irish rocks, and certain herbs growing in Irish bogs. They fought with each other of the same English blood, exactly as the native Irish tribes and chiefs had always fought with each other. They had the same feuds—becoming in some cases just as hereditary and continuous—as in the well-known case of the Geraldines and the Butlers.

I am afraid, too, that we must go farther in our account of this decline from a comparatively high, and certainly a rising, civilisation, to the depths of a barbarism which had been getting deeper and deeper for a thousand years. There is nothing more indicative of this scale among any people than their established usages and rules of war. Giraldus Cambrensis, a contemporary Anglo-Celtic historian, tells us that the Normans in his day habitually gave quarter to the vanquished, and held their prisoners to ransom; whereas the Celtic Clans gave no quarter, struck off the heads of the vanquished as trophies, and allowed no one to escape. Did the English settlers demean themselves by adopting these Irish habits too? Except as regards the utterly savage practice of carrying off the heads of the slain as trophies, there is only too much evidence that they did. Indeed, it is obvious that the natural law and necessity of reprisals would compel them to do so. Men cannot fight under totally unequal conditions as to the consequences of defeat. Moreover, it is certain that they did adopt that most fatal of all the peculiarities of Irish war—the peculiarity of fighting, not for any worthy aim, or even any definite political object whatever, but for the plunder and devastation of the territory of some hated local enemy. In short, the Ersefication of the English settlers was almost complete. Under those circumstances, it is a gross perversion of historical facts to pretend that Ireland, after the nominal conquest of 1172, was under the Government of England even in the "last resort," and the phrase which assigns for English dominion the period of "seven hundred years," which Mr. Gladstone adopts, is seen to be an inflated fiction indeed. Still more specifically false is the assertion of Daniel O'Connell that Ireland became the prey of the English Colonists, who alone, or who principally, clung to Irish usages against the earnest entreaty of the native Irish to be allowed to come under the protection of English law.

One rich source of the most authoritative evidence against this fiction is to be found in the contemporary Irish Annals. If any man will take the trouble, and undergo the really revolting task of reading consecutively through those Annals for the period of nearly a century and a half which elapsed between the Norman invasion of 1170-2, and another invasion which forms a new epoch in the history of Ireland in 1315, he will find that of the interminable wars, predatory incursions, slaughters, plunderings, and treacherous murders there faithfully recorded,[*] a comparatively very small number belong to any racial hostilities or any contests between the native Irish and the English settlers; and that the vast majority of these atrocities are specially recorded as yearly incidents in intertribal contests between the native Irish Septs, or clans, or "bloods," amongst, and against, each other. These were continued exactly as they had been continued through the whole range of preceding Irish history. The names given of the conquerors and the conquered,—of the slaughtered and the slaughterers,—of the plunderers and the plundered,—of those cruelly murdered, and of the treacherous murderers, are all, in the immense

[*] "Irish Annals," "Four Masters," vol. ii.

majority of cases, purely Celtic names. It is not prominently a record of any destructive war between the Irish and the English. It is savage fighting between the "Kinel Connell" and the "Kinel Owen;" between the "O'Donnells" and the "O'Rourkes;" between the "O'Briens" and the "MacArthys;" between the "O'Neills" and the "MacLoughlins;" between the "O'Donnells" and the "Clan Dermot;" —it is of these pure Irish Celts, and a host of others with unspellable and unpronounceable names, that we read—tearing at each other's throats, ravaging each other's territories, slaughtering each other, men, women, and children, and leaving each other, so far as they survived, to perish with hunger in the bogs and woods of a ravaged land.

It is perfectly true that after 1170 we do find the English barons and people also warring and fighting more or less like those among whom they lived, and whose habits and manners they so unfortunately adopted. But on this head there are at least three general conclusions established by the Irish Annals, which are remarkable as bearing on the crowning fiction put forward by O'Connell and constantly repeated by Irish declaimers. The first is that, as already said, the old intertribal savagery between the native Irish is enormously the preponderating element in the list of horrors perpetrated and endured. The second is that, in almost every case in which the English settlers fought against

F

native Irish, they did so in close alliance with other Septs of the same race, who were often the instigators in the quarrel, the directors of the attack, and always the fiercest destroyers of the vanquished. The third is that, so far from the English settlers being able to dominate the native Irish as they pleased, or being the only one of the two races who could exercise and profit by the hereditary plundering usages of Irish warfare, it appears on the contrary that in numerous cases they were defeated by the native clans, who routed them often with great slaughter, and sometimes even succeeded in taking and burning their new castles of stone and lime. The truth is that not only during the century and a half succeeding the invasion of which I have been now speaking, but for the whole period of the five hundred and thirty-one years which elapsed between that event and the accession of James I. in 1603, the native Irish, partly by the Ersefication of the Colonists, partly by their own strength of arm and the difficulties of their country, not only held their own as regards the prevalence of their own old usages, but gradually recovered ground which they had lost, and at last succeeded in excluding English law from the whole of Ireland except a very small area near the Capital well known in Irish history as the Pale. All the classes, both native and English, whose rule and habits determined the condition of life for the people of Ireland over nine-tenths of the Island, had thus been combined—partly by passive resistance partly by conscious effort—in keeping up the desolating usages of their country against the continual but vain desire of English Sovereigns, and against their repeated attempts on various points, and at various times, to counteract the worst evils of the native system, and to protect its people from their effects.

So far, then, as this period of time and this ground of accusation against England is concerned, we have as clear an answer to give to Mr. Gladstone's question, "Who made the Irishman?" as we had for a like period before the invasion. It was Ireland and its usages that not only "made" the native Irishman, but to a large extent "made" also the Anglo-Irish who were settled in that country, and which reduced both races to a lower level of civilisation than that which prevailed in any other country in Europe. There were, nevertheless, even in such miserable conditions, a few symptoms of that immeasurable superiority in English laws over Irish usages and habits and traditions, which is the only element of truth in O'Connell's representation of the facts. There were at least some Anglo-Normans who did good service to their adopted country. Even in the building of their castles—bad as the use was to which those castles were often turned,—the very worst of them introduced an element of advance on the squalid houses of mud and clay which alone had sheltered even the native kings. But they did more and better than this. We have already seen how to their Danish cousins, and not to the native races, Ireland owes to this day all her principal commercial cities; and we are next told by the same truthful Irish historian that to the first great Anglo-Norman barons Ireland owes, not less, a large number of her existing towns of the second class. Those barons did not confine themselves merely to the creation of sub-feudatories. They also to a very large extent attempted to found municipal towns, and granted numerous charters in the hope of attracting colonists. "Thus Kilkenny and New Ross received the first charters from the great Earl Marshall. Galway and Clonmel were founded as towns by the De Burgs, Fethard by the Butlers, Athenry by the Berninghams."* This is a fact which implies a great deal. It shows that, in spite of all the demoralising influences under which the Anglo-Normans fell, owing to contact with a form of barbarism which offered to them many charms, because many temptations in the exercise of licentious power, the English settlers did nevertheless sow in Ireland the seeds of all that in other countries are the recognised indications of at least one of the beginnings of civilisation. To this must be added the important fact that the one thing on which the English Sovereigns did always insist was the right of appointing the Bishops of Irish Sees. In this way they established more and more, from the very first, the Anglo-Norman Church, to the gradual extinction of the semi-barbarous Celtic eccle-

* Richey's "Short History," p. 170.

siastical organisation. There are archæological sentimentalists, and there are theological parties, who may think this a matter of regret. I am not Protestant enough to deny, or to doubt the immense part taken by the Latin Church in the growing civilisation of Europe; nor am I sentimentalist enough to fancy in the Celtic or "Culdee" theology any elements of real value in its differences with Rome. The balance of advantage as regards all civil or secular affairs cannot be doubted. It is certain that, in that age at least, the English power was in this matter exercised for the best in the interests of the Irish people.

CHAPTER III.

EFFECT OF NATIVE IRISH LAWS AND USAGES.

BUT we must not forget that the charge of Mr. Gladstone against England is not the same as the charge which we have dealt with in the mouth of O'Connell. The two charges are the same only in the one fundamental assumption—which is not true—that subsequent to 1172, England governed Ireland in a sense which made her responsible for the domestic and economic condition of the Irish people. But beyond this fundamental assumption, those two Counsel for the prosecution take lines of argument which are not only different, but are diametrically opposite and contradictory. O'Connell's charge is invaluable in the broad assumption which it makes, and on which it entirely rests, that it was the Irish laws and usages which were the bane of Ireland, and that England's sin lay, not in imposing her own law, which was the highest and best, but in even permitting the old Irish customs to continue, and still more in so far as she may have winked at that continuance when clung to by her own colonists. Mr. Gladstone, so far as I know, has never taken this line of argument. The instincts of the adroit debater, and the necessities of his own new policy, have, indeed, not only held him back from admitting this great truth which underlies O'Connell's accusation, but they have led him to adopt the opposite and far more ignorant contention, that the crime of England lay in forcing her own "foreign" law on a people to whose condition it was not adapted, and whose ancient usages ought to have been conformed to and respected. Mr. Gladstone knows that this is by far the more popular idea of the two—the one which best lends itself to passionate declamation,—to the separatist policy, and to inflated fable. It would never do for him to admit that the law and usages of England, if universally established and resolutely enforced, would have been the salvation of Ireland in the twelfth century. It would never do for him to recall, as O'Connell did, the repeated occasions on which portions at least of the Irish people, both natives and settlers, had earnestly appealed for the protection of English law against the miseries to which they were exposed from what may be called the systematic anarchy and oppression of native usages. And so, on repeated occasions, his language has strictly conformed to the exigencies of his immediate position, and has repeatedly dwelt on the alien character of English legislation, and on the consequent woes it has entailed. Demonstrably true as the opposite doctrine of

O'Connell is, and founded as it was on his own knowledge as a lawyer, it was not the view which at all suited Mr. Gladstone's purpose. Moreover, the opposite contention being vague and general in its terms, and harmonising with popular passion and popular ignorance in Ireland, had this great advantage—that even the best and most temperate of Irish historians have used a great deal of wandering language which involves the same notion, and is more or less inspired by it.

Fortunately, here again, there can be no dispute about the facts. The only question which can arise is as to the terms and words in which those facts can be most consistently described. In dealing with this it is well to remember what the temptation is to which Irish writers are inevitably exposed. Apart altogether from the natural feelings of a local patriotism, there is in our time, perhaps in all time, a sentimental sympathy with primitive conditions of society, and along with this a great liability to mistake for conditions really primitive, other very different conditions which were not primitive at all, but, on the contrary, were the later products of a long development of corruption. And this is exactly what has happened in the case of Ireland. There is a vague almost incoherent notion that the conditions of society in Ireland in the twelfth century had continued to be those of what is called the "tribal" system, whereas the Anglo-Norman system is known to have been what is called the "feudal." And upon this supposed distinction an immense superstructure of inflated fable is erected. The sentimental imagination always goes back, on the very mention of the word "tribal," to those conditions of society in which every association of men, having even the semblance of a separate individuality, were brothers or cousins in blood, and all equal in such possessions as might belong to the group. Unfortunately, these are conditions of which we have no authentic record later than the Book of Genesis. And even that information is imperfect. We do not know how long it lasted. The charming pictures of Patriarchal times are vaguely identified with it, and then we think of the old tribes of Israel, or the early tribes of Latium. A hazy notion of universal brotherhood and equality is the attraction here. And no doubt, as compared with this assumed and theoretical past, the regular grades of subordination, and the rude dependence of everybody on some Lord or Chief, which we associate with the Feudal System, offers a very wide, and even an apparently violent, contrast.

But the moment we begin to inquire into the system prevailing in Ireland in historic times, which has been called "tribal," the whole conception on which this contrast is founded breaks down and vanishes like a dream. The real facts cannot be better stated than in the words of Dr. Richey: "The Irish tribe, at the earliest date at which we possess any distinct information upon the subject, had been altered from its original form: it had then reached the stage at which wealth, representing physical force, had become the acknowledged basis of political power and private right, and the richer members of the community were rapidly reducing the poorer freemen to a condition little better than serfdom; and at the date of its extinction, the tribe had been finally supplanted by the military retainers and tenants, or serfs, of the chiefs." * The condition of things among the Irish during all the centuries which belong to history before the Norman invasion, was a condition of Feudalism of the coarsest and rudest kind. That is to say, it was a condition of things in which every man held everything on which his life depended on the condition of absolute subordination to the chief, or lord, under whom he lived. The nobler part of feudalism, indeed, was wanting—the roof of the whole—the cope-stone of the building. Under the perfected feudal system of the Normans, the Chief himself was subordinate to some central Sovereign, to whom his relations, as well as his own relations to those below him, came more and more to be fixed and defined by an advancing system of Jurisprudence and of Law. In Ireland, this golden link of subordination to a central authority, and to common principles of limitation and definition in all rights and obligations—this link was wanting.

* "Short History," p. 42.

Each petty Chief was a law unto himself. His power was practically absolute, and the theoretical "tribesmen"—really clansmen—were entirely at his mercy—until in extreme cases extraordinary vices may have induced rebellion and civil war.

As to the notion of any equality amongst the mass of the Irish people,—such as fancy imagines between brother tribesmen,—such a thing did not exist in Ireland. The whole constitution of society was intensely aristocratic—full of men whose condition was abject, of others who were little removed from it, and of others, again, who were graded and ranked below and above each other strictly in proportion to their wealth in the rudest scale of semi-barbarous Possession. Deeply aristocratic in the value set on lineage, and in the power it enjoyed, it was next, and almost equally plutocratic in the privileges which comparative wealth conferred. The one possession in which almost all wealth consisted was that of cows. And such was the miserable poverty of the country, that the possession of even eight of the small cattle then known in Ireland was enough to place a man at once on at least the first rung of the aristocratic ladder. A man rich enough to have twenty-one cows "of his very own," as our children now say, was by comparison a Prince in the Irish Israel—for by virtue of that wealth he was reckoned among the "lords" of Irish society. "Aire" was the Celtic word by which that rank was designated, and as in this, as well as in all other branches of Aryan speech, the old root of "Bos" or "Bo" was the name of an ox or cow, so in the Irish terminology the possessor of twenty-one cows was entitled a "Cow-Lord" or a Bo-aire. And so on, up the ladder of power and wealth on which all political privileges depended in Ireland, the "Aires" or Lords were ranked one above another in consideration and importance.* It might be called a Bo-ocracy, under which the great mass of the people were actually serfs, or but little removed above that condition.

This is the condition of society which Irish factions, and sometimes English ignorance and declamation, have combined to imagine and represent, and mourn over as a condition of "Tribal" simplicity and equality which was cruelly broken up and oppressed by Anglo-Norman Feudalism. The looseness of thought, the indefiniteness of meaning, with which many men write and speak of what they call the "feudal system" is indeed extraordinary. Some politicians now habitually apply the expression to everything in old, or in existing laws, which they themselves disapprove and dislike. The universal and necessary dependence of men upon each other in all the relations of life—the dependence of the borrower on the lender in money, or in land, or in anything else which is not our own, but which we may need to hire—the dependence of ignorance upon knowledge—the

* Professor O'Curry's "Manners and Customs of the Ancient Irish," vol. ii. pp. 34-38.

dependence of labour upon capital, which is the dependence of value upon demand—the dependence of weakness upon strength,—all these forms and kinds of interdependence of some men upon others, are often stigmatised and denounced by anarchists as Feudalism. But, without turning aside to confusions such as these, we have to encounter continually in writings of just repute, a laxity of use as to what is called feudalism, which vitiates the most important practical conclusions. Thus, even Dr. Richey says that no two systems of social organisation can be more widely separated than the Feudal and the Tribal. This is quite true, if by "Tribal" we understand the Patriarchal as slightly developed into larger family groups, held together by the bonds of a near blood-relationship, and living together in security and in peace. But it is absolutely untrue, if by "Tribal" we mean such a condition of society as that which had prevailed in Ireland since before the dawn of history—a system of clans and septs recruited from all quarters, holding, in large numbers, serfs and bondsmen—themselves in vassalage under others—and living in a state of perpetual and internecine wars. That condition of society was "feudal" from top to bottom, and as different from the ideal state of primitive tribes as it is possible to conceive.

The essence of the feudal system is a very simple matter indeed. It is the necessity of protection on the one hand, and of service and allegiance as its price upon the other. This relation always is, and always must be, the foundation-stone of all societies which exist under conditions in which everything depends upon the sword—the sword for the defence of everything that is held,—the sword for the recovery of everything that has been lost,—the sword for establishing protective power,—the sword for destroying enemies, and for repelling aggression. Of course, in every nation that has ever existed, as regards the ultimate necessities of self-defence, this principle has been represented in its military organisation. But in great and powerful states it does not come home to individual men in their social, or even in their political, relations to each other. In all Empires, moreover, properly so called,—that is to say, in great monarchies, with subject and tributary states under them,—the same principle has always received a marked development in directly feudal forms. It was so under the Babylonian and Assyrian Empires. It was so in the Persian, Turkish, and Indian Empires, where it largely survives to the present day. Imperial Rome herself had taken a long step in the same direction when she endowed barbarian soldiers with lands on condition that they would defend the frontiers of the Empire. But in mediæval Europe its more full and detailed elaboration was due to the long absence of any adequate central authority, and the subdivision of power practically supreme among the many chiefs who led the northern nations. This intensified the universal sense of dependence on the sword. It brought it home to every man's door. In Ireland this subdivision was carried to the uttermost limit, and beyond it, of human endurance, for there it was coupled with hereditary enmities between clan and clan, sept and sept, which made the whole Island a constant pandemonium of savagery and destruction. Under such conditions the dependence of every man upon some lord or chief who could alone defend him, became, of necessity, more absolute than in any other country in Europe. To talk of tribal simplicity and equality among men in such a country would be an absurdity, even if we knew nothing of the details which contradict it. The more tribal it was, and the less national—that is to say, the more the depositories of power were not great kings but petty chiefs, each practically independent and unrestrained in his own country—the more intense and helpless must have been the feudal subordination and dependence of the great bulk of the people,—the more unmitigated by any general law, which could define rights or limit obligations.

Such, accordingly, we know to have been the fact, and such is the only, as it is the full, explanation of the assumption of O'Connell that the greatest crime to be alleged against England is that she did not sooner enforce her own higher and more regulated feudal organisation on the Irish people, to the complete supercession and abolition of their own feudalism, which was so desolating, because so unlimited and unrestrained. Dr. Richey says, truly enough, that what the English settlers practised in Ireland was not the feudal system at its best, but at its worst—severed from those higher elements of the system, which not only redeemed it from coarseness, but converted it into the greatest agency of civilisation and of law. But when he says,—or rather implies, for he hardly asserts it distinctly,—that the coarser feudalism was introduced into Ireland by the Anglo-Normans, he wanders widely from the fact, as given both by himself and by a crowd of the most purely native witnesses. What the English barons did was simply to rest more than satisfied with the feudalism which they found to have been long established in Ireland—a feudalism which vested in them a degree of power over their subordinate people which had many legal and customary restraints in England. The facts on this subject are notorious. They are the whole burden of the song of every Irish writer who undertakes to describe, however superficially, the condition of the people. We have only to look at that single obligation on the one side, and of privilege on the other, which became proverbial as specially Irish, the practice of "Coigne and Livery." This was the acknowledged right, habitually exercised, of every Irish Lord to quarter himself and his followers to an unlimited extent upon those who occupied land within his territory. It is perpetually referred to as a typical example of many similar usages which depressed the condition and perpetuated the poverty of the people. But it is not less a typical illustration of the principle on which all feudalism was founded, and of the rude necessities out of which it came to be. Its historical origin, and the only basis of justification on which it ever rested, was tersely and forcibly expressed in the proverbial motto of the poorer classes in Ireland, "Spend me, but defend me." This means, "All that I have depends on your protection:—I must give you as much of it as you like to take."

It would be difficult to put into fewer words the very essence of feudalism—that dependence of every man on some lord for all his possessory rights, which is the central idea of the whole system. Even therefore if it had been true that the words, and terms, and phrases, by which feudal relations were popularly expressed, had been unknown in Ireland, it would be an accountable error on the part of Irish historians to fail in recognising the identity of facts, and above all to confound such a system of not only subordination, but subjection, with any supposed primeval equality of men grouped in patriarchal tribes. But when we come to examine the evidence supplied by the best-informed Irish writers, we find that not only are the essential principles and conditions of feudalism the determining elements in all Irish history, but also that even the very root-words which represent those conditions, are of Celtic origin, and were familiarly used in Ireland to designate

G

the corresponding orders of society. The very word "Vassal," embodying, as no other word can do, the fundamental idea of the feudal relation, is a purely Celtic word, and was used to designate the most devoted dependants on Irish Chiefs. It is a word which expressed in English ears, as it still in a measure does, all that was most associated with the abuses of feudalism,—all that was most raw and crude in its beginnings and in its less fortunate developments.

I know that I have entered upon a thorny subject in taking a single step into the bypath of Celtic etymology. But at least the one step I have thus ventured upon has been taken under the very safest Irish guidance. Two eminent Irish Professors, in the Catholic University of Dublin, full of Irish patriotism in its best form, have combined their labours to present to us all that can be traced and known by the most laborious and learned investigation on the ancient habits and manners of their country. The "Lectures" of Professor O'Curry, together with an elaborate Introduction by Professor Sullivan, leave nothing to be desired in the picture they present of mediæval Irish life. As regards the mere language of feudalism, not only does Professor Sullivan identify, without doubt, the word "vassal" as purely Erse, but even the word "Feud" itself, respecting which there have been so many theories, he has equally little doubt in identifying with an ancient Celtic word, "Fuidirs," which, passing through many stages of meaning, came to designate specially men of native races who had been conquered, and who became, under victorious Chiefs, holders or occupiers of land at the will of their lords.* To a very large extent indeed they became Serfs bound to the soil. Speaking of the name attached to this class of men, "Fuidirs," Professor Sullivan says, "I have no doubt it was the true origin of the word 'Feodum,'" † adding that languages foreign to the Celtic adopted the word in forms variously modified "to describe almost the very same kind of tenure already existing among the people where the word 'Feodum,' and all the other forms of that term, came first into use."

But this is not all. No writer has torn asunder more ruthlessly the inflated fictions which represent the system of society under the Irish septs and clans as one which had even the slightest flavour of the supposed simplicity and equality of primeval tribes. He depicts and describes in detail, on the contrary, a condition of things in which division, subdivision, inequality, subordination, and subjection penetrated society through and through. In the first place, the Irish clans in the twelfth century, of whom he speaks conventionally as being the natives, were nothing but a victorious aristocracy, who held an older and a conquered population in bondage. They were not, any more than other races, autochthones. They were not even

* O'Curry's "Lectures," Introduction, pp. 224, 225.
† Ibid., p. 226.

indigenous since times that are wholly unknown. The details of the conquest effected by the dominant Irish Clans, anciently called Scoti, are indeed obscure. But traditions, which rest on much historical corroboration, have compelled the substantial agreement and assent of the most learned writers on Irish history, to conclusions which make it certain that the Irish Clans, as we know them in the Middle Ages, had exactly the same title, but no other and no better, to the possession of their country, than the title of any other invading and conquering race in Europe, or than the title of any yet later invaders who might succeed in repeating the same process. Moreover, the same evidence and the invariable results of the like causes have convinced the same writers that the numerical proportion of the subject races to those who ruled over them came to be so large that, in fact, the great bulk of those who would now be called the people of Ireland, were reduced to serfdom—to the condition, that is to say, of holding everything that belonged to them on conditions of tribute, or of service, or of both, together with the usual status of serfs—that of being bound to the soil.

But this universal cause and origin of inequality in the social and political condition of every country in Europe, was reinforced in Ireland by the most elaborate system of distinctions of rank and wealth between individuals among the dominant race itself, which do not seem to have had any parallel elsewhere. When we try to follow Professor Sullivan, for example, through his learned and careful analysis of the good old Irish society before the pretended conquest, we find ourselves lost in a perfect maze of names and designations for the different grades into which men were divided, and subdivided, under and above each other. Those names are not only unpronounceable, and unspellable, —which would be a small matter as the result of the mere linguistic peculiarities of the Celtic tongue,— but, what is much more remarkable, they are almost as untranslatable. The English language and the English mind, labour in vain to follow the number and variety of degrees under which Irish human beings could be separately ranged and ranked in a society which was even nominally one. But wherever a translation of those names can be effected through evident points of comparison and of contact with the other military societies of Mediæval Europe, we find substantially the same elements out of which the system of Feudalism arose—only with this difference, that they were much less civilised—much less modified by the influence of that splendid jurisprudence of the Roman people, which even its barbarian conquerors had learnt to respect, and the great monuments of which had been largely translated into their own tongue.

The Celtic Clans in Ireland, cut off from this great source and fountain of organic power, and a prey to continual feuds and fightings, went on for centuries developing nothing except all those more and more savage conditions of society, which are the inevitable result of everything depending, not only on the sword, but on the sword in the hands of nobody more important than petty Chiefs, and Kinglets. And so it comes out, as the net result of Professor Sullivan's account, that those Irishmen, who were in the enjoyment of such political and social rights as then existed at all in a so-called Irish Tribe, were a mere fraction of the people,—all others living in various degrees of subjection down to the lowest serf. Thus Professor Sullivan's account of the "Different Classes of Society in Ancient Ireland" occupies some twenty pages of closely printed matter devoted to explain the position of some nine classes, of which only three "could be said to have political rights, that is, a definite position in the tribe;" * and all these classes, without any exception, we are expressly told, were equally under the protection, as retainers, of the "Flaths," or Chiefs—the very highest of these classes, who were called "Aires," holding their lands of their lords in lieu of suit and service rendered, and the payment of certain feudal rents.†

It is true that these graded classes were not castes in the Indian sense of that word:—that is to say, a man might rise from a lower to a higher class. But it was equally true that he might fall from a higher to a lower grade. And it is farther true that

* Introduction, p. 129. † Ibid.

the process of falling was much more easy than the process of rising. The system, besides being intensely aristocratic, was almost as predominantly plutocratic. A man's wealth almost alone determined his position. And as there was, among the ancient Irish, practically but one form of wealth—the primitive one of cattle—the system may be described as a Cow-ocracy, or, as we have seen, it was to some extent even actually called a Bo-ocracy. There is no doubt as to the meaning of the class of nobles called Bo-aires in the old Irish social classification; because the very same word, with the same root-meaning, survives to this day in Scotland, where it is the custom in some counties for one man to hire a whole dairy of cows from another man who owns them as a farmer, and to undertake the marketing of the produce for a stipulated rent per head of the cows. This man is locally called the Bo-er, corrupted into "Booer," and it is possible, perhaps probable, that the common word for a Dutch farmer, Boer, is nothing but another survival of the same word. However this may be, the essential fact as to the ancient Irish is that the social and economic, and even legal condition of every man was mainly determined by his wealth in cattle, and that the predatory habits of the clans as against each other must have made the tenure of rank, depending on this profession, a tenure of extreme precariousness. Accordingly, Dr. Sullivan explains* that as a necessary

* Introduction.

consequence of continual ravages all over the country, the constant gravitation of all men downwards from comparative wealth as estimated in those days, to the greatest poverty, was a never-ceasing force dragging down all the subordinate classes into more and more abject dependence on the Chiefs, who alone could possibly protect them.

Such is the system which many Irish agitators, and some deluded English politicians think, or pretend to think, was a system of charming tribal sympathy and equality, which " we " broke down by the introduction of what they call feudalism into Ireland. Dr. Sullivan and other really learned and honest Irish historians are not responsible, except by occasional and inconsistent observations, for this gross delusion. He says emphatically, "that the state of things in Ireland was no exception to what conquest has always produced among nations—privileged classes and serfs or slaves, —may be inferred, not only from the number of distinct immigrations which our legendary history records, but also from the complete development of a tribal system, *aristocratically organised*."* Nor does he fail to show how in Ireland, even in the oldest and most primitive days before the succession to chiefry had become hereditary, eligibility to the position of Chief was an eligibility attached to birth. It was only out of a limited number of families, to whom legend attributed a divine origin, that the Chiefs could be elected;" †

---

* Introduction, p. 79. † Ibid., p. 100.

and Dr. Sullivan goes the length of saying that, "properly speaking, it was only the noble families that were *of* the Clan—the tenants and retainers, when not related by blood to the Chief, only *belonged to it.*" Neither does Dr. Sullivan deny—on the contrary, he fully admits—that whatever original elements of inequality existed in the very nature of the clan system and organisation, were aggravated in Ireland by its perpetual wars—during the course of which a larger and a larger portion of the whole people did of necessity fall lower and lower, from the enormous losses of property which they entailed, and from the increasing need which all men felt for placing themselves under complete conditions of service and dependence.

But the most inveterate part of all this delusion about the old "tribal" system of the Irish, and the part of it which is most hugged and cherished, is that which is identified with the delusion that private property in land was unknown till " we " introduced it at the supposed conquest along with the rest of the " feudal system." Dr. Sullivan and Dr. O'Curry both repudiate and expose this delusion—as well they may. Some of the most patent facts in Irish history are sufficient to contradict it absolutely. There is a handsome volume called "The National Manuscripts of Ireland," in which we find, in regular feudal form, three Charters of land given by Irish Chiefs and Kings, and written in the Erse or Gaelic language. One of these is a

Charter,—a grant of land—to a family of monks, given ninety-two years before the invasion of Henry II. And we know that in all countries the first granting of land in the form of written Charters was always the mere beginning of formal records, and not at all the beginning of the transactions thus for the first time recorded. All the first Charters were, and purported to be, a mere recognition, in a new form, of rights and practices of immemorial usage and antiquity. As regards Ireland, it is notorious that Dermot, King of Leinster, who invited the first Anglo-Welsh adventurers, granted to them land as part of his treaty-obligations with them for their aid in recovering his own possessions.

Irish writers, indeed, pretend to find fault with this grant as having been beyond the right of any Irish King. But in this contention, they found only on theoretical and purely imaginary conceptions about ancient tribal rights in Ireland, which are without any sound historical evidence, even as regards the earliest times, and are wholly inapplicable to the usages which, in the twelfth century, had been long established. The grants given by Dermot to the first of the Irish Geraldines, were obviously made in pursuance of those rights of disposal over landed estates which had been exercised and recorded, nearly a century before, in favour of the Monks of Kells in Meath. Nothing can be more definite, nothing can bear more clear evidence of the transaction being one of a familiar kind, than the grant by Dermot to Maurice Fitzgerald and Robert Fitzstefen of the town of Wexford " and two cantreds of land in its neighbourhood."* Moreover, we know that these grants by Dermot were afterwards recognised and sanctioned by the titular King of all Ireland, who seems to have still retained some shadow of a recognised authority in such matters. Farther, we see incidentally, from these authentic Irish Charters, that land had then commonly become possessed by individuals, and had been bought and sold for definite sums of money. In the Charter of 1080, the title given by it to the grantees proves by the careful record of the fact that it had been the property of an individual, who sold it and had held it "as his own lawful land." †

There is, moreover, much older written evidence than this Gaelic Charter of 1080. The "Book of Armagh" is one of the greatest treasures of Irish Archæology. The writing in which we now have it has been pretty clearly identified as belonging to the ninth century, and it is known to have been then only a copy of an older manuscript of the seventh century. In any case, whatever its precise date may have been, it contains much of the very oldest contemporary evidence we possess on the condition of Ireland in what has been called its "heroic

---

* "The Earls of Kildare," p. 5.
† "National Manuscripts of Ireland," part iv. p. 45, and No. lix.

age." Yet in this Book we have the following entry—"Cummen and Brethan purchased Ochter-n-Achid, with its appurtenances, both wood and plain, and meadow, together with its habitation and its garden."* This is clearly the purchase of an Estate precisely like the transactions recorded in Charters of four hundred years later.

But, in truth, such formal evidence is superfluous. The exclusive right of use over certain areas of land vested in groups of men, and within those groups, in the individuals of which the groups are composed, according to the different kinds of use prevalent at the time and place, has been the universal claim and possession of mankind, whether savage or civilised, since the world began. For this right they have always had to pay, often heavily, by some sacrifice or some exertion. Under whatever name this payment passes, and to whatever kind of use it is applied,—whether hunting, pastoral, or agricultural,—the principle is the same in all cases. Some organised defence of this right is a necessity of its enjoyment. The imaginary condition of tribes, patriarchal and pastoral, feeding their flocks upon a vacant land, with "none to make them afraid," is a vision and a dream. It certainly is as wide as the poles asunder from the condition of the Irish Celts from the earliest dawn either of history or tradition. The particular organised system of defence upon which in Ireland

* Sullivan's Introduction, p. 89.

every man depended for all he had, and for life itself, was a system which made the heaviest demands upon him. Unlimited exactions were the price of any tolerable security. Constant liability to be "eaten out of house and home" was the permanent and paramount condition. With those who wielded this supreme power, the supreme disposal of land necessarily rested. This fact could not fail to be recognised in the practical transactions of life. Accordingly, those Irish historians who have been really learned in the ancient lore of their country, have felt that in the whole structure of Society as the oldest literature and tradition present that structure to their view, there are to be recognised all the same essential conditions which marked corresponding stages in the barbarism and in the civilisation of the other northern races.

It is now thirty years since Dr. Sullivan wrote his elaborate Introduction to the "Lectures" of Professor O'Curry upon the ancient Irish. Since that time much has been written and much has been clearly ascertained, which is at irreconcilable variance with the prevalent but vague impression about the communal ownership of land among the various barbarian races who overwhelmed the Roman Empire. Yet Dr. Sullivan, from his intimacy with the facts of the earliest Irish history, has anticipated much of the results which have now been well established. In our own Island the researches of Mr. Seebohm, and more recently the nearly exhaustive investigations of Mr. Fustel de Coulanges, in France,—researches which extend over the whole of Europe,—have made it evident that whatever may have been the state of things in ages which are quite beyond the reach of history—ages when all our ancestors were nothing more than nomad families—it is certain that the division of ownership into individual possession had been established, and often highly developed, at the earliest dates of which we have any certain knowledge. Moreover, the amended doctrine, now generally accepted on this subject, reconciles to a great extent the real facts with the mistaken interpretation which had long been put upon them.

That mistake lay in confounding communal occupation and communal methods of cultivation, with communal ownership. But these are wholly different things. Communal methods of cultivation, communal pasturages, and communal customs, even as to the little ploughing that was practised in the wretched agriculture of the early Middle Ages, were indeed almost universal. The individual property of most men consisted chiefly of cattle, and these grazed of necessity, when there were no enclosures, in common with the cattle of all neighbours in the same township. But this has nothing whatever to do with the question, whether all these men did not owe their common right of pasturage—common as among themselves, but exclusive as regards all outsiders—to the grant or leave of some common lord or supreme owner. It is these two questions which have been long confounded. Individual ownership has been denied merely because there was little or no individual pasturing, or even continued individual cultivation. But on close investigation it comes out clearly enough that in all cases every man had to pay for his share in the common rights to some chief, or lord, or king, some dues, or services which were in the nature of rent, and which very often represented a far larger share of the produce than is, or can be paid, by a modern tenant farmer. The payment of these dues and services is a universal fact in the earliest history of Ireland. They are inseparably connected with the idea of that exclusive right of disposal over certain areas of land, whether small or large, in which individual ownership consists.

Accordingly, Dr. Sullivan says, "I believe that the right of individuals, among the Irish and so-called Celtic inhabitants of Great Britain, to the absolute possession of part of the soil, rests upon as certain, perhaps more certain, evidence, than among the Anglo-Saxon and other Germanic peoples; and farther, that, as might have been anticipated among so closely allied branches of the Aryans, the general principles of the laws regulating the occupation of land were practically the same among all the early northern nations, whether called Celts or Germans."* "In Ireland," he farther

* Introduction, p. 138.

tells us, "the ownership of land constituted, as it does now, the special characteristic of the 'Flath' or lord." That there always was and always must have been a part—and a large part—of the territory of the whole Sept not occupied by the Chief himself, with his more immediate retainers, is true. But Dr. Sullivan tells us that even over this part he held "dominion," and considering what "dominion" meant in those days, and among a people so dependent on the supreme military power—considering that all that we now think of as the State was then concentrated in the Chief—considering, too, that tribute and rent seem to have been a universal condition of life to all,—we can well understand how little that distinction came to on which antiquarian theorists lay so much stress. But so far as the communal habits of pasturage and of cultivation were concerned, they remained the same in all cases. Under the man, for example, whose lands were bought, and given to the Monastery of Kells,—and of which it is expressly said in the Gaelic Charter of 1080 that they were his "own lawful" lands,—there may have been, and there no doubt were, occupying tenants of the various grades into which Irishmen were then divided, according to their birth or their wealth in cows, and these must have lived under the same communal usages, which were universal in the Middle Ages.

But perhaps the most extraordinary delusion about Irish land is that which dwells upon the idea of irremovability as attaching to such subordinate tenures as were possessed. It is an idea, indeed, largely founded on some very certain and very obvious facts. And yet it is extraordinary because of the equally obvious misinterpretation of those facts. It is true that the poorer classes in Ireland, in the early Middle Ages, were to a large extent stationary, because they were to a corresponding extent in a condition of bondage. They were bound to the soil, and bound not less to render dues and services for the protection which they enjoyed under a bondage which was often voluntarily adopted. This was one great reason and cause for the irremovability which has been made so much of. But there was another reason and another cause equally powerful, and even more wide in its operation. In the military ages men were valued for nothing except their hands and arms as usable in fighting. There was generally no reason in the world why any chief or landowner should prefer one man to another, except for physical strength; and some average number of weaklings had to be counted on in every population. In those days and under those conditions of society, there was nothing whatever that could induce a chief or great landowner to move his poorer dependants. One man as well as another could employ a serf to herd his cows. One man as well as another could employ the same agency to take his turn in such miserable ploughing as was then known among the people. The great aim and object

H

of every territorial lord was not to have poor dependants whom he could remove, but to have such dependants who could not even remove themselves. On the other hand, those dependants themselves had nowhere to go to except to place themselves, as soon as they could, under the same kind of service and correlative protection under some other chief. Nevertheless it is a curious fact that even in ancient Ireland there seems to have been a large class of what we should now call agricultural, or rather pasturing tenants, who were not only theoretically removable, but were actually and systematically removed whenever, from any cause, it was convenient for the owner or chief to change his tenants. This was the very large and ever-increasing class of men who were too poor to have any cows of their own. They hired the cows as well as the land, and Dr. O'Curry tells us that the term of their tenure was only seven years, at the end of which term they had to give up both the cows and the land—the cows in undiminished number and quality.* In short, he says that within the tribal territory then, just as within all national territory now, "individuals held inclusive property in land, and entered into relations with tenants for the use of the land, and these again with under-tenants, and so on, much as we see it in our own days." †

This testimony from one of the most learned writers on the ancient constitution of Irish society, effectually

* O'Curry's "Lectures," vol. ii. p. 34. † Ibid.

disposes of the vague declamatory language held by politicians on this subject. The truth is that in Ireland the mass of the people were not better off, but greatly worse, in all these economic conditions, than any other people in Europe. In Ireland, because of the long endurance of lawless conditions, the steps of development were from a comparative personal freedom to more and more universal subordination and relative servitude. The wonderful thing about popular Irish oratory upon the subject in modern times, is that the best Irish historians have here also, as in other cases, seen and stated clearly enough the facts which demonstrate the absurdity of transferring the language and ideas of the nineteenth, or even of the seventeenth century, to the conditions of any of the centuries between the Christian era and the Norman invasion. Thus Dr. Sullivan very significantly says that the irremovability of the poorer classes from the home of their birth or of their enlistment, and even of classes far above the poorest, was the inevitable result of the immediate interest which the Chiefs had in keeping up their military force. "Adscription to the Glebe," he says, "only gradually grew up in Europe from the difficulty the lords experienced in keeping tenants." *

In the rest of Europe, indeed, in proportion as ancient towns and municipalities revived, or were anew created, freemen might be easily tempted to move away from the territory of oppressive lords. In Ireland, there

* Introduction, p. 114.

was no such resource. But on the other hand the universal prevalence of imminent danger to life and to such property as existed, made the condition of removability from the soil as little coveted on the one side, as it would have been thought of on the other. "All freemen," says Dr. Sullivan, "in the olden time in Ireland, not even excepting the privileged crafts, such as goldsmith, blacksmith, and some others, as well as professional classes and Bo-aires (Cow-owners), were retainers of the Chiefs or Lords."* Theoretically, indeed, "freemen" were free: but even they had the conditions of dependence imposed upon them by the circumstances of society in Ireland during all the centuries of its early history. For it cannot be too emphatically repeated that the historical evidence for the perfect continuity of its miserable history from the earliest times, is as overwhelming as it is authentic. If the "Annals of the Four Masters" stood alone, they would be enough to prove the facts. But these Annals do not stand alone. In the "Book of Leinster"—another of the most ancient Gaelic Manuscripts of Ireland, transcribed from much older documents in the twelfth century, we have a collection of the antique historic tribes of the Irish Celts. They go back to the Christian era. They have been classified under the following heads—the titles of which tell their own tale:—"Destructions," "Cattle-Spoils," "Wooings," "Battles," "Incidents of Caves,"

* Introduction, p. 110.

"Voyages and Navigations," "Tragedies and Death Feasts," "Sieges," "Adventures," "Elopements," "Slaughters," "Expeditions," "Progresses," and "Conflagrations."* Such was the whole history of Ireland for twelve centuries and a half before the Normans came, and such it continued to be with little or no mitigation for three or four centuries later—until the country was at last really conquered, and the Irish were admitted to the same external influences to which all other European nations owe their final civilisation.

To speak of irremovability from the soil, as it existed in Ireland, as a boon to the people, or as an indication of happy conditions which were subsequently lost, is one of the strangest misconceptions which has ever arisen, even from that most fertile source of confusion—the transfer of words and phrases from modern times to an older world in which they had a very different significance. The more clearly Irish orators can prove the late date down to which the idea and the practice of irremovability attached to the poorer classes in Ireland, the more clearly they will prove the very late date at which two of the first conditions of civilisation were established in their country. The first of these two conditions is the recognition of personal freedom as regarded military services. The second is the recognition of personal merit as regards the pursuits of industry. In the battles of spears and shields, irremovability was the badge of bondage. In

* "National Manuscripts of Ireland," part ii. p. 30.

agriculture, it was the badge of stagnation and of the absence of all improvement. There is no evidence, however, that in this matter the Norman invasion did either good or harm. In so far as a new element of strength was added to Irish chiefry, it did probably tend to improvement, because each chief in proportion to his strength was better able to defend his own territory, and so to afford some better opportunity to such settlers as may have introduced some elements of knowledge and skill into the archaic agriculture of Ireland. But not much stress can be laid on this— because even in England, in those ages, both pastoral and agricultural industry were in a very rude stage. All that can be said with certainty is that nothing was made worse, and some things must, of necessity, have been made a great deal better.

The moment we come to examine any of the specific cases in which the English Government is said to have been the cause of any injury to the condition of the people, as compared with their former state, the accusation breaks down completely. There is one case in which this charge has the support of Dr. Sullivan, which is an excellent example. It is a charge founded on the fact that the English law never recognised the archaic usages of succession to property in Ireland, which were akin to the old usage of Gavelkind in Kent. Yet Dr. Sullivan himself, as usual, supplies all the facts, and even a good many of the arguments, which prove that the Irish usages, in this matter, were in those ages always injurious to the people amongst whom they had become established, and were especially injurious in Ireland. In very rude and prehistoric conditions of society, such as those which prevailed among the northern nations before their great migrations,—when no property existed except some cattle, household utensils, and weapons of war,—the subdivision of such property indiscriminately, or with complicated discriminations, which were perhaps worse, might possibly be comparatively harmless. Yet Dr. Sullivan explains very truly that even then the system could only be worked by a resort to that extensive emigration in quest of new settlements which was the one great relief, in those times, to hunger and poverty at home. He explains how, as regards the Teutonic tribes, upon the Continent, the inconveniences of increasing subdivision were early arrested by the adoption of primogeniture. He quotes the opinion of a distinguished writer on the Anglo-Saxons, who thinks that the long survival of the ruder custom among them, had so weakening an effect that it facilitated their conquest by the Normans.* He confesses that we only know the Irish custom in a much more archaic form than even among the kindred races, and he gives such an account of it in detail as to show at a glance how incompatible it must have been with any progress in wealth. But in his candour as an historian he goes farther than this. He

* Introduction, p. 179.

frequently admits that "the custom of gavelkind, by the great subdivision of property which it effected, tended to deprive the majority of freemen of all political rights under a constitution where property was an essential element of political power." *

Yet in spite of these truthful representations of the historian, the feelings of the Irish sentimentalist prevail again; and in referring to the fact that English law never did, as indeed it never could, recognise those Irish usages, and, in 1605, did at last expressly repudiate them,—he breaks out into the usual and most illogical declamation—averring that this repudiation "more than any other measure, not excepting the repeated confiscations, injured the country, and gave rise to most of the present evils of the Irish law system." † Wonderful as this sentence is in contrast with what has gone before, it is perhaps even more curious in connection with some additional historical facts which he adds in the same paragraph. One of these is this emphatic testimony to the weakening and impoverishing effect of the Irish gavelkind— that when the Protestant Parliament was inventing weapons of offence against the Roman Catholics, they pulled this most effective of all weapons out of the old Irish armoury, and enacted, as one of the Penal Laws, that the Estates of all Roman Catholics should be made subject to the old Irish custom of Gavelkind for the very purpose of preventing their acquiring

* Introduction, p. 183. † Ibid., p. 184.

wealth, or founding families. Another fact Dr. Sullivan records in the same connection, with apparently an equal blindness to its significance— namely this—that in Wales also, as well as in Kent, the custom of Gavelkind was abolished by Statute under Henry VIII.; and he adds this significant observation: "But the rights of the tenants do not appear to have been injured by the new legislation." Of course not. It was not better, but a great deal worse for the poorer classes, who were only tenants, to be placed under petty landlords rather than under greater landlords. The uncertain exactions, which were the great curse of Ireland, were of necessity more oppressive and ruinous to the mass of the population in proportion to the weakness of their landlords—to their poverty—to their inability to defend their dependants against the raids of enemies, and to their own dependence upon, and need of exhausting contributions.

We could have no better example than this of the inveterate unreasonableness of even the best Irishmen in ascribing all the evils of their country to external influences and causes, and of their blindness to those which were of purely native origin. Dr. Sullivan is no mere declaimer—no mere mob-orator—no mere unscrupulous or passionate party leader. As an historian he is in the highest degree capable, exact, and honest. He gives us all the facts. He tells us of the custom of inheritance to property—that known as Gavelkind—which every other European race abandoned as soon as a settled civilisation began to be established. He shows how it operated in weakening the social and political organisation wherever it was suffered to remain. He tells us how it was deliberately abolished, where it still lingered in England, at the request of those who were most immediately affected by it. He tells us how it was at the same time abolished universally in Wales, and specially notes that the abolition of it had no injurious effects on the condition of the people. Passing to his own country, he shows how disastrous its operation had been there in breaking down all natural barriers against the oppression of arbitrary power, and reducing the people to one dead level of helpless poverty and dependence. He tells us that those effects were so thoroughly recognised and known that the revival of this ruinous custom and its special application to Roman Catholics was one of the sources of the Penal Laws. And yet in the face of all these facts and inevitable inferences, he suddenly turns round in a passing observation to blame England for not having kept up this custom, so penal in its effects against the whole people of Ireland.

In comparison with this charge against England, O'Connell's contradictory charge is reasonableness itself,—the charge, namely, that she had not, centuries before, applied to Ireland the benefits of her own higher law and civilisation. And although, for other reasons already stated here, this accusation can be repelled, yet as regards this particular Irish custom of succession it is true that when England did at last, at the close of the sixteenth and beginning of the seventeenth century, really conquer, and begin to govern Ireland, on the principles recommended by O'Connell, her statesmen saw and denounced this old native custom as one of the main causes of Irish poverty and of Irish stagnation. Sir John Davies, in his celebrated Report, declared it to have been a custom which would have been enough to ruin Hell, if it had been established in the kingdom of Beelzebub. And it is a curious fact that all individual Irishmen whose interests or whose intelligence had led them to look at this, and other closely related customs of the country in respect to property, had long been unanimous in their desire to escape from the whole system. Especially did the Irish ecclesiastics of all divisions of the Church, whether Celtic or Latin, bear unconscious but striking testimony to their sense of the ruinous character of all the native customs, and invariably made a point in all the charters of land which they accepted to stipulate expressly that the land was to be held free from all the "evil customs of the Irish"—or as it was tersely described in Latin, "absque omnibus malis consuetudinibus Hibernicis."

If Irishmen in our day have no other accusation to make against England than that she would not sanction those "evil customs" when she did get the power of government into her own hands, we may well be satisfied with the result, and may turn with good hope to the work of dealing with the extraordinary delusion of men, even so eminent as Dr. Sullivan—that what are called the evils of the Irish "land system" have had any connection whatever with the abolition of customs which have been admitted by Irishmen themselves, in so many forms of action and confession, to have been barbarising and ruinous in their effects. To this subject I shall return—in thorough agreement with O'Connell's opposite contention—merely observing here that Mr. Gladstone has adopted the easy method of all declaimers—that of denouncing England for having introduced "foreign" and alien laws, without any attempt to prove or to trace any rational connection between the alleged cause and the effects. In the mean time, and before returning to this subject, I claim to have established the fact that, so far as concerns the domestic government and social condition of the Irish people, the great operative causes continued to be, after the pretended conquest seven hundred years ago, precisely what they had been for twelve centuries before that date—causes deeply seated in the customs, manners, and political divisions of the Celtic Clans, and that, so far as these causes are concerned, they have nobody to blame but themselves, and those outward circumstances of geographical position which isolated them from the main stream of European civilisation, of race-mixtures, and of conquest. That every people should be governed according to its own ancient usages and customs is a general proposition which may be plausible. That all old usages and customs are good for the people amongst whom they have come to be established, considering the corruption of mankind, and the way in which man has tortured himself all over the world, is a proposition that is, on the face of it, absurd. That the very same Irishmen who admit the disastrous effects of the old customs of their country, should nevertheless ascribe all later evils to the conduct of England in not upholding them—this is an exhibition of inconsistency which may be interesting and even pathetic when we trace it to the national influence of a vague patriotic sentiment. But when we find this sentimental nonsense passionately expressed by English politicians, who have no similar excuse, it is high time to expose its true character.

CHAPTER IV.

HISTORY CONTINUED FROM A.D. 1172 TO THE END OF THE FIFTEENTH CENTURY.

But now at last we come to a cause of Ireland's later woes which does stand in close connection with the events of 1172. But it is a close connection forged mainly—in one aspect forged entirely—by Irish hands. That connection is simply this—that, from the moment that the King of England became the Feudal "Lord of Ireland," all his enemies were tempted to attack him on his Irish side. If the Irish had been loyal to their Liege, according to the code of honour and obligation admitted in that relation and in those ages, this temptation on the part of the enemies of England would have done no harm to Ireland. The Island was practically inaccessible from the European continent; and Ireland would have remained far more unconquerable by the enemies of the King of England than she was by that King himself. Obviously therefore the danger could only arise out of the complicity of the Irish, or of some considerable part of them, with the enemies of the Sovereign to whom they owed allegiance. Or if we choose to say that it is absurd to claim as against the Irish any duty of allegiance, even although they had accepted it and sworn to it;—if we choose to say that —looking to the habits of those military ages—the Irish had a right to throw off their allegiance if and whenever they could, and to lend themselves to the enemies of their acknowledged King,—even thus, the case remains the same. There is much to be said for this view. Those were not the days of Peace Societies, and Courts of Arbitration. Everything, all over the world, hung upon the sword. But if this is the view taken, it must be taken consistently. If the Irish had a right to ally themselves with the enemies of England, at least England had the corresponding right to do her very best to defeat and punish all such alliances. Nor in the light of history and of reason as applied to all the results to civilisation which were involved, can it be doubted for a moment that this was, on the part of England, as much a duty as it was a necessity and a right. She bore in her hands a great future for mankind in government and law. The Irish bore in their hands no interest whatever of this kind—so much so that even their greatest leading advocate in our own time, Daniel O'Connell, could say nothing worse of England than that she had not enforced her own system of jurisprudence at a time when she could not possibly effect any such design. I lay stress on this matter here, because, as we shall see, it is the key to the whole history of the relations between England and Ireland from the twelfth century down to the middle of the eighteenth—from 1172 to 1750. It is even the key to the traditions, as well as to the thoughts, and feelings, and anticipations which affect, and legitimately affect us still.

The first occasion on which this great cause and source of evil is seen working is an occasion typical of all its worst effects. For nearly a century and a half after Henry II. had received the homage of the Irish Chiefs, the five succeeding Kings of England had no enemy who was in a position to attack them through Ireland. On the contrary, England was in a position to use the Irish for her own aggressive purposes. The Anglo-Norman element, both fresh settlers and old Ersefied settlers, was on the whole gaining ground in Ireland by reason of its inherent superiority in many ways. The native Irish were always ready to lend themselves to any fighting. The English Kings continually called on the Irish Barons for aids and military services in all their foreign wars.* And so it happened that when Edward I. undertook the conquest of Scotland he was able to draw upon Ireland for a very large contingent to his army. No less than ten thousand foot, besides cavalry, was his summons in 1295. Such a force

* Richey's "Short History," p. 181.

could not be raised out of the English Settlers alone, who must have themselves relied largely on their native Irish retainers. The Irish of both breeds did their very best to rivet the yoke of England on the rising kingdom which had been established in Scotland by the happy union and common allegiance of both the Celtic and Teutonic races there.

When, after Edward's death, his feebler son tried to complete his father's enterprise, the same combination defeated him in the signal overthrow of Bannockburn, in 1312. And it is a curious and significant indication of the perfect consciousness of both kingdoms as to the weakest points in their respective armours, that when peace was made on the footing of the independence of Scotland being recognised, both Sovereigns pledged themselves not to assail, or to intrigue against each other through alliance with the Celtic Clans. For England these were represented by Ireland taken as a whole. For Scotland they were represented by the Hebridean Islanders. And so accordingly, the moment quarrels and war broke out again, the English monarchy and nation was at once attacked through Ireland. The Irish themselves were excited by the exhibition of English weakness. The Scots were excited by the possibility of wresting from their old enemy that country which had helped him to subdue them. The Scoto-Norman knights, one of whom had become King of Scotland, were not less excited by the hope of founding a New Kingdom in the

West. But there was one fatal flaw in this conspiracy against England. And it was a flaw due to the ineradicable effects of the old Irish character. Scotland had won her independence by a thorough and hearty union between the strongest and best of her many races, and by the noble ambition of setting up a central and a civilised government. The Irish proceeded, as they had always done, by falling back upon racial animosities, and a fierce desire to expel the very best of the materials out of which alone they could build up a civilised government.

Dr. Richey tells us that the native Irish chieftains entered into their agreement with King Robert Bruce for the purpose "of expelling the English;" and in their long letter to the Pope they expressly mentioned the Celtic blood of Edward Bruce as the natural explanation of their choice. They describe King Robert as "a descendant of some of the most noble of our own ancestors."* If we are to allow ourselves to be irrationally affected in our readings and judgments of history, by either racial, family, or even the lower forms of national sentiment, I should heartily sympathise with the famous attempt of Edward Bruce to do in Ireland a work at least superficially like the great work his brother had done in Scotland. Scotchmen who, like myself, have the same special share that he had in the ancient Celtic blood of the Irish Scoti—who admire as we all do the heroic character

* "Short History," p. 195.

of "The Bruce"—who are disposed to remember with resentment the ready help which Irishmen then gave, and often have since given, to the enemies of Scottish liberty,—we might be tempted to cherish a natural sympathy with the invasion of Ireland by the Bruces in 1315. But for those who look in History, above all things, for the steps of human progress, and who desire to know the causes of its arrestment or decline, it is impossible to be guided by such childish sympathies. It is, indeed, as idle to blame the Scottish King, as to condemn the Irish chiefs and clans. If indeed we were to carry the judgments of our own time back into the history of the past, it would be impossible not to denounce the war that followed as having been, on the part of the Irish, a war quite as wicked as it was disastrous to themselves. At the same time it must be observed that although it must be so judged as regards the Irish, it is impossible to deny that King Robert the Bruce had a legitimate cause of war even according to the most civilised rules of modern times. Dr. Richey very fairly says that one object he must have aimed at was to cut off the supplies of men on which England depended for a large part of the forces with which she fought against the Scotch. The real truth, however, is that to blame Irishmen in the fourteenth century for rebelling against their Liege Lord, or for fighting against him with anybody or for anything, would be as absurd as to blame one gamecock for flying at another, and inflicting the most bloody injuries upon him.

Let us therefore put praise and blame equally out of the question on both sides, and look at the matter simply as one of cause and of effect. Whatever defence or justification may be pleaded for either the Irish or for the Scotch, it is certain that no defence or justification is needed for the English. It cannot be denied that England was not only entitled but bound to fight with every weapon she could employ against the setting up of a new and hostile kingdom on her flanks—a kingdom to be founded on the defeat and expulsion of her own sons, who had been settled in Ireland for a century and a half, and held their possessions by the same title as the Irish themselves:— a kingdom which would be animated by the fiercest hostility against herself, and under the sway of a family which had proved its formidable military genius. The rout of a great English army at Bannockburn only three years before had made as deep an impression upon the English as upon the Irish mind. And the reality of the danger as it must have appeared to Edward II. may be measured by the fact that only a few years later King Robert the Bruce did actually repeat the process, not in Scotland, but in England itself. At Bannockburn it could at least be said that Bruce had the advantage of a position chosen by himself, and one which hampered the deployment of so great an army as that of Edward.

But a few years later all those advantages were on his own side, when in the heart of a great English province he awaited the attack of King Robert at Byland, in the heart of Yorkshire. Yet there again he was disastrously defeated by the Scots.

Although this event was still future when the invasion of Ireland took place, the very possibility of such a military power as the Scotch had already shown, being made the basis of a hostile kingdom in Ireland, must have appeared at that time a very formidable danger. It was therefore a necessity of life for England to put down the Irish insurrection, and the Irish must have known it to be so. The disastrous results must consequently be laid entirely on them. All historians are agreed that the two years of war during which the Scotch and native Irish fought a desperate and devastating war with England on the soil of Ireland, was a great and terrible epoch in the miseries of that country. The war lasted no less than three years and five months—from May 25, 1315, till October 5, 1318, when Edward Bruce was killed in the battle of Dundalk. And as during all this time the contest was waged over a great part of Ireland, as far south as Limerick, with all the ferocity and all the devastating practices of the Irish tribal wars themselves; it may be easily conceived what a terrible effect it must have had upon the country and upon the people. An eminent Irish authority is quoted by Dr. Richey, with full adoption, as saying, that the barbarism and weakness of Ireland during the rest of that century, and the whole of the succeeding century,—that is to say, for one hundred and seventy years, from 1315 to 1499,—were due by consequences, direct or indirect, to the Scotch invasion brought about expressly by Irish invitation. And one of the indirect consequences is explained to have been simply that aggravation, or at least continuance of that very old source of Irish woes, the increasingly arbitrary power over all below them which wars always do and always must place in the hands of those who retain any power at all.*

Now let us note in passing what the result of these acknowledged facts is upon the inflated fiction, which is so ignorantly but so constantly repeated about the seven hundred years of English Government in Ireland. We have before seen it to be admitted that there was no real Conquest of Ireland till the beginning of the seventeenth century—or the accession of James I. to the English throne in 1603. But real responsibility begins only with real power. The whole interval between the date of the nominal Conquest in 1172 and the real subjugation about 1603 is four hundred and thirty-one years. Of this we have now seen that, during the period up to the Scotch invasion, or one hundred and forty-five years, the condition of Ireland was determined by a mere prolongation of her own indigenous customs, against which England

* "Short History," pp. 198, 199.

had no means whatever in her hands to struggle with success. Next we have seen it acknowledged by Irish historians that after the Scotch invasion, for another period of one hundred and seventy years—down to the year 1500—her condition was mainly determined by the effects of that war which the native Irish had entirely brought upon themselves. These two periods make together three hundred and fifteen years out of the whole four hundred and thirty-one years before the real Conquest came—thus leaving only a little over one hundred years to be still accounted for, as regards the internal condition of Ireland, before the real Conquest was effected, and the real responsibility began. This makes a large hole in the clap-trap seven hundred years—reducing it from the "seven centuries" to little more than three hundred years—even if we had not one word more to say upon the subject.

But we have a great deal more to say. In the first place, before parting with—to use a very Irish phrase—the long reign of anarchy for three hundred and fifteen years from the nominal Conquest down to the end of the fifteenth century, we must go back upon some instructive incidents which demonstrate the injustice and inconsistency of the chief charges laid against England by many Irishmen, and by the new school of English declaimers. The agents for the prosecution against England must make up their minds as to which of the two opposite and contradictory pleas they intend to urge—that of O'Connell, or that of a host of other Irishmen, now backed by Mr. Gladstone. Have we to defend England against the charge of trying cruelly to force "foreign" and unsuitable laws upon a people who had happier laws and customs of their own; or, on the contrary, against the accusation which charges her with having refused to Irishmen the protection and advantages which English law would have afforded against their own ruinous and desolating usages? I have already pointed out that this last form of the attack is by far the nearest to the truth, inasmuch as it at least admits that most important portion of the truth which recognizes the indisputable evidence we possess against the Irish customs. I have also pointed out that, with the true instinct of all declamatory rhetoricians as to dangerous admissions, Mr. Gladstone takes the opposite line of attack. But the really instructive exhibition is to see one and the same writer adopting both charges—the one when he is engaged in responsible narrative, or in deliberate reasoning, and the other when he makes passing comments under the influence of a local sentiment.

Such is the exhibition which we have in that excellent Irish historian, Dr. Richey, in connection with an event which happened fifteen years after the defeat and death of Edward Bruce, when the English King —that great sovereign, Edward III.—had to face the utter disorganisation and ruin into which the Scotch invasion had thrown the whole miserable framework of Irish society. The Norman colonists—the "degenerate English," as Dr. Richey himself calls them—had been almost reduced and degraded into the condition of the Irish Clans. They were fighting with each other fiercely. The old Irish Septs were recovering strength only to use it as before. In 1329 retaliating massacres and murders were the order of the day. At last England was aroused to the dreadful condition of the country—dreadful to the Irish of all races, and shameful to England, in so far—but only so far—as she had any power to effect a reform. And so she turned to that only remedy,—which Daniel O'Connell blamed her for not having adopted from the beginning,—the remedy of applying the principles of English law at once to the whole of Ireland. The odious distinction of races was, as far as possible, to be abolished. Accordingly, in 1331, Acts were passed in England providing that one and the same law should be applicable to both English and Irish. Such elementary principles as the keeping of good faith in truces between combatants received statutory embodiment. No landowner was to keep bands of armed men on his estates other than were needed for mere self-defence. The barons were to reside upon their lands. In short, England tried to do what was obviously needed to lay even the first foundations of a civilised government in Ireland. The righteousness of that policy is not denied. The trueness of aim with which, so far as it went, that policy struck at the root-evils of Ireland for a thousand years, is not denied. Yet Dr. Richey allows himself to describe the new measures thus:—" The policy of those ordinances may be called Imperialism. They attempted to establish English ideas and laws among a totally dissimilar people—to bring about a unity of the two countries by extending and enforcing in Ireland, English law and government."* A dissimilar people! Yes—fortunately for the world. But surely to make them "similar" in the elementary ideas of civilisation was the one great work to be done.

Dr. Richey, however, soon recovers himself from this relapse into nonsense. He proceeds to say what is quite true, that this policy could only be successful if founded on, and enforced by effective conquest. Was this physically possible at that time, and with the resources at the disposal of the English sovereign? Let us look at the event that followed.

Within five years of the Statutes which, if obeyed, would have effected a great reform, Edward III. found that Irish disorganisation had gone too far to encourage the faintest hope that the country could be reclaimed by mere authority not enforced by arms. One of the greatest of the Norman Feudatories, who had remained loyal to the English Crown, was murdered, and his great remains of power were usurped by relatives who ostentatiously renounced the hereditary policy of their House,

* "Short History," p. 201.

and, as the symbol of new enmity, threw off their English dress, and donned habiliments of the Irish "saffron." Edward sent his son Lionel to Ireland to re-establish, as far as was possible, the authority of the Crown over at least some remnant of the kingdom. Then followed, in 1361, the famous "Statutes of Kilkenny," passed by an Irish Parliament, under the influence of the Prince, the whole object of which was to leave the native Irish to themselves, and to limit the authority of the English law to that small area of country, which was still inhabited by Anglo-Normans, loyal, in the main, to the English monarchy. No part of Irish history has been more obscured and more grossly misrepresented than this episode. Inflated fable has been riotous and rampant on the subject of the Statutes of Kilkenny. Plowden, one of the most prejudiced and clamorous of Irish writers, breaks out in the most violent language against the policy of "antipathy, hatred, and revenge" which animated the code.

There seems, indeed, to have been some unusual excuse for this ignorant language in the fact that the text of the Statutes was hidden away and lost, and only recovered so late as 1843. Dr. Richey analyses the clauses or sections, as now known, with perfect candour, and with this remarkable result—that he not only excuses, but he defends them all, and actually praises some. The new Statutes do, indeed, denounce the old Irish customs as the cause and source of the fatal degradation of the English settlers; and in this they did but speak the words of truth and soberness. But the prohibitions of the Statutes against Irish customs were confined to those whose duty it was to maintain nobler laws against the invasion of surrounding savagery. "A fair analysis of the Act," says Dr. Richey, "leads to the conclusion that the English Government, at this time, abandoned the prospect of reducing to obedience the Irish and the degenerate English, and, adopting a policy purely defensive, sought merely to preserve in allegiance to the English Crown the miserable remains of the Irish Kingdom."* As usual, the one only substantial fault, which Dr. Richey finds with England, is her want of power or energy to enforce her wise and civilising policy. "The policy of the Act, if steadily carried out, might have been advantageous to both the English and Irish in Ireland, but it required a vigorous executive." This is true; and it brings us back again to the truth implied in O'Connell's reproach to England that she did not conquer Ireland more effectually, and give it all the blessings of English law.

But now let us see what was the next remarkable step taken in this strange and monotonous history of the effect of savage customs entrenched behind an inaccessible geography. If indeed we could legitimately judge of the conduct of men in the fourteenth century by the principles both of duty and of policy,

* "Short History," p. 214.

which would be acknowledged without difficulty or doubt in the nineteenth, the blame to be cast on English Sovereigns for several generations would be heavy indeed, not specially or alone in respect to Ireland, but quite as much in respect to England and Europe generally. Their long, bloody, and exhausting wars to establish a separate kingdom in France were, in the light of our day, not only useless, but mischievous and even wicked. If they had only spent one-half the energy, thus worse than wasted, in completing the civilisation of their own country, and in effectually establishing their authority over Ireland as an integral part of their dominions, the gain to themselves, and so far as we can see, to us even now, would have been untold. But such judgments and speculations are worse than idle—unless, indeed, we take them as lessons in the mysterious course of human follies since the world began. But it is a curious incident in this connection that it is said to have been due to this very ambition of English Kings to become great continental potentates, that Richard II. was at last induced to make no less than two considerable efforts to conquer and to civilise Ireland. The first was in 1394; the second in 1399, the last of his reign. This may be a bit of gossip from the Middle Ages—but it was believed by Sir John Davies, early in the seventeenth century, and it is adopted by Dr. Richey as if it were true,—that Richard had hoped and intrigued to be elected Emperor, as successor of Charlemagne, and of the far-off Emperors of the Western World. His pretensions are said to have been ridiculed, and one of the jibes against him was that he could not even hold his own against the wild tribes of Ireland.

This may or may not be true. If it was true, it is the earliest specimen we have got of that element in our controversy with Ireland on which Mr. Gladstone has often dwelt effusively—namely, the vague impressions of foreign spectators. In this case, they seem to have been a great deal more intelligent than Mr. Gladstone's modern friends; because they do not seem to have blamed Richard or his predecessors for having asserted a sovereignty over Ireland, but, on the contrary, for not having made that sovereignty practical and effective. However this may be, another motive assigned by other Historians is, perhaps, more probable—namely this, that the small tribute of revenue which had ever been reaped from the Irish kingdom had now been stopped. And so followed one of those expeditions to Ireland which prove how really great, if not insuperable, were the difficulties of a mediæval sovereign in effecting such a lasting and effectual conquest as could alone be of the least use in Ireland. The expedition of Richard II., in 1394, was almost an exact repetition of the original invasion of Henry II., two hundred and twenty-two years before. He went with great pomp, and a formidable feudal array—four thousand men in armour, and no less than thirty thousand archers. Whereupon the Celtic Chiefs, exactly as they had done with Henry II., flocked to Dublin, and, in a "humble and solemn manner," did homage to their Liege Lord, and swore fidelity. The evidence appears to be that there was not a chieftain or lord of an Irish Sept but submitted himself in one form or other. But, just as before, the moment Richard's back was turned they all returned to their old life, and to their inveterate predatory habits—specially directed against the newly established "Pale." And so, enraged by this conduct, the unfortunate Richard again collected his army, and, in the last year of his reign, re-landed in Ireland. In a very short campaign against one of his sworn Anglo-Irish Vassals, he was victorious—of course. But the Irish had only to retreat into their bogs and forests, drive away their cattle, and leave the invading army to be starved. Such, accordingly, seems to have been very nearly the fate of Richard's armament, which was only saved by the timely arrival of the English transports to take them home.

This brings us to the close of the second out of the four centuries—the fourteenth—which elapsed before that complete conquest of Ireland which could alone attach any real responsibility to England. We have seen how false it is that the government of the country was in her hands even in "the last resort." We have seen how false it is that she had intentionally tried to withhold the benefits of English law from Ireland; we have seen how equally false it is that the Irish, as a people or a nation, were willing to accept it at any time. We have seen that the miserable condition of the country was the natural and inevitable result of Irish habits and Irish conduct in each conjuncture of those times. Two centuries more, out of the four we have still to account for—the fifteenth and the sixteenth—remain to be considered; and never has the perfect continuity of great historical causes been more signally displayed. There is no other change whatever than such as was due to the same identical causes—only operating with fresh intensity because of additional circumstances of outward provocation. Human history in this way is often very like a pendulum, which may swing a long time with equal beat; but if any synchronous movement reaches it from outside, then the swing will rapidly become excessive, and may break all bounds imposed by the mechanism which contains it.

During the whole of the fifteenth century England was so situated as to leave her no time to deal seriously with the condition of Ireland. Her foreign wars in France, and her civil wars of the Roses, due to a disputed succession to the throne, made it impossible for her to govern Ireland even in "the last resort." We have seen how the pendulum was swinging at the close of the fourteenth century. It was swinging towards the complete reconquest of the whole island by the native chiefs,—by the degenerate English who had been amalgamated with them,—and by the desolating usages of Clan feuds and fightings which were inseparable from that condition of society. Even the narrow territory of the Pale which Richard II. and his Irish Parliament of Kilkenny had tried to define and to keep within the marches of civilisation—even this Pale was being invaded perpetually by incursions and robbery, and still more fatally by the infusion of Irish usages. During the reign of Henry V., at the very time when the power of English arms was being shown in the historic glories of Agincourt, and an English King became Regent of France, with the right of succession to that kingdom, the English Colonists in Ireland were reduced to such misery that they were emigrating in crowds back to England; and England could only endeavour to force them to return again to Ireland. At last,—close to the end of the century,—that last refuge of feebleness was resorted to—the refuge of actually erecting a fortified embankment and ditch against the Irish enemy, round the nucleus of the Pale in the immediate neighbourhood of Dublin.*

But even this extreme result of Ireland being left practically to herself is not the most important lesson which the events of this fifteenth century impressed upon the English mind, and which explain and largely vindicate her conduct then, and in later times. We have seen the inevitable tendency among the Irish Clans, and among the degenerate colonists, to take part with any external enemy of England who might heave in sight over the troubled waters of those stormy times.

* "Short History," p. 229.

This tendency had been exhibited in a terrible manner in the fearful wars brought upon Ireland by the invited invasion of the Scotch in the beginning of the previous century. But now we have to note the same danger in another form. Whenever any faction might arise in England—above all, when there came to be a disputed succession to the throne,—the inevitable temptation of the Irish was to take sides with the claimant—whoever he might be—who did not succeed in England. To set up a separate and a rival kingdom had been their object, so far as Irish Septs ever had any object at all, in inviting Bruce. But obviously the same purpose might be as well or even better attained by choosing a king for themselves, who had failed to establish himself on the throne of England.

Accordingly, when the Wars of the Roses broke out, the Irish, in so far again as they ever acted together, or on any principle whatever, embraced the cause of the House of York against the great Lancastrian sovereigns who had succeeded Richard II. They had some temporary and personal temptation to do so. In the middle of the century with which we are now concerned, the fifteenth, the Lancastrian Henry VI. sent over to Ireland, in order to get him out of the way, Richard, Duke of York, as Viceroy. This shows that the new danger was not then foreseen or expected. But it was immediately developed. Duke Richard at once set to work in that body which was called a Parliament, but which represented nothing but the narrow limits and the degenerated occupants of the Pale, in order to establish for himself an independent position. The first step was to get that Rump of a Parliament to declare itself independent of England as representing the whole of Ireland. It asserted what Dr. Richey calls the complete independence of the Irish Legislature, and all those constitutional rights, which,—as this excellent Irish writer significantly says,—" are involved in the existence of a separate Parliament, but had not hitherto been categorically expressed." * It took up the position, in fact, in the middle of the fifteenth century which was afterwards taken up by Grattan's Parliament towards the end of the eighteenth century in 1782. The spirit and intention with which this was done, and its political significance to the English throne and nation, is sufficiently shown by the fact that the Irish Lords took an active part in the civil war and fought for the House of York in several of the battles of the Roses.

It is not the least necessary to blame the Irish for this course. It is quite enough to consider it as only natural—in the sense in which a great many things are natural which are nevertheless inseparably connected with causes working to the most ruinous results, even for those who are under their influence and controlling power. But for those in later generations who look at those causes in the light of their origin and effects,

* "Short History," p. 232.

it is impossible not to see that Irish independence in the fifteenth century would have given free play to influences which had shown their disastrous action in Ireland for more than a thousand years; and that as regards England it would have been a serious political danger. We have only to ask ourselves, which of those two communities of men was most freighted with good influences for the world, to have that question answered in favour of England with a shout—as much of reason as of sympathy. At all events, if we are to judge of the conduct of men merely according to that which we see it was both right and natural for them to do in the circumstances of their case as it appeared to them, we must apply the same standard to the conduct of England and her sovereign. Nothing can be more certain than that when the Wars of the Roses had closed on the field of Bosworth in 1484, and the rule of the Tudor Sovereigns began with Henry VII., he was absolutely called upon, by his duty to the great monarchy of England, to put an end to the danger of an independent kingdom in Ireland, founded as it would be on the claim of a small section of the whole people of Ireland to choose its own dynasty, its own sovereign, and to maintain its own half-Ersefied usages and laws. This is the full and adequate explanation and defence of one of the most celebrated and determining episodes in Irish history—the enactment of the Statute known as Poyning's Law, from the name of the Viceroy or Lord Deputy who induced the same Parliament of the Pale to pass it in 1495. This was an Act which acknowledged the Irish Parliament to be a strictly subordinate legislature—not to be summoned and not to act except under the supreme authority of the English Crown. It is needless to say that this was nothing but the full realisation of the duty which O'Connell charged England with having so long neglected. As Dr. Richey says, "English legislation was introduced *en bloc*." All English statutes then existing in England were by the same statute made of force in Ireland. If only this measure had been made effectual, it is the universal testimony of Irish historians themselves, that it would have been the greatest of all reforms.

It is perfectly intelligible that Irish historians, if they can manage to throw off from their minds the bearing and significance of every one of the great facts which they themselves narrate, or are compelled to admit,—and if they can imagine themselves to be citizens of a state, or subjects of a monarchy which had a great past, and might otherwise have had a great future,—should deprecate or even condemn this attempt on the part of England to make her old suzerainty a real and effectual dominion. But it does indeed require a strong effort of imagination to conjure up a vision and a dream so utterly at variance with all the realities of the case. Yet Dr. Richey, speaking in this sense, says of the

Poyning's Law, "This, the most disgraceful Act ever passed by an independent Legislature, and wrung from the local Assembly of the Pale, bound future Parliaments for three hundred years." That the body, which he now discovers to be not in any true sense a Parliament of Ireland, but only "a local Assembly of the Pale," was under the supreme influence of the English Lord Deputy is likely enough. But they had been equally under the influence of the Duke of York when, thirty-six years before, in 1459, they had taken the opposite course of constituting themselves an independent Legislature and of supporting the family of a Pretender to the English Crown. It is not rational to speak of this body as representing an Irish nation when it acted in one way, and then to disparage it as a mere "local Assembly" when it acted in another way. In both cases it was the same body— with the same restricted character—with the same disabilities, and liable to the same influences of personal favour or of corruption. Probably, whatever of wisdom and of public spirit it enlisted, it was stronger in the later action which clung to the English law and power, than in the earlier action which asserted its own separate independence. We know how much the Colonists of the Pale suffered from the wild Irish around them, and, in setting up an independence which they could certainly not have maintained alone, they must have been acting from mere impulse, and with great ignorance of the true interests of their country.

From an English point of view,—which is the point of view identified with the civilisation of the British Islands,—there can be no doubt whatever of the duty of the Sovereign to act as he did. But even in that point of view which looks solely to the interests of Ireland, it is difficult to conceive how any reasoning man can regard the so-called Parliament of the Pale in the fifteenth century as having been one whose separativeness and independence can now be regarded as even a possible source of good. Such a prospect could only be founded on one or both of two things—either on the fitness of the Anglo-Norman Colonists inside the Pale at that time, to exercise such powers well and wisely not only in its relations with England, but in its relations with Irish tribes all over the Island;— or else on the possibility at that time of the Irish tribes reinforcing that Parliament with better elements of its own, and so forming gradually a really national Parliament likely to govern the country well and wisely. Neither of these alternative suppositions has one single element of plausibility or even of possibility. And it is only doing Dr. Richey justice to observe that he supplies us with the most definite and conclusive information against them both. As regards the first,—the capacity of the English Colonists of the Pale to govern well even the small portion of the country which they precariously held,—the experiment was actually tried. Henry VIII., having no army of his own to enforce his policy, resolved to trust the

Government of Ireland to the oldest and noblest representative of the first Norman Settlers. He confided his powers to the Geraldines, the Earls of Kildare, who were the lineal descendants of the men who preceded Henry II. three hundred years before. The Pale was thus to be governed under the English Crown through the greatest of its own Magnates—a family which had been so long settled, and had so identified themselves with the Irish people, that it was their boast to be called "More Irish than Irish." And what was the result? Let us hear what Dr. Richey says. He tells us that the Geraldines had many of the personal characteristics which distinguish men in rude ages. They were brave, enterprising, courteous, and generous. But they were totally devoid of any of the qualities requisite for the character of a statesman. They had no higher views than the maintenance of their position as chiefs of the most powerful Irish Clan. Accordingly, during the time of their supremacy from 1489 down to 1535 the Government was utterly perverted to their private purposes, and the Royal banner was carried in a great battle in which sixteen Irish chiefs were defeated by the forces of the Pale in alliance as usual with other Irish Septs from the north. Here we have a perfect and indeed a typical specimen of what Home Rule had always been in Ireland, and what perhaps more than ever it would have been under a "local Assembly of the Pale." We have the head of the Geraldines, representing the authority of the English Crown, quarrelling with a member of his own family, his son-in-law, and in alliance with a fighting mixture of De Burghs, the O'Briens, the Macnamaras, the O'Carrolls, and other southern Septs, fighting a desperate battle with the O'Reillys, Mac Mahons, O'Farrells, O'Donels, and other chiefs of the north.* Such is the spectacle presented by the best specimens of that English Pale which ought—it is suggested—to have been allowed to declare itself independent of the power and civilisation of England.

Then let us turn to the condition of the "Irish enemy," as they were called,—the native Septs and Clans occupying all the rest of Ireland. Here, again, Dr. Richey not only does not deny the facts, but states them most explicitly. He admits that the Celtic Clans were not only as bad, but considerably worse than they had been three hundred years before. "In the twelfth century," he says, "the Irish Celts were in a state of political disorganisation, but they still had a feeling of nationality, and had the form at least of a national monarchy. Justice, criminal and civil, was administered among them according to a definite code of law. At the commencement of the sixteenth century there remained no tradition of national unity—no trace of an organisation by which they could be united into one people. The separate tribes had been disorganised by civil wars, and the

* "Short History," pp. 233, 234.

original tribesmen were suppressed and supplanted by the mercenary followers of the several rivals for the chieftaincies." * Such is the description we have of that other portion of the Irish people whose abstract interest in an independent Irish Parliament was to supplement what was wanting in the degenerate English of the Pale!

So closes the fifteenth century—the third of the four centuries for which we have to account before England had effected that real conquest which could alone give power to remedy the desperate evils of the Irish clan system. In describing the once happier condition of the Irish people in the words here quoted, Dr. Richey can only be criticised for having given an almost purely ideal sketch of the condition of things even in the twelfth century. The native Annals testify against the truth of it. The stages of descent through which the Celtic clans had fallen in Ireland had reached, even in the twelfth century, a lower point than Dr. Richey in this passage admits; and every farther step in the same descent was confessedly due to the continued operation of the same causes,—all being of purely native origin. England's only blame was the fault which consisted in her want of power,—a want which was due quite as much to insuperable physical obstacles as to ambitions, pursuits, and policies which were the common heritage of all the European races in the military ages.

* "Short History," p. 238.

CHAPTER V.

IRELAND UNDER THE TUDORS DOWN TO THE DEATH OF HENRY VIII.

LET us now pass on. The sixteenth century in England, as we all know, was wholly occupied by the rule of the Tudor sovereigns. No less than eighty-one years out of the hundred were passed under the two single reigns of Henry VIII. and of his daughter, Queen Elizabeth. The intervening short episodes of Edward VI. and the "bloody Mary," lasting together only for eleven years, contributed nothing of lasting importance to that side of British history with which we are concerned here. But in those two reigns England was, to a very large extent, made what she continued to be; and Ireland was at last brought for the first time within the influences of one supreme dominion. The first nine years of the century, during which Henry VII. continued to reign, brought no change as regards the Irish. Neither did the first twenty-six years of the reign of Henry VIII. Nothing particular happened except that which was then happening always, and had been happening with a perfect continuity of causation for a thousand years, namely, the deepening of anarchy, the development of corruption from the more complete abandonment of all classes of Irishmen to themselves. At last a crisis occurred, out of which a new life began for Ireland. The Geraldines rebelled. The best and noblest representatives of the early English Pale—the very chiefs and heads of those whose rule was carried on in the shape of a local Parliament—broke from their admitted allegiance to their Sovereign, publicly and formally renounced it, and rode out from Dublin shouting the Celtic watchword of their family—now converted into a mere Irish Sept. It marks with poetical fidelity the influences which were supreme with the rebellious Lord-Deputy Fitzgerald, that he was incited to this course by the rhapsodies of a native Irish Minstrel; and that among his own retainers with whose aid he seized the Castle of Dublin, and invaded the Council Chamber, not one of them could speak the English language, or could even understand the speech of the Chancellor, who tried to dissuade them from a course so disastrous.

This event happened in 1534—when the second quarter of the century had been well advanced. And it is universally recognised as an epoch in the history of Ireland. Dr. Richey says it marked the close of the Middle Ages, and the beginning of those conditions which belong to the modern world. Dr. Richey accordingly takes this as an opportunity for summing up the condition of Ireland as it was found to be, when England was then compelled to take up the gauntlet thrown down by the same Geraldines who had preceded Henry II., and had been now for a number of years the King's Deputies in Ireland. Here once more we meet with that marked discrepancy between the language of the sentimental Irish patriot, and the language of the Historian. Counting up the years between the pretended conquest of Ireland in 1172 and the year 1534, he finds the interval to be three hundred and sixty-two years—and he proceeds to call this period "three hundred and sixty-two years of English so-called government." In the same strain he says the "English government had collapsed, leaving nothing but the misery it had caused." This language from an historian whose account of the facts is, as we have seen, so honest is all the more strange, and all the more pathetic, because at this juncture we find it in juxtaposition with a special exhibition of candour. As an Irishman he puts the question to be answered, and he answers it as an Englishman and a philosopher. "To what condition was Ireland reduced by the first three hundred and sixty-two years of English rule?"—this is the question—and it could not have been put in any form involving a more thorough traversing of the facts of history. It is a form worthy of an Irish stump orator, or of Mr. Gladstone in his more recent phase. But how does the honest Dr. Richey answer his own question? He says he will not answer it himself, nor will he take his answer from any native Irish historian. And so he replies in the words of the first of the State Papers addressed to Henry VIII. when the minds of English statesmen were first brought really to bear upon the state of Ireland—now become really urgent, and from external causes likely to become alarming. Dr. Richey quotes *in extenso* this Paper, which, from beginning to end, is one long indictment against Irish native usages, and one long demonstration that the miseries of Ireland were due to them alone.

Of course the only logical escape for Dr. Richey and for those who speak in the spirit of his question, is to point out that England was to blame for the very reason that Irish usages had been so long allowed to act almost without a check. But no one has explained better, as we have seen, than Dr. Richey, the insuperable difficulties which had made it practically impossible for England during those centuries to conquer Ireland and enforce her own law by arms. Besides which, even if we set aside this consideration, it will be at least a great step gained if we recognise what were the positive, and not merely the negative causes of the desperate condition to which human society had been reduced in Ireland. The State Paper quoted by Dr. Richey leaves nothing to be desired on this head. It tells us that there were more than sixty distinct divisions of the country, which were in the possession of the native Irish Septs —every one of them ruled by some chief who assumed various titles, from Kings and Dukes, and Archdukes and Princes, down to Chiefs and Lords—and every one of these was independent of the other—exercising the whole powers of government within his territory, and all also exercising constantly the right of peace and war against each other. Those other parts of Ireland, which were nominally English, were similarly divided between thirty more rulers completely Ersefied, and all exercising similar powers and jurisdictions. Nor was this all. Within each chieftainship, the succession was not regulated by any fixed law or even custom, but was practically determined by the power of the strongest to seize upon it. Whence it followed that many parts of Ireland were a prey to intestine factions, and to the constant fighting of still more petty chieflets. Then as regarded the condition of the poorer and dependent classes we hear once more of the desolating usages, purely native, of "coigne and livery," and of the consequent devastation of the country. They who wished to be peaceful were flying from the island. The Pale was perpetually invaded and ravaged, and few parts of Ireland were more miserable. Such was Ireland—not under the rule of England even in "the last resort"—but under Irish Home Rule, and the operation of the identical causes which we have seen to be in operation with more or less severity for many centuries. Nor is Dr. Richey less honest when he resumes his own narrative, and tells us in his own words what was the condition of Ireland, and who had been its rulers, as well in the first as "in the last resort." "The Celtic Tribes," he tells us, "had for above two centuries enjoyed a practical independence." * But "more than two centuries" before 1534 are words that take us back to some undefined date before 1334—in fact, to the great Scotch invasion which those tribes had invited and brought upon their country in 1315, in the reign of Edward II. But why stop here in the retrospect of years during which the Irish tribes enjoyed a practical, and for themselves a disastrous, independence? Was it not with special reference to the preceding period of one hundred and forty-three years between the pretended conquest of Henry II. and the Scotch invasion, that Dr. Richey himself explained the physical impossibility of England effecting any real subjugation of Ireland? And have we not the testimony of the native Celtic Annals as to the perfect continuity of the characteristic habits and usages of the Irish?

But here again we have nothing to say against the perfect honesty of this Irish historian. No sooner has he quoted the graphic account of Ireland in 1534, which is given by the Statesmen of Henry VIII., than he

* "Short History," p. 244.

proceeds to quote, with the same fidelity, the account to be gathered from the native Irish Annals. Casting aside all the pleas which have been advanced by other Irishmen against taking the testimony of those Annals as a fair picture of the state of society in Ireland as it really existed, Dr. Richey says, "It is but fair to judge the Celtic tribes by their own historians;"* and then he proceeds to give the following result of the yearly jottings for the thirty-four years from 1500 to 1534,—and this for one part of Ireland only: "Battles, plundering, etc., exclusive of those in which the English Government was engaged, 116; Irish gentlemen of family killed in battle, 102; murdered, 168—many of them with circumstances of great atrocity; and during this period, on the other hand, there is no allusion to the enactment of any law, the judicial decision of any controversy, the founding of any town, monastery, or church; and all this is recorded by the annalist without the slightest expression of regret or astonishment, and as if such were the ordinary course of life in a Christian country."†

Even much more marked ebullitions of a local patriotism might well be pardoned in an historian who is so splendidly honest as to pen this powerful description of the condition of Ireland at the close of some five hundred years of "practical independence." But Dr. Richey's candour is not exhausted. It is helped, no doubt, by the curious idea that he can

* "Short History," p. 247. † Ibid., pp. 247, 248.

assign to the English Government, as a cause, all the evils which his facts, and his narrative alike, attach by an inseparable connection to that Irish independence to which he confesses freely. But his genuine historical instincts are not satisfied even with such confessions as these. He returns to the subject again and again, and explains in the greatest detail the operation of those purely native usages which were sinking the people deeper and ever deeper into the miserable condition which he has described from their own native historians. He tells us how unceasing civil wars had tended more and more to degrade the whole people into mere armed retainers of predatory soldiers: how, within each tribe or clan every ambitious member of the tribal house sought the chieftainship, which tended to fall into the hands, not of the elected, but of the strongest and most unprincipled member of the house:"—how the future was as hopeless as the present and the past were terrible, inasmuch as "neither chiefs nor followers had any aspiration for, or idea of, a higher state of society:"—how the "Hibernicised Norman Lords" were as bad as, or worse than, the Celtic chiefs around them, just because they were so completely Hibernicised; and because even their own Estates were largely repeopled with a native or a bastard race, "ignorant of the freedom of the Saxon tenant," but devoted to their lords with absolute and unscrupulous devotion:—how even the few centres of a possible civilisation in Ireland, the walled towns on the seacoast, or on the great rivers, had betaken themselves to the same lawless habits, and in 1524 "the cities of Cork and Limerick carried on a war against each other by sea and land, sent ambassadors, and concluded a treaty of peace." In short, civilised society did not exist in Ireland, nor was there the smallest hope of its restoration from any internal centre of resurrection or reform.

Yet even after all these confessions, Dr. Richey cannot help again returning to his patriotic misconceptions of the true solution to the question which he asks: What was the cause of this most miserable condition? English writers, he says, would only assert that it arose from the uncivilised and untamable nature of the Celtic nation. But this is not the solution of English writers. What they did and do assert is not that the Irish were untamable; but that the process of taming had to be begun by submitting Ireland to the same process which had effected the civilisation of all the rest of Europe—namely, conquest by a fresh race, and a higher and an older civilisation. But here again, as usual, Dr. Richey's unfairness is only momentary. His most erroneous account of the only thing that "English writers would say" is immediately contradicted by his own quotation of what Henry VIII.'s Irish Council did actually say in 1533: "As to the surmise of the bruteness of the people, and the incivility of them, no doubt, if there were justice used among them, they would be found as civil, wise, and polite, and as active as any nation." This is the truth. But what did the hingeing condition in this sentence mean: " if there were justice used among them "? It meant government established, and law enforced. Dr. Richey's own question, however, is very different. Assuming for a moment the poor part of a declaimer instead of the nobler part of an historian, he asks two questions in a breath—as if they were practically the same. But they are absolutely different—one of them to be answered with a decisive "yes," the other to be answered by an as decisive "no." He asks—(1) " Were the Celts a nation hating all rule and order; and (2) by destiny given over to chaos and degradation?" Again the answer to the first of these two questions is his own. What did he tell us of the causes which led to the failure of a native sovereign, King Brian, more than five hundred years before, who had for a time established something like a civilised monarchy? He says that "a truly national government of this description found its bitterest enemies among the provincial chiefs who longed to restore anarchy, and were willing to league with the foreigner for that purpose."* So it had been all through; and so it was when Henry VIII. was at last compelled by the rebellion of the Fitzgeralds to begin the real conquest of Ireland.

As to Dr. Richey's second question—all the eminent men of the Tudor period, both in Henry VIII.'s

---

* "Short History," p. 116.

time and in that of Queen Elizabeth, attribute the ruin of Ireland, not to anything incompatible with civilisation in the nature of Irishmen, but to the nature of the indigenous, social, and political system under which they had so long lived. All of them who have a natural opportunity of doing so, repeat in various forms the same testimony to the many elements of natural genius and virtue in the Irish character. All of them unite in placing these elements in startling contrast with the actual condition to which the people had been reduced; and all of them "point the moral and adorn the tale" by dwelling, as Dr. Richey himself repeatedly does, on the traditional habits which made all their natural gifts fruitless in building up the edifice of a civilised society. Dr. Richey's question about "destiny" is on a level with Mr. Gladstone's celebrated ascription to his opponents of an idea that the Irish have "a double dose of original sin." The question is not about original sin, but about developed corruption. The germs of that corruption are thickly sown in the natural soil of all races; and it has often happened to nations, as it has often happened to individuals, to fall into positions, both physical and moral, out of which they cannot rise without some help from outside themselves. From no other quarter could that help come to Ireland than from England—from that country and nation, which through the fire of many conquests, and the intermixture of many breeds, had enjoyed advantages and opportunities which she alone could now afford to Ireland, by the long-needed and long-desired enforcement of her own great dominion. At all events we have at this juncture as clear an answer as before to Mr. Gladstone's question, " Who made the Irishman ? " The Irishman had made himself—through many centuries of a practical monopoly in that business. And the only blame that can be cast on England is that she had so long allowed that " making " to have its way, and produce its own deplorable results.

But now we enter upon a broader reach of the great stream of history: and it is impossible to speak too highly of the truth and candour with which Dr. Richey treats the subject. The thrones of kings have never been first established on abstract theories of duty; nor has the dominion of great nations ever been founded on mere philanthropy. They are the result of impulses and instincts which are the common heritage of mankind, and we have to judge of them by the fruit they bear. Moreover, as regards the actors, in every case we have simply to remember that in proportion as they have had really great and permanent interests to defend or to sustain, in the same proportion they must be credited with a more or less conscious and responsible recognition of the real greatness of the cause which they may happen to represent in the history of the world. It will not be denied by any sane Irishman that the cause of the English monarchy was in the sixteenth century a great cause—perhaps the greatest cause which then depended on human action and on human conduct in any part of the world. No man can compare with that cause the separate causes of the ninety petty chiefs of Irish Celts, and of degenerate Englishmen, all " Hibernicised," who fought, and slaughtered, and robbed, each other all over that poor land of Ireland, without one thought or aim which could grow up to be even the germ of a prosperous or a civilised nation. And what has to be clearly seen, firmly grasped, and frankly admitted—is the unquestionable fact that the very existence of the English monarchy, and the place of England among the nations, was now at stake in the Irish contest.

The Fitzgerald rebellion was declared, as we have seen, in 1535. But in the year before that memorable date the whole history of Europe had taken a new turn. Henry VIII. had finally quarrelled with the Pope, and along with the Pope had a quarrel forced upon him with the German Emperor, and with France, and with Spain. From that moment began the great combination, and standing conspiracy of the Continental Catholic Sovereigns to subdue England and to put down her reformed religion,—a conspiracy which for more than two hundred years never ceased to exist more or less in fact, and never ceased to inspire Englishmen with a determined spirit of sleepless watchfulness and of active resistance. From that moment, too, Ireland became the cherished hope of

England's enemies, as the joint in her armour where she was weakest. Let it, then, be clearly understood and universally admitted that nothing that England might really find it needful to do—however severe it might be in itself—in order to keep out her foreign enemies from Ireland, and in order to secure her own dominion in it,—can now be considered in any other light than as the necessary steps in a long battle for self-preservation and for life. We may leave to their own operation all those sources of feeling and of sympathy which may lead men to take part in the past, as they continually do in the present, with the worse instead of with the better cause. We may leave Irishmen, as such, to identify themselves in imagination, if they really can, with the ninety petty chieftains who alone represented Ireland at that time, and were living a life of perpetual war and hopeless anarchy:—we may identify ourselves, and leave Roman Catholics, as such, if they can, to identify themselves with the endeavour of their co-religionists all over Europe to extinguish in blood at home, and by conquest abroad, the liberty of the Christian Church to reform itself. We may even leave political anarchists of all kinds to cherish a universal sympathy with all rebellions: but we can at least demand from all those types of mind the recognition of the plain fact that England was now not only entitled, but called upon by all that has ever determined the conduct of mankind, to establish her own complete dominion over Ireland by every means at her disposal. All men who can rise above the pettiest temptations which pervert the judgment, must see something more and higher in the actual conduct of England at this crisis than simply the natural and inevitable action of universal human instincts. They can see that English statesmen and the English Sovereign had a clear and a noble consciousness of the great interests with which the cause of England was identified in the world, and at the same time a clear, intelligent, and even generous perception of their own duty towards the people of Ireland. Such was unquestionably the language, and the conscious motive of all the great statesmen of the Tudor period.

Now, it is precisely in those conclusions that Dr. Richey does rise above the level of mere provincial feeling in the discharge of his duty as an historian. He not only admits, but he lays stress upon the fact that since the Irish factions—just as they had done two hundred years before—had again begun to intrigue with the foreign enemies of England, and since those foreign enemies had also begun to lay their plans accordingly, the contest into which Henry VIII. was compelled to enter, by the rebellion of the Geraldines, was a contest of life and death for England. So early as twelve years before this date, the Irish Earl of Desmond had actually negotiated a treaty with the King of France for the invasion of Ireland by a French army; and five years later, he received a letter from the Hapsburg Emperor, asking for a similar alliance.* Every enemy that the Pope could stir up anywhere in Europe was sure to take part, sooner or later whenever opportunity might arise, in the contest. England, as Dr. Richey says, was then entering on a "struggle for existence."† England found that she must entirely conquer Ireland, or herself succumb in the struggle. A full admission of this is all that, on behalf of England, we need care to demand. If the cause of England had been laden with as many woes for humanity as it was, in our opinion, laden with many blessings, the admission would be enough to justify her in every step she took to assert and enforce her sovereignty over Ireland. But we can demand much more than this. We can assert, on the clearest evidence, that the statesmen of the Tudor period were wise and foreseeing men, who knew the real greatness of their cause, —the place it had in the highest politics of Europe,— and the bearing it must have on the permanent interests of the inhabitants of Ireland. And all this, too, Dr. Richey admits, and more than admits. He breaks out into a splendid eulogium on the statesmen who acted under Henry VIII., and on that Sovereign himself. "The study," he says, "of his official correspondence, especially the letters and instructions relative to Irish affairs, gives a much more favourable impression, not only of his abilities, but also of his moral character. Like all his contemporaries, he was impressed with the

---

* "Short History," p. 303.   * Ibid., pp. 234-239.

permanent necessity of maintaining law and order,—he had a deep sense of his own responsibilities,—a sympathy with the poor and weak who were exposed to the oppression of the powerful or insolent,—and a sincere dislike to shed the blood of, or to use violence towards, the masses of the people. His own subjects understood him better than his historians. He was all through supported by the masses of the people. The violent and despotic acts of which he was accused, were done by a monarch who had no standing army, scarcely even a bodyguard, and who resided close beside, almost within, the powerful and turbulent city of London. As regards his Irish policy, his State Papers disclose a moderation, a conciliating spirit, a respect for the feelings of the Celtic population, a sympathy with the poor, which no subsequent English ruler has ever displayed." Nor is this all that Dr. Richey admits. He admits further that under this Sovereign,—compelled at last to assert his sovereignty, and aided by Statesmen on whom he bestows praises as large and generous,— a policy was thenceforth adopted, "honest in intention, noble in its aspirations, and persistently pursued." So much for matters of historical fact. Then comes the usual expression of a purely sentimental feeling, "but founded on principles radically erroneous." *

Let us now bring this sentimental feeling to the test of reason. What was the Tudor policy,

* "Short History," p. 268.

as described by himself? The first aim was to establish the Sovereignty of England both in reality and in name, and to repudiate as its basis the grant of a mere Lordship over Ireland, by a Pope of the twelfth century? Was this "most erroneous"? Another aim was to effect a financial reform, and to secure a revenue from Ireland sufficient to pay the costs of its own Government. Was this "most erroneous"? The third was to substitute the civilised laws of England for the barbarous anarchy and the desolating usages which had been the curse of Ireland for a thousand years. Was this "most erroneous"? Is there a rational being who can dispute either the political necessities, or the imperative demands of wisdom and of justice by which all the links of this chain of policy were welded and twined together? It is too little to say that it was only natural,—or that it was defensible,—or that it was on the whole the best. It was all of these; but it was more,—it was the only possible policy. There was absolutely no alternative. There was no other law than the law of England to which Henry VIII. could resort. The old Irish Brehon Law, even if it had been really operative at all, was no law at all in the modern sense of the word. It was a mere collection of archaic precepts and usages wholly inapplicable to the conditions of what we understand by civilised society, and with no machinery for judicial application. But even that law was not really in force. Each one of the ninety Chiefs and Kinglets in Ireland was a law unto himself.

Henry VIII. went to the heart of the whole question when he said, in an excellent letter to his Lord Deputy, that it was not so much a question whether the Irish should be compelled to live under the law of England, but whether they should live under any law at all—of any sort or kind. There is, therefore, neither justice nor common sense in any of those complaints made against the Tudor policy towards Ireland, which harp upon the old story of the evil of forcing upon any people laws which were strange to them. And accordingly the result is that when we ask reasonable men like Dr. Richey to condescend to details, and to specify what particular instance they can give of violent or unjust legislation in Ireland, they are obliged to fall back upon one so trivial in itself as the prohibition for the future of the Irish dress and of the Irish habits of personal adornment, such as the mode of wearing beard or moustaches, or of cutting the hair. Let all this be conceded, as inexpedient and practically useless, not only because it could not possibly be, and was not, enforced; but also because the abandonment of barbarous personal habits would necessarily have followed in due time the establishment and enforcement of the weightier matters of the law. But even in this trivial question we must not forget how it really stood in the eyes of both Englishmen and Irishmen in those days. For centuries the Irish dress and habits of personal apparel had been the symbol and flag of repudiated allegiance to the acknowledged Lord of Ireland. Whenever an "Hibernicised" Englishman wished to declare his rebellion, the "donning of the Irish dress and accoutrements" was the regular accepted form of abjuration and rebellion. The step, therefore, of denouncing and prohibiting the use of such symbols was a perfectly natural part, however well it might have been omitted, of the new policy of reducing Ireland to order and to law. And even if it had been true—as O'Connell audaciously asserted in 1834—that the Irish people had been eagerly desirous in previous centuries to enjoy the advantage and protection of English law, and if they were now even hostile to such a change,—this could only prove the immense decline which had taken place in the intelligence of the people, and in that poor degree of political consciousness which they had ever possessed, but which they had lost through long familiarity with chaos.

But whatever may be the aberrations from common sense upon this subject which may be due to a misplaced national sentiment, there is one broad fact which stares us in the face as we follow the acts and the language of Henry VIII. and of his successors in respect to Ireland,—and that is the fact that every year brought more and more home to the mind of England that, in fighting for her secure hold over

Ireland as an integral part of the dominions of the English Crown, she was fighting for her own life. Every year, more and more, Ireland became the focus of intrigue, and the hoped-for basis of actual invasion, against England, by the Catholic continental sovereigns, and by Scotland, then under the same influences. Moreover, the serious difficulties which Henry VIII. encountered in putting down the Geraldine rebellion, and in establishing his authority in Ireland, throws a clear light on the ignorance of historical conditions, which can alone account for the blame thrown on England for not having undertaken the work of conquest much sooner. During the long period of the wars with, and in, France, and also during the civil wars of the Roses, England was in no condition to accomplish a task so beset with physical difficulties and almost insuperable impediments. Even in the later days of Henry VIII. it was more than a year, from March, 1534, to June, 1535, before England could provide and equip an army capable of battering down the single Geraldine Castle of Maynooth; and it was no less than seven years before, in 1542, Henry could summon a Parliament professing to represent the whole of Ireland, which he could trust to pass the Act which should transmute his old hereditary feudal title of Lord of Ireland into that of King, with all its authority and honours.

Yet even this date of 1542 does not mark the complete subjugation of the country, which still lay more than sixty years in the future, and was only accomplished by Queen Elizabeth in the last year of her life, 1603. This last, accordingly, is the date which, as we have seen, Dr. Richey specifies as marking the first full sovereignty of England over Ireland, and therefore the first full responsibility for the government of the country. This calculation at once strikes off four hundred years from the "seven centuries" which is the stereotyped period of inflated declamation; and as during the whole of our own present century, and during eighteen years of the last century, Ireland has had either a native Parliament with full powers, or a full share in a united Parliament in London, the period of English responsibility would be reduced to the period from 1603 to 1782, or exactly one hundred and seventy-nine years, instead of seven hundred years, as usually represented. Inasmuch, however, as Henry VIII. had unquestionably conquered at least a great part of Ireland in 1542, when this kingship was declared and acknowledged, and inasmuch as from that date, England did unquestionably enforce her own laws and policy wherever she could, and inasmuch, farther, as her power did actually prevail wherever any semblance of law or civilisation existed at all in Ireland, we may well take that earlier date of 1542 in any argument either in defence, or in accusation of English action in Ireland. That leaves exactly two hundred and fifty-eight years instead of seven hundred years for the period, in any sense, of the responsibility of England—as regards the condition of the people—even to repeat Mr. Gladstone's phrase "in the last resort." Let us now proceed to deal with the great cause before us, in respect to the conduct of England during this period, as clearly as we can.

In the first place, then, there is one imperative demand which we must insist upon on behalf of England—and that is that we do not assume the applicability to her conduct of the rule which we now understand as the law of perfect equality and freedom in matters of religion. We must repudiate that assumption, not only on the ground that nobody then admitted it for a moment, but also on the farther ground, too much forgotten, that the Roman Catholic Church,—wholly in the sixteenth and seventeenth, and partially even in the eighteenth century,—was not a mere religious body or communion, but was more or less actively one great political organisation of the most formidable kind. For myself, I must at once declare that I do not admit the sacred doctrine of religious freedom and toleration to be applicable at all, unless what is meant by "religion" is defined. If, for example, a man says that his religion demands that he should be free to resort to human sacrifices, he must be told that we shall not allow it. If another man tells us that it is part of his religion to acknowledge the supremacy over his conduct of some priest, whether at home or abroad, he must be told that we shall not allow him to translate his belief into act, if

M

it leads him to transgress one iota of our laws. If another man tells us that it is part of his religion to obey a spiritual Potentate, who pretends, or who inherits the tradition of pretending, to influence his allegiance to our laws, he must be told that we will hold him in perpetual suspicion, and take all necessary precautions against him, until we have good reason to believe that his doctrine has been either formally abandoned or has died a natural death from the changed conditions of the world,—a change which may make all such pretensions harmless and even ridiculous. The whole of this demand, or claim of right, with all its consequences, cannot be stated too broadly. It may appear an abstract doctrine to us now, although even in our own days we have occasional warnings that cannot be disregarded. But we must fully realise and take in that, during the later half of the sixteenth century and the whole of the seventeenth century, this doctrine was not abstract at all, but ever present in the most concrete of all possible forms. The Roman Catholic Church over the whole of Europe was one great standing conspiracy against the English monarchy, and the liberties of England. With nations, even more than with the individual, the instincts, duties, and rights of self-preservation are absolute and supreme. We may think as we please of the origin of the quarrel between Henry VIII. and the Pope,—we may sympathize as we please, with either the Catholic or the Protestant cause, as each emerged out of the dubious personal motives in which the separation began. But we must all acknowledge that the highest interests of mankind and of nations were from the first involved, and we must acknowledge with perfect frankness the necessity under which England lay to use every old, and to forge every new weapon that could be serviceable in her own defence.

Farther, let us remember that at the time of which we are now speaking, those weapons against the Catholic Church in Ireland which are now known specially as the Penal Laws, were not in question. Those penal laws lie as yet a century and a half ahead of us. So far as the arbitrary conduct of Henry VIII., in ecclesiastical matters, is concerned, no just distinction can be drawn in principle between his conduct in Ireland and his conduct in England. In his time the purely theological rebellion against Rome was not yet fully developed, and, so far as it was seen at all, it is not probable that his proceedings were regarded with more general suspicion in Ireland than in England. It does so happen that in matters ecclesiastical, all the English Sovereigns since Henry II. had taken an active part in the maintenance of their rights over the Latin Church in Ireland. There was, in fact, in this matter a close alliance between the two branches of the English Government. The Irish people had been accustomed for many centuries, as we have seen, to see an antagonism between two Churches—both nominally Catholic—which hated each other with a mortal hatred. They had been accustomed to associate the Latin Church with its historical origin as introduced first by the Danes, and then upheld and extended by the Norman English. The rebellious Irish had more or less resented the original Papal gift of the Lordship over Ireland to the English Sovereign, and had, not very long before, addressed a laboured remonstrance to the Holy See against its legitimacy and justice.

Thus, all things considered, the conduct and policy of Henry VIII. in ecclesiastical matters had much more an aspect of natural continuity in Ireland than it had in England; and it should never be forgotten by Catholics even now that whatever share they may be disposed to claim for their Church in its influence over the Irish people, was a share due to the continual support and patronage of the English Kings against the anarchical and even degrading influences which had been long exercised by their own native and tribal ecclesiastical organisation. So far as the Irish rebels are concerned, whom Henry VIII. was called upon to suppress, it would be absurd to credit them with any motive connected with what is now called Catholic doctrine. It is indeed a significant circumstance, as indicating the real nature of that rebellion,—as it had been of all previous rebellions in Ireland,—that one of the very first things the Geraldines found it convenient to do, was to

murder the Archbishop of Dublin and his chaplains.*
There was absolutely no religious element, properly so
called, in the rebellion, and whatever ingredient there
may have been at a later time, which pretended to
the name of religion, was an ingredient involving
a permanent hostility to all that then concerned the
very existence of the English Government and nation.
In the days of Henry VIII. there was not even this
pretence. He found no difficulty whatever in procuring from the Irish Chiefs, without apparently any exception, a willing agreement to renounce the authority of
the Pope, and to acknowledge the Royal supremacy.
"The renunciation of the Pope's pretensions"—says
Dr. Richey—"was made a necessary article in the
submission of the local rulers. None of them seem
to have had any hesitation upon this subject. The
instruments still remaining are such as to forbid our
considering this arrangement less than universal." †

Nor is it less striking to find the explanation, given
by this excellent historian, of the causes which led, in
the course of some fifty or sixty years, to a change, as
regards this great test of Catholicity, in the attitude
of the native Irish. "They did not become ardent
Catholics until an intimate connection with Spain, at
the end of the sixteenth century, taught them that
the cause of Celtic independence, in order to be successful, must be united with the Catholic Church."
In other words, the Irish did not become ardent

* "Short History," pp. 304, 305. † Ibid., p. 363.

Catholics at all, until they found that, in the interests of their own rebellions, they must identify themselves with the declared enemies of England on the Continent of Europe. It follows from these facts, which are indisputable, that no condemnation can be passed on Henry VIII.'s conduct towards the Church in Ireland, except on grounds which would condemn equally, or even far more severely, his conduct in England. Dr. Richey does indeed indicate an opinion "that the monastic bodies in Ireland, at least those belonging to the Latin Church, were not as corrupt in morals as their brethren in England were alleged to be." This, we may or may not believe. There is no adequate evidence on the subject. But on the other hand there is abundant evidence of the utter uselessness of those bodies in Ireland for any of the great aims of Christian civilisation. They had become almost as tribal and ferocious in their habits as the degenerate representatives of the old Celtic Church of St. Patrick and Columba. They did nothing to maintain a religious life among the people—nothing even to restrain the most cruel crimes. "In an age," says Dr. Richey, "of lawlessness and violence, they never came forward to protest, as Christian priests, against the tyranny, robbery, and murder rife around them: their Bishops were, to a great extent, agents of the English Government; and the mass of the clergy were split into hostile parties, and participators in the national animosities and lawless violence of those times."* Nay, more than this :—the monastic clergy were often the most insensate instigators of the old intertribal hatreds. Abbots and monks would appear in arms, invade and slaughter the Irish people, and yet celebrate their Masses notwithstanding, and with hardly an interval of time to mitigate the desecration. They maintained no learning. They kept up no piety. They promoted no culture. So far from the intellectual condition of Ireland advancing with that of the Continent, it had retrograded continuously from the date of Edward Bruce's invasion; and its condition in the sixteenth resembled more that of the twelfth than that even of the fourteenth century." † In short, we may say with certainty that the practical independence of Ireland for so many centuries had ended, in spiritual matters as in secular affairs, in one universal scene of chaos and of crime, and that when "We"—England— began for the first time to "make the Irishman," we had everything to begin anew if the very foundations of civilisation were to be laid at all.

* "Short History," p. 295. † Ibid., p. 297.

CHAPTER VI.

THE EPOCH OF CONQUEST AND COLONISATION.

Passing now from the religious or ecclesiastical grievances of Ireland to that other great alleged source of grievance, the agrarian policy of the Tudors,—let us see how this stands. Irish Nationalist writers, and their new sympathisers in England, go on repeating that England forced upon Ireland her own "land laws," which were totally unsuited to the people, and have been the fountain of innumerable woes. Those who use this language never take the least trouble to define even to themselves what they mean by the "English system" of land tenure. Do they mean the size or extent of the Estates which were granted to new settlers? If so, they mean something which has no relation to the facts. There is no evidence that the new owners under the Tudors held their rights over larger areas of land than the old Celtic chiefs. Quite the contrary. Doubtless there were large grants in some cases. But they were generally, if not universally, the mere transfer to a new set of owners of great territorial estates held by the Celtic or Ersefied English who had rebelled. The general tendency was undoubtedly the other way —to cut up the old larger territorial possessions of the Irish chiefs into a greater number of comparatively limited estates. What then is meant by the English land system? Is it the system of rent-paying on the part of the peasantry, and rent-receiving on the part of the Proprietary class? Was there anything new in this? Is there any Irish writer—even a Nationalist—who will venture to deny that, under the old Irish system, rent or its equivalents were universally paid by all the occupiers of land? But more than this—can they deny that the equivalents for regular rent, in the shape of services and exactions of all kinds, were infinitely more oppressive under the old Celtic usages than under what they call the English system? Nothing can be more certain and more universally admittted by Irish historians and Annalists than the fact that the Chiefs habitually, and as part of the known usages of the country, could live upon their agricultural tenants by unlimited exactions— "eating them out of house and home," to use the expressive phrase adopted by that intense Irishman, Mr. Prendergast.

The one grand distinction between the English system and the Irish was precisely this—that whereas in Ireland there was no limit to feudal rent-exactions, except the possibility of getting them, under the

English system, the rent or dues were always limited and definite in amount. This was the one feature of English law which from the beginning had been attractive to some Irishmen, and had induced them to seek its protection, and even to buy it with large sums of money. But in this lay the whole wide difference between utter barbarism, and even the possibilities of civilisation. It is worse than a merely inflated fable—it is a direct opposite of the truth—that, in this fundamental matter, the Irish system was better for the people than the English system. It was not only worse, but it was worse in an immeasurable degree. There is no comparison at all between the two systems. The Irish system was incompatible with the very beginnings even of agricultural prosperity. The English system, on the contrary, was one which assured that prosperity in those gradual degrees which were proportionate to growing skill, and growing capital.

What then can be meant by the English system which has been the source of Ireland's woes? Usually that system has been identified with the custom—belonging to a later time,—under which the proprietor builds the houses on a farm, and encloses the fields, and drains the land. But, even in England, this custom came later than the sixteenth or even the earlier part of the seventeenth century, and was merely one of the natural and rational developments of the system of definite rents paid for definite privileges which were lent or let. Not that—even in Ireland—some analogies with this custom were wholly wanting. On the contrary, one very close analogy was common. The Irish peasantry—even the larger occupiers—were often, as we have seen, too much impoverished by centuries of desolating wars, to be able to provide "capital" in the only form in which it was known in those days, namely cattle. Consequently all over Ireland the ownership of the cattle had fallen almost wholly into the hands of the Chiefs who were the strongest, and they supplied to their dependents, at a rent, the whole stock, without which land had no value whatever. Hence we see the meaning of the Celtic eulogy on a great chief that he was a "great distributor of cows." Not in any other form was capital ever laid out on the land in those days—at least in Ireland. The houses of the whole people were nothing but huts and hovels. Even in England, down to a much later date, the rural population built their own cottages of wood and clay. Nothing else was thought of. But in the ownership by the chief of the only equipment of land which was known in those days,—the cattle—what is called vaguely the "English system" had its exact counterpart in Ireland as a necessity in the nature of the case. The one only difference which was essential was that in England all rents had been made definite and limited, instead of being, as in Ireland, indefinite and unlimited.

What other meaning, then, can there be in the inflated fable about the English land system? If it be that change in an agricultural system, which put an end to an absolutely sedentary population—never moving except when called to fight, or except when robbed and decimated, or even exterminated by a victorious enemy on the war-path—then indeed this was a change, not specially English, but world-wide, wherever peaceful industry began to be established instead of the universal profession of arms. When the new object and aim of life was to improve and cultivate the soil,—to produce better corn and better cattle,—then, of necessity, men came to be valued for their ability and industry in this happier pursuit. And just as men fared hardly in the military ages who were weak or cowardly, so, when the industrial ages began, men who were bad cultivators had to give place to better. The best interests of society,—and amongst other interests, that one of paramount importance, the increase of the food of the people,—were absolutely bound up with this great change. But it was not a change peculiar to England. It was European. And in those stagnant nations of the East where a sedentary population has been stereotyped by the survival of primitive conditions,—as in half-Oriental Russia—we now see, in our own day, nothing but extreme poverty, indebtedness, and frequent famines.

But next we come in the category of inflated fable

which ascribes all Irish woes to England, to the well-worn phrase of " frequent confiscations." Considering the unquestionable fact that a very large part—indefinite in numbers and equally indefinite in distribution—of the existing population of Ireland are the direct descendants of those to whom the land was given, and not of those from whom the land was taken,—this historical reminiscence does not seem to be very relevant. Considering the farther fact that the whole population of Ireland, without exception, have inherited whatever rights they possess in land from either the new race of owners who got the land for the first time, or from the old owners who were not disturbed in their possession, it does seem to be an " Irish idea " indeed to connect any of the evils which now exist or which have arisen within the last three hundred years with the " confiscations " of the sixteenth, or the early part of the seventeenth century.

But there is a great deal more than this to be said about the Irish confiscations. They are not generally or expressly referred to, and they cannot be referred to, as justifying or accounting for any sense of personal grievance in any portion of the mixed population which in Ireland, as elsewhere, is now a mongrel breed between those who gained and those who lost, at a time removed from us by so many generations. They are referred to for no other purpose than that of heaping up epithets, which may give the flavour of continuous wrong to all that was done by England against Ireland. It may be well, therefore, to point out the indisputable facts which show how thoroughly justified were most of the territorial confiscations upon every ground which has been universally acted upon by all nations and governments in the history of the world. There is not a civilised people now existing in Europe which is not living on "confiscated land." The confiscation may be more or less remote. But the fact is universal. There is not now such a thing in existence as aboriginal possession: and, for that matter, the Irish of the mediæval centuries were themselves conquerors, dispossessors, and enslavers, within a time still at least traditionally remembered. But, without going back to those fundamental facts of all our modern civilisation, there were special circumstances, in the case of Ireland, which, even in the light of modern law and practice, are a special justification and defence of the Irish confiscations three hundred years ago. If there were frequent confiscations, it was only because there were also frequent rebellions, and all of them more or less closely connected with the danger of foreign conspiracy and invasion. Then, besides this, there was the still higher ground for the confiscations, that the lands confiscated were almost universally in a barbarous condition of neglect and waste as regarded all the uses to which they were put.

As to the cultivation of the soil—there was none. The truth is that, when we come to look into the evidence furnished to us by Irish historians themselves, the only wonder is that confiscations on a large scale were so long delayed, rather than that some such confiscations were seen to be an absolute necessity at last. And it is indeed a memorable fact that they were not made when resentment against rebellion seemed most natural, and when, as a mere form of punishment, they would have been most amply justified. Nor were they dictated, as is often supposed, by any connection with religious persecution or even antagonism. Both Henry VIII., in spite of his quarrel with the Pope, and Edward VI., in spite of his more pronounced Protestantism in theology, dealt most gently with the conquered Irish rebels, and systematically avoided territorial confiscations. It was a Catholic Sovereign, —Queen Mary—who began those confiscations and adopted on a considerable scale the policy of Plantations in Ireland. Mary, indeed, was a Catholic, but she was also an English Queen, and she was a Tudor. Whatever she might believe as to the Mass, or even as to the supremacy of the Pope in matters of spiritual belief, she was not willing to abate one iota of her Sovereignty, or to sacrifice the interests of England as a Nation, or as an Imperial Government. The Irish Chiefs, on the other hand, did not care at all either for her religion or for their own; and, despite her Catholicism, her accession to the crown was at once marked by a revival of their rebellious habits. Farther than this —there was the urgent fact to be dealt with,—that a great district in Ireland,—close to the old English Pale, within easy reach of the Capital, and commanding access to other parts of Ireland, lay in the hands of certain chiefs who kept it in a state of absolute waste, and valued it only as the inaccessible harbourage of the armed bands with which they raided the surrounding provinces. The continued possession of it by them made any progress towards even a decent civilisation impossible in a region lying close to the very heart of the kingdom. Never, therefore, in the history of the world, could there be a more thorough justification, or indeed a more absolute necessity for the action of any Sovereign than that which was taken by Queen Mary, when she erected the great territory held by the O'Mores and the O'Connors into the civilised districts ever since known as the Queen's County and King's County.

Dr. Richey as usual admits all the facts, and as usual also gives way to the most incongruous sentiments of censure and regret. He admits that "no Irish tribe had been the cause of such constant annoyance to the English Government." He admits that the territory they held was "theoretically,"—that is to say legally,—a part of the territory of the arch-rebel Geraldine, who had been the cause of the war in 1553, and whose lands were justly forfeited by rebellion. He admits that it was simply "a wild pathless tract of forest and bog, almost inaccessible to the forces of the Crown." He admits that it menaced the Pale, and threatened the communications between Dublin and Kilkenny. He admits that the tribe was so wild and lawless as to be a perpetual danger to the Government, and that they had been the most active supporters of the Geraldine rebellion—in short, he admits every fact which establishes not only the fullest justification of the action of Queen Mary, but the absolute necessity for it in the interests of her kingdom and people. He further admits that after all the Queen did not wish or propose to expel the whole native population, but only to make a division of the land between them and new settlers, who could, and who would improve the country, and keep the peace. Nay more,—he admits the triumphant success of the first Plantation—how the country became improved—how the dense thickets were removed—how the bogs were reclaimed—how wealth and comfort were established,—where nothing but savagery and poverty had held sway for centuries. Yet he cannot help inserting the qualifying epithet "material" before the word "wealth"—as if any spiritual or intellectual wealth had flourished in the woods and bogs of a tribe of lawless freebooters! But the most candid admission of all is that which this excellent historian makes as regards the general result of the Plantation. He says that result was such as to satisfy alike "the statesman, the lawyer, and the economist." Surely under one or other of those three categories every consideration may be brought which ought to determine the conduct of civilised and Christian Governments. Let us admit—if this be demanded of us—the right of the O'Mores and the O'Connor tribesmen to fight for the continued possession of their old wasted lands—as we are told they did go on fighting for their woods and bogs until they were either expelled or exterminated. We may even sympathise with them in such a struggle, just as we sympathise with any other wild creatures whose habits and whose traditions are incompatible with the very elements of civilisation. But at least do not let us commit the double absurdity and injustice of blaming the Sovereign, or the nation, which was compelled to assert its own supremacy, or of pretending that the existing population of those two Irish counties have been injured by the conquest of their barbarian predecessors, or by the civilised laws which they now enjoy.

Nor is it enough to stand on the defensive in this great question as regards the conduct of England towards Ireland. Of the seventy years that passed between the time when Henry VIII. undertook, in earnest and at last, an effective subjugation of Ireland under the English Crown and the English law, every year was marked by some step more or less sure, however slow, towards the great end of securing for the first time some measure of prosperity and civilisation among a people who, for more than seven hundred years, had been the prey and the victims of their own desolating tribal wars. The remaining years of Henry's own life, the seven years of his son Edward VI.,—the five years of the Catholic Queen Mary—had all seen substantial progress made, in spite of many difficulties, in one part of the island or another. The forty-five years of Queen Elizabeth's reign were full of events which more than ever impressed upon the English people the life-and-death character of the struggle which she had to maintain in Ireland, against foreign as well as domestic foes. The half-century of the Spanish Armada was one which burnt this great lesson into the English heart and mind. Elizabeth found on her hands a war with France and a war with Scotland. She could barely afford to keep up a little force of fifteen hundred men in Ireland. The "Ersefied" Geraldines were again meditating rebellion, and a renewal of the alliance with the old Celtic rebel chiefs. The North of Ireland was being rapidly "planted" by invaders from the Celtic Hebrides, as hostile to England as the Irish tribes whom they had exterminated or driven out.

It was under these circumstances that Queen Elizabeth at once indicated her determination to pursue her sister's policy of Plantations—that is to say, of colonising appropriate parts of Ireland with loyal and industrious subjects, and especially that part of the North of Ireland which was then being actually "planted" by men who were at once exterminators of the native Irish and, at the same time, inveterate enemies of England. Thus so early as the very first year after her accession, the Plantation of Ulster, subsequently effected with such triumphant success, was deliberately planned by Queen Elizabeth, with the view, as she expressed it, "of peopling some parts thereof (Ireland), and especially the North, now possessed with the Scots."* But next followed the War of Shane O'Neill, one of the last of the contests between the English Crown and a great Irish rebel chief. It is useless and irrelevant to lay any stress on this man's personal character. Dr. Richey implies that English writers have exaggerated the blackness of its features. But his own account of it may well satisfy the most hostile writer who has ever painted the characteristics of that kind and type of man. Dr. Richey admits that he "was a murderer;" that he was "bloodthirsty and merciless;" that he was "false and treacherous;" that he was "profligate in his life;" that he was a "drunkard;" that he was a "tyrant;" —that he was "barbarous in his manners." But against all those admissions Dr. Richey sets off counter-accusations against the personal character of many of his enemies. With all this we have really nothing to do. What we have to do with is the much more important admission of Dr. Richey that "Shane O'Neill," whose family and clan had accepted the Earldom of Tyrone from Henry VIII., was aiming in his war at no object short of that of making himself King of Ulster."† What we have to do with is his

* "Short History," p. 451. † Ibid., p. 461.

farther admission that England under Queen Elizabeth —the "We" of Mr. Gladstone—acted under the one "fixed idea" that this was not to be allowed. What we also have to do with, as a subordinate fact and consideration, is this—that Dr. Richey admits, farther, that Shane's ambition was not at all in the interest even of his brother Celts in Ireland, inasmuch as it was no object of his "to unite the Ulster Chiefs, but to crush them beneath him." What we have to do with—in short—are the conclusions admirably expressed by this writer himself in the following words, giving a summary of the whole war: "The leading native Chief aimed at establishing his ancient supremacy in utter disregard of the changed condition of things, and uninfluenced either by patriotism or religion—staked his existence in the attempt at once to resist foreign dominion, and crush into obedience his traditional vassals: (whilst) the lesser chiefs, equally regardless of country, sought only to maintain their local independence, and hailed the English as deliverers."* At last, in 1567, Shane O'Neill was defeated, and took refuge with the Hebridean Celts who had devastated a great part of Ulster. By them in a drunken brawl, and in revenge for old injuries, he was in true Irish fashion hacked to pieces, along with all his immediate followers who had not time to mount their horses and escape.

Next and last came the "Desmond War"—one of a

* "Short History," p. 489.

similar kind, but contemporary with other events of high significance in judging of the conduct of England towards Ireland. There is one method of looking at history which may often be most usefully adopted. It is the method of looking back on the conduct of men very much as we look on the actions of the lower animals, or of the inanimate agencies of nature. On this method we do not read of, or look at, events with any reference either to praise or blame. We do not even think of conduct as determined by reason, but only of action as determined by causes. Reason, of course, is in itself not only one cause, but the very highest and noblest of all causes. But men cannot be considered always as purely reasoning beings. They are governed by feelings and impulses which are comparatively in the nature of mere physical causes. It is in this aspect that—more or less consciously—Irish historians are apt to take up the defence of their countrymen in the past centuries. We are summoned to consider what was only natural and inevitable in their conduct—they being what they were. This is quite fair—so far as it goes,—and it is an aspect of every historical question which ought never to be altogether neglected.

But if this criterion of judgment be adopted as regards the conduct of the native Irish during the sixteenth and seventeenth centuries, or in any other century, we have a right to demand that it be equally applied to the conduct of the English Government and people at the same epochs. And this, with his usual candour, Dr. Richey admits. He is honest enough to conceal nothing, although he treads lightly sometimes on the tremendous significance of the contemporary events of that memorable time of thirty-six years, which elapsed between the suppression of Shan O'Neill's rebellion in 1567 and the end of the reign of Queen Elizabeth in 1603.

That was the time when England stood almost alone in Europe, not only as the bulwark of a theological Protestantism, but as the one great mainstay and defence of all the liberties, political and intellectual, of the civilised world. It was the time of the great Catholic reaction—of the counter-Reformation—of the cruel and sanguinary wars in the Low Countries carried on by the armies of Spain under Alva—of the organised attack on England by the Spanish Armada. It opened with the promulgation in 1569 of a Bull of Excommunication by the Pope against Queen Elizabeth—an instrument which was expressly intended to release all her subjects from the duty of allegiance and which, it was specially hoped, might rouse the native Irish, who were all Catholic, to reinforce foreign invasion by domestic treason and rebellion. We may try to conceive—perhaps it is difficult now to do so adequately,—so far off do those times seem to be—with what feelings of indignation, exasperation, and defiance, those events must have inspired all Englishmen in defence of everything that they held most sacred. This is enough not only to account for all they did, but also, at least as regards their aim and motive, to justify their conduct and even to make it glorious. The danger was great, imminent, and perpetually renewed. There was hardly a year of that long generation when there was not some dark cloud on the horizon—some threat of invasion—some fresh intrigue with Irish rebels, or even some alarming successes of those rebels to keep up the national excitement, and to warn England that she must strain every nerve to secure her safety by keeping whole the integrity of her dominion. Spanish correspondence and intrigue was always going on. Spanish ships were constantly hovering round the coasts of Ireland. The Desmond rebellion arose in the Province of Munster—suppressed indeed easily as regards military operations, but at great cost and trouble. This was followed by another of those Plantations which gave to Ireland the only prosperous populations she had held for centuries. Then came a renewed rebellion on the part of the great clan of the O'Neills, represented by the Earl of Tyrone.

So formidable was this rebellion at one time that, in 1598, the Queen's army was defeated with great slaughter, including the Marshal in command, and eighteen out of twenty-three officers of rank. England was at last thoroughly aroused and alarmed. An army of twenty thousand men had to be poured into the country; castles were stormed, the territories of the enemy were wasted with fire and sword. Forts were established, and the country occupied by an army of men, many of whom had seen the butcheries of the Catholic party in the Low Country. Then followed another signal proof of the real danger to be feared. A Spanish fleet arrived on the Irish coast in 1601. It landed a force at Kinsale; and called on all Irishmen to rise in the name of the Pope. "I speak to Catholics," said Don Juan de Aquila, the Spanish General, "not to froward heretics." Another force of Spaniards soon landed at Castlehaven, and then at once the Irish Chiefs of Cork and Kerry rose and joined their allies. Nothing could so well serve to burn into the very heart of England the inseparable connection between Irish rebellion and the utmost peril of her own destruction. The joint Spanish-Irish army was defeated with a slaughter aggravated, as usual, by the ferocity of the Irish element which was in alliance with the English army. Yet so far was the conduct of England from being unreasonably vindictive after her victory, that it may well astonish us to recollect that Tyrone was ultimately allowed to retain his possessions almost on the same terms which he had himself proposed several years before. Well might Tyrone "burst into tears" when he heard of the death of Queen Elizabeth, as he rode into Dublin in 1603. For, unlike the Queen herself, neither her English nor her loyal Irish subjects could bear to see a man treated with honour and kept in great local power, who had done his very best to bring down upon Ireland the dominion of Philip of Spain. New Catholic conspiracies, as is well known, real or believed, speedily inflamed still farther the fears and the passions of all who were filled with the spirit of a natural and justifiable distrust; until at last, in 1607, the last of the Irish Chiefs, who had so long kept up the traditions of anarchy, violence, and rebellion, fled from Ireland, and the real conquest of the Island was at last crowned by the Plantation of a half-empty and desolated Province, by James I.

But now let us again proceed in our review of the centuries of Irish history. The dominant facts and considerations, by which we are bound to judge of the conduct of both parties engaged in the wars of the concluding years of the sixteenth century, are the same facts and principles by which we must continue to judge of them during the whole of the seventeenth. Religion and politics were inseparably interwoven. That Christ's kingdom is "not of this world" was a doctrine neither accepted nor even understood by anybody. The great contest lay between the cause of Rome and despotic governments on the one side, and the cause of Protestant England and constitutional liberty on the other. Ireland was only one of the battle-fields on which this great contest was carried on. By all means, let the conduct of both parties be considered as "only natural." But let this doctrine be equally applied. Even if the principle of perfect religious toleration had been admitted by either of them, it would not have been applicable to the case. Catholicism did not represent religion—pure and unmixed. It represented, in a pre-eminent degree, politics in its most fundamental principles. It represented ambitions of dominion—fierce hatreds and antipathies—and resolutions of violence fortified by the flavour of religious fanaticism. The English Government and people, on the other hand, represented in an intense degree the spirit of a proud nationality, and all the passions which are naturally aroused by the danger or by the fear of losing it. Looking at events in this point of view, it is quite idle to blame either party. What we ought to do is to make due allowance for both in respect to personal conduct, and above all to associate our sympathies with whichever cause we can best identify as representing the lasting interests of mankind. In this point of view it is quite possible, or ought to be possible, for us now to cast aside all thought of the questions of mere theology which distinguish the Roman from the Reformed Churches. But let us always remember that a great nation is a thing of infinite value in the history of mankind—of a value altogether immeasurable as compared with rude local tribes such as the Irish, with an almost unbroken history of anarchy and barbarism for more than a thousand years. We have only to look at the conduct of Mary Tudor,—an intense Catholic in her personal religious belief,—to see this great natural connection, and the universal instinct of it, translated into corresponding action. The Protestant Sovereign, James, who succeeded the half-Catholic sister of Mary Tudor, pursued exactly the same policy, and with as complete justification in Ulster, which Mary Tudor had pursued in the district of the O'Mores and the O'Connors. Nor can it be questioned that the Plantation of Ulster was even more successful. To this day it is the most industrious and peacefnl part of Ireland. In respect to that Plantation we may use the words of Dr. Richey in respect to the Queen's and King's Counties by the Catholic Queen Mary Tudor—that "the statesman, the economist, and the lawyer may alike be satisfied."

CHAPTER VII.

THE SEVENTEENTH CENTURY.

WITH the "Flight of the Earls," the last of the great Irish Chiefs,—with the death of Queen Elizabeth, and the Plantation of Ulster,—we enter on the full current of that seventeenth century which was everywhere an epoch of civil and of foreign wars and of political troubles—all of them animated with, and some of them entirely dominated by, the fiercest religious passions. They were prolonged and destructive over almost the whole of Europe. They caused much suffering and distress in England, still more in Scotland. But in Ireland it may be said with truth that the whole century presented the spectacle of a veritable Pandemonium. It was truly a hell upon earth. Each party when dissecting the conduct of the other can truthfully describe it in the blackest colours of injustice, violence, and the most savage cruelty. For this period we lose the guidance of that historian, Dr. Richey, whose perfect fidelity to fact we have seen to be wholly unaffected by his occasional outbursts of inconsistent sentiment. But it is more than a full compensation that we come instead under the guidance of another Irish historian of the highest rank in English literature, Mr. Lecky. In tone and balance of mind he is quite as judicial as Dr. Richey, and, if there is any bias due to nationality, it takes the better and stronger line of protesting against the somewhat rough partisanship of Mr. Froude. In dealing with the dreadful massacres of Protestants with which the great Irish rebellion of 1641 began, Mr. Lecky has proved, I think, to demonstration that at least the extent and number of them has been greatly exaggerated. In dealing with the causes which led up to that rebellion, he has laid an amount of stress on the feelings of exasperation roused by the policy of conquest and of Plantations which tends, I think, to obscure our memory of the preceding condition of the country, of its utter anarchy—of its chronic poverty, of its decimation by other enemies, and of the hopeless waste of its naturally fertile lands by the most barbarous systems of native exactions. But Mr. Lecky's great point is one in which he is indisputably right—namely, this—that the Catholics in Ireland had the best reason to be convinced that, in a yearly increasing degree, the Government, and especially the Parliament of England, was aiming at, and was determined to effect, the complete suppression of their Church, which was to them the whole of their religion.

In the time of Henry VIII. this had not been true. Considerations of policy, and not of religion, had been supreme with him. This was still more evident and was made indeed conspicuous in the conduct of Mary Tudor. Even Queen Elizabeth was but a half-hearted Protestant in theology. But, during the reign of James I., and still more during the reign of his successor, Charles I., that torrent of Protestant passion, which—in the form of Puritanism—had been gathering head for many years in England, burst through all restraint, and obtained complete possession of the English people and of the English House of Commons. Mr. Lecky is fully justified in pointing out this great historical fact, and in putting prominently forward, in mitigation of the conduct of the Irish, that to a large extent they were then a "half-savage" people whose native soil had been invaded, conquered, and planted by those whom they regarded as hereditary enemies, and whose religion was directly threatened with extinction.

It is quite fair to remember all this. But what is imperatively demanded, if we take the philosophical line in judging of human conduct, is that we should apply it equally all round. I am not quite sure that in trying to redress one side of the balance, Mr. Lecky always recollects the other side. If Ireland had good reason to believe that Protestant and half-Puritan England was determined on the suppression of their Church, most assuredly England had equal reason to be convinced that the Catholic party, both in Ireland and all over the Continent, was one vast and ever-active conspiracy to overthrow Protestantism in England, and to crush her liberties under both a political and a religious despotism. The Irish Catholic party was known to be in constant communication with the implacable enemies of England; and the only course for a philosophical politician to take is to consider two great questions, first—which of the two great contending parties in Europe began the course of religious tyranny, intolerance, and savage cruelty;—and secondly, which of those two parties was, on the whole, most freighted with the principles and beliefs on which the progress of the world depends. To some extent, of course, the last of these two questions may, even still, be a matter of opinion. There may be men surviving in the nineteenth century who think that it would have been better for the world, and for Christianity in particular, if Ireland, and England too, had been subjected to the Government of Philip of Spain, or of Louis XIV., and if Protestantism had been put down by such measures as Alva used in the Low Countries, and the French monarch adopted in the revocation of the Edict of Nantes. But as to the first of the two questions above indicated—which of the parties began persecution—there can be but one reply. It is a matter of historical fact, and not at all a matter of opinion. The abominable doctrine, that men's religious convictions were to be put down by force, and that heresy was to be quenched in blood, was then the favourite doctrine of the "Catholic" Church. Nor was it a doctrine only. It was put in practice and enforced all over Europe in the very sight and hearing of those who in England came to identify the Catholic cause in Ireland, and everywhere else, with the ruin of all that was dear to them in life. And even if they had not been Protestants they had at least the same interests and inducements connected with an Imperial dominion as those which dictated the conduct of Mary Tudor, the Catholic Queen of England.

And then, is there not another aspect of the whole case which is forgotten in Mr. Lecky's excellent chapter on the history of Ireland during that dreadful century—the seventeenth? If we are to be really philosophical historians, is it possible to avoid the questions which arise when we weigh in the balance of a higher morality, and of a higher knowledge, the comparative character of the many motives which have been the cause of man's fearful "inhumanity to man"? How stand the ferocious hatreds and the cruel deeds of clan and intertribal wars as compared with those which have their origin in conviction, however false and misdirected, as to the duty of enforcing religious truth? Which has the nobler elements of the two? Which of them stands nearest to the dawn of a rising day? Yet it is undeniable that the miseries of Ireland,—and they can hardly be exaggerated—during at least a thousand years, had been due entirely to that lowest form and stage of perverted human instincts. Men who fight, and spoil, and massacre under the fierce incitements of religious bigotry, or of the pride of a great national dominion, have at least some great object in view. Men who do the same under no other incitement than hereditary feuds, or the plunder of cows, have nothing in view that can be even called a cause in the progress of humanity. Mr. Lecky holds up to just condemnation the conduct and the language of Cromwell when he put to death a number of helpless Catholic captives after he had stormed the city of Wexford. And yet, on a smaller scale, and under no similar fanaticism, such massacres had been constant in the fights between native chiefs and tribes during many centuries. Then, again—as regards the lower motives of cupidity on which Mr. Lecky dwells in the conduct of the English in Ireland, we may well ask whether is it worse to covet land for the purpose of planting a higher civilisation, than to covet cattle for no other purpose than that of mere plunder and robbery? This had been the most constant and predominant of all motives in the Irish native wars; and it often involved not merely the most abject poverty to the vanquished, but the extreme consequences of actual famine. Then lastly—if we are to be philosophical,—is it fair to forget that the very feelings of indignation and of horror with which we now read the words of Cromwell, in respect to the massacre of rebellious Catholics, are feelings which have arisen out of the very conquest he effected, and even out of the triumph of the special sect to which he belonged. The Independents—threatened with persecution by both Episcopalians and Presbyterians—were the first Christian sect to proclaim the doctrine of religious toleration; and the inconsistent conduct of Cromwell towards the Roman Catholics is one of the many proofs that throughout the seventeenth century and, as we shall presently see, down to a much later date, the Catholic Church was never in that century thought of as a mere theological or religious sect, but as a great political power, acting under the most determined motives of political domination, and armed with the most formidable means of military strength.

But the main lesson to be enforced from the history of Ireland, during the whole of the seventeenth century, is to establish the conclusion that it must be withdrawn absolutely from our reckoning of the time during which Ireland was, in any proper sense of the term, under the Government of England. It was a century mainly occupied by the completion of the necessary work of conquest. That work, even if it had been conducted most humanely, instead of being conducted as it was under every possible inducement to the most passionate indignation, was in itself a work incompatible with the exhibition of the settled and peaceful policy of an established government. Consequently any charge against England, which is founded on the omission or forgetfulness of this cardinal fact, is liable, in proportion to the injustice of the terms in which it is conveyed, to the condemnation of being a serious misrepresentation. And nothing, accordingly, can be more grossly unfair and unjust than the language used on more than one occasion by Mr. Gladstone, when, for political purposes, it has been his object to heap up odium against England, under the plausible appearance of candour by the use of the pronoun "We." Thus, for example, the employment of foreign mercenaries in putting down the rebellion by King William has been referred to as aggravating the sins of England in the vindication of his sovereignty over Ireland,—a reproach which implicitly, although not explicitly, implies the glaring injustice of assuming that the invocation of foreign intervention was the special and peculiar iniquity of England—whereas it is notorious that foreign intervention had been the one hope and the one strenuous endeavour of all Irish rebels since the invasion of Edward Bruce in the fourteenth century: had been resorted to repeatedly during later centuries — was most conspicuous and most dangerous to England during the whole of the century then running,—and, in the final struggle at the Battle of the Boyne, was visibly represented by the presence of some ten thousand men of the best troops of France. This sort of misrepresentation is a great deal worse than merely "inflated fable." That phrase may mean nothing worse than great exaggeration. But the ripping up, by a minister of the Crown, of old animosities by a special accusation, which of necessity implies a total misrepresentation of historic truth, is a far worse offence than any amount of mere exaggeration.

Then there is another item in Mr. Gladstone's language about Ireland which is open to an objection almost equally serious. He has denied that the Irish Catholic party has ever shown any disposition to persecute the Protestants. It is, of course, true that as the purely religious element did not, as we have seen, enter much into the inducements to Irish rebellion until the beginning of the seventeenth century, and as, moreover, the Catholic party had no general ascendency, except for a moment, at the end of it, the odium of religious persecution attaches most visibly to the Protestant and not to the Catholic cause. But, besides and in addition to the close alliance of the Irish Catholic party with those foreign Governments who were pre-eminently persecutors, when, at the Revolution, a moment did come when the Irish Catholics gained a complete ascendency, then the disposition towards religious persecution blazed forth in overt acts of the utmost violence and injustice. Mr. Lecky has indeed, fairly enough, protested against the one-sidedness of the dark pictures drawn by Macaulay of the deeds of the Irish Parliament of 1699. In the same spirit of philosophic equity in which he has pleaded in palliation of the Irish massacres of 1641-2, on the ground mainly of intense provocation, he has also pleaded in palliation of the forfeitures and attainders of Protestants by this almost purely Irish Parliament. I have not a word to say against this view of the case when it is equally applied. But it must be so applied to be at all compatible with truth and justice. And when this application is made, it remains undeniable that the doctrines of religious persecution were then the doctrines of the Catholic party, and its practice, too, whenever it got the power.

The truth thus comes clearly out, as the result of the historical facts which I have now traced, that we must practically subtract the whole of the seventeenth century from the time during which England has been fully and really responsible for the Government of Ireland. Her assured and complete dominion did not begin until the close of that century, or rather the beginning of the eighteenth century, when William III. finally accomplished the suppression of the Irish rebellion.

Our investigation into the course of Irish history has now established the conclusion that, so far as those causes are concerned which determined the domestic and economic condition of the people, they lay entirely outside the power of the earlier English "Lords," or of the later English Kings of Ireland. Those causes lay not only predominantly, but almost exclusively, in the persistent survival in Ireland of native habits, usages, and traditions, some of which had indeed been common to the earlier stages of society in other countries, but the whole of which in Ireland had yielded to no process of development except the development of increasing barbarism and destructiveness. The seventeenth century was almost wholly occupied by civil wars incidental to the indispensable work of establishing English sovereignty, and of repelling the danger of a foreign dominion over one of the three kingdoms. With the concluding ten years of that century, and with the opening years of the eighteenth, we for the first time enter upon a time when England did become more or less responsible for the government of Ireland in so far as the possession of full dominion, and of supreme political power, were concerned. This condition of things, however, lasted only till the year 1782, when a virtual independence was conceded to a native Parliament. From that moment any supreme power was lost, and with it any supreme responsibility; so that, as one striking result of all these indisputable facts, we see that the inflated fable of "seven centuries" of English rule over Ireland becomes reduced in sober truth to a period of rule less prolonged than that of many a single human life. And, although, no doubt, it is conceivably possible to do much harm even to a nation in the course of a single human life, it is plain that we begin our farther investigation of this fractional period in a closely consecutive history of more than a thousand years, with a presumption of tremendous force that the influences and tendencies which had gathered strength during that long lapse of time, did not at one fixed date suddenly cease to be, but, on the contrary, that they must have continued to exert a more or less powerful influence for the ninety-two years which followed the nine hundred years preceding. Only in the case of the complete extermination or the complete expulsion of any people can such a complete break be effected in the continuity of social causes; and in the case of Ireland, much as we all talk of the confiscations and plantations of the Catholic Queen Mary, of Queen Elizabeth, of James I., and of Cromwell, yet, after all, the great bulk of the Irish people were comparatively unaffected, and remained in a great deal larger numbers and in greater force than was sufficient to carry on the old habits and traditions of the race to which they belonged, with all the peculiar social and political conditions which had made them what they were.

When, therefore, Mr. Lecky says that no Government has ever had more complete or more uncontrolled power over any people than England had over Ireland from the battle of the Boyne, which completed the conquest in 1690, down to 1782, we may accept this assertion implicitly without any sacrifice of our right and our duty to examine very carefully the limitations under which alone it can possibly be true. It is true in all senses except that in which any political power is supposed to be independent of the nature of things—of surrounding facts—of the influences which these facts must necessarily exert upon the minds both of governors and of the governed—of the purely physical materials it has to work upon—and of the universally accepted doctrines of men in the epoch in which that power is exercised. Mr. Lecky, as we shall see, fully admits these limitations, at least in general terms, although I do not think he quite sees some of them, or fully appreciates the full force of others which he does see and does specify.

In the first place, then, let us recollect what was the physical condition of Ireland at the close of the long and exhausting civil wars, which were at least as destructive as—although they could hardly be worse than—her own old intertribal, continual, and internecine fightings. All Irish historians are agreed that the destruction of human life, and especially of property, effected during the civil wars which followed the great rebellion of 1641, was only to be compared with the similar devastations of the Island produced by the invasion of Edward Bruce in the fourteenth century, and from which Ireland is said not to have recovered for many generations. The population was reduced to the lowest ebb both in number and resources. The Island was still covered with bogs and forests. No beginnings even of agricultural improvement had been possible, or were even conceivable to the people. They were sunk in ignorance and superstition. The only form in which capital had ever been known in Ireland, namely, the form of cattle, was as nearly exhausted as was compatible with the bare maintenance of life among a scanty population, ignorant even of the commonest expedients for keeping cattle alive during the winter months. Mr. Lecky, in justly deprecating extreme censure on these poor people when they broke out in deeds of cruelty and massacre against the Protestants who were suppressing their religion and occupying their lands, calls them "half-savages," And this is the plain truth—implying no disbelief in the high capacities of a quick-witted and imaginative race, but simply describing the condition as to the very elements of civilisation in which centuries of their own native misgovernment had left them. But if this was the admitted condition of the people, and of the country, it must be admitted, not for the purpose of one particular argument alone, but for all the arguments which it may effect. Such was the physical condition of the country, which for the first time fell into the hands of England to be governed, and such was the economic and the intellectual condition of the great mass of its people. One immediate and insuperable consequence was this,—never now sufficiently thought of or considered,—that even as regarded the mere physical or material improvement of the country—the drainage of bogs, the clearing of forest thickets, and the reclamation of other kinds of waste land, for the mere production of human food in any tolerable sufficiency—the sole reliance of England, and of Ireland herself, lay in the new planters, whether as owners or as mere occupiers, who brought at least some knowledge, some skill, some industry, and some capital into the island. We have only to follow up this fact and this reflection to a few of its most immediate consequences to see how much they practically involve. They indicate that inseparable connection which exists between the natural action of human instincts and the ultimate welfare of mankind. The instinct of nations in respect to the security of their dominion, and of individual men in respect to the security of whatever property they may have acquired, is a universal and insuperable instinct; and we see how in abstract economic reasoning both those intincts, which are indeed one, must have co-operated with increased intensity in Ireland from the moment that the suppression of rebellion had been accomplished by William III.

The next step follows as a matter of necessary consequence. The head and front of the offending of England against Ireland at this time is most truly identified with the two great systems of policy and of law which the English Government brought into new operation. One of these was the system of Penal Laws against the Irish Catholics, and the other was the system of Protective Laws against the commercial freedom of all Irishmen, whether Catholic or Protestant. Nothing can be more true than that these were for a while, if not the dominant, at least the most conspicuous, features in the new government of England. Yet if we look at each of them in turn we shall see, as Mr. Lecky most fairly admits, that the conduct of England, in respect to both of them, was dictated by motives, and under conditions, of almost insuperably coercive strength.

In the first place, both Dr. Richey and Mr. Lecky—pattern historians in recording facts—admit explicitly that the Irish Penal Laws, which were enacted between 1700 and 1709, were nothing but the echo and rejoinder, on the part of Protestant England, to the innumerable persecuting laws and practices of the Catholic party all over Europe wherever it had the power. "The celebrated penal laws," says Dr. Richey, "are the reflection of the equally detestable legislation of the Bourbons." * I attach no importance to Mr. Lecky's notice and admission of the fact that the penal laws of Queen Anne were passed through the instrumentality of the Irish and not of the English Parliament; because, as the English Parliament was supreme, the ultimate and the substantial responsibility may undoubtedly be laid upon it. But I do attach great importance to the fact, as admitted by Mr. Lecky, that, at that time, "over the greater part of Europe, the relations of Protestantism and Catholicism were still those of deadly hostility." * I attach

---

* "Short History," p. 132.
† Lecky's "History of Ireland," vol. i. p. 241.

still greater importance to the more detailed and specific admission of the same conscientious historian, when he informs his readers that the Irish penal laws "were largely modelled after the French legislation against the Huguenots; but persecution in Ireland never approached in severity that of Louis XIV.; and it was absolutely insignificant compared with that which had extirpated Protestantism and Judaism from Spain." *

But this is not all—it is not even the strongest fact that is to be remembered in judging of the conduct of England at this time. It would have been indeed an irrational and a purely savage proceeding, to revenge upon the Irish the iniquities of foreign Governments, if no urgent danger, and hardly any risk even, would arise in Ireland from this universal temper of Catholicism towards Protestantism in general, and towards England in particular. But the matter is wholly altered, and the whole complexion of the question changed, the moment it is admitted that England still was, or at any rate conceived herself to be in imminent danger, from year to year, from the old Catholic conspiracy against her among the Continental States—certain to make use, as they had always done, of Catholic disaffection in Ireland for the suppression of Protestantism and the overthrow of the English Monarchy. Now, it is on this very question that Mr. Lecky, with his usual fairness, gives emphatic, though somewhat scattered, testimony. In

* Lecky's "History of Ireland," vol. i. p. 137.

the first place, he makes at the very outset of his history of the eighteenth century, this striking statement:—"The position of the new dynasty was exceedingly precarious, and its downfall would inevitably be followed by a new revolution of property in Ireland." The only defect in this statement is, that it rather seems to limit the consequences of the overthrow of the Protestant Monarchy in England to a revolution in respect to "property." It is needless to say that it would have been a revolution in everything else—to all that Englishmen hold dear in law, liberty, and life.

In harmony with these facts, and in an inseparable connection with them, Mr. Lecky fully admits that the Irish penal laws were "not mainly the product of religious feeling, but of policy."* Again, he says, "Besides, there was in reality not much religious fanaticism."† And, yet once more, in connection with his distinction between the safety of property and the safety of all on which property depends, he says, "The penal Code, as it was actually carried out, was inspired much less by fanaticism than by rapacity, and was directed less against the Catholic religion than against the property and industry of its professors."‡ All these are but different ways of expressing the unquestionable fact that the Irish penal laws had essentially a political origin and a political aim, and that this aim was nothing less

---

* Lecky's "History of Ireland," vol. i. p. 137.
† Ibid., p. 168. ‡ Ibid., p. 152.

important than the security of the Protestant religion, and of the English Government and nation. Not only are all the historical facts connected with these Acts consistent with this explanation of them, but they are inconsistent with any other. The penal laws did not prohibit or proscribe Catholic religious worship, pure and simple. On the contrary, they expressly permitted it, and provided for its lawful celebration by registered Priests, and in registered Chapels. What they did strike at and prohibit was the entry into the kingdom, not of parochial priests, but of the Regular Orders and of the Bishops and higher dignitaries of the Catholic Church. The reason for this distinction is clear. Neither the Monks nor the Bishops were essential to the ordinary ministration of the altar or of the Confessional; whilst, on the other hand, the Monks were considered as the soldiers, and the hierarchy as the commanding officers, of the great Papal army. How thoroughly justified was the English Government in those assumptions, comes out in a strong light indeed from a discovery, which Mr. Lecky tells us has been made in documents recently brought to light. For from these documents it appears not only that all the Catholic priests in Ireland were in sentiment and opinion adherents of the Pretender, but that he actually held from the Pope the personal privilege, during the whole of his life, of appointing his own nominees to the Catholic bishoprics in Ireland.

This remarkable discovery only reveals what was practically known or correctly presumed at the time, and is a complete vindication of conduct on the part of the English Government which has been falsely called, and attributed to, religious intolerance and persecution. If a religious communion chooses to act the part of a political conspiracy it must take the consequences. The same interpretation of the whole aim of the penal laws is enforced by the nature of those provisions which have naturally attracted most attention because of their exceeding oppressiveness and injustice from every other point of view. These provisions were specially directed to prevent Catholics from acquiring wealth, or from attaining official positions which could give them the least political power. Especially were they directed to impede them in the retention or acquisition of that form of wealth which, in those days, was most connected with political and territorial influence—namely, landed property. Although far less bloody and ferocious than the contemporary action of Catholics in the persecution of Protestants on the Continent, the Irish penal laws seem specially odious from the very fact that they were apparently connected with a permanent civil policy, and contrast so hideously with even the pretence of toleration.

So much for the evidence to be found in the Acts themselves. But the time and circumstances of their enactment are equally, or still more, decisive. They were enacted in years immediately following a Revolution which had been needed to relieve England of a Sovereign who had apostatised to Popery, and who was endeavouring to restore it under the guise and shelter of a pretended desire for toleration. They were passed, therefore, at a time when the very name of religious toleration was the symbol of concealed designs for the restoration of Romish tyranny. They were passed under the fresh recollection of an Irish Catholic Parliament, which had resorted to measures of confiscation and attainder against all Protestants in Ireland which were passed under circumstances of special violence and hypocrisy. They were passed under all the excitement of the suppression of the Irish rebellion, when it was still fresh in the minds of men that an army of French soldiers, ten thousand strong, had just been combined with Irish rebels in defending the passage of the Boyne against an English army. They were passed in a series of eight or nine consecutive years, during the whole of which it was known that the great and powerful French Monarch was entertaining the Roman Catholic Pretender to the English throne, and was prepared at any moment to assist him actively in his attempts. It is impossible for us fully to realise or even to conceive the frame of mind, and the natural and legitimate motives, which were then operating on the Parliament of both countries, in England and in Ireland. Intense alarm and passionate indignation—an attitude of just and vehement suspicion and of vigilant guard against an imminent danger to the highest interests—were the motives and incentives called into action by all the circumstances of the time.

But if this almost purely political interpretation of the penal laws is thus justified by all the facts connected with their enactment, and with the nature of their provisions, it is, if possible, still more clearly proved by all the circumstances attending the measure of their enforcement, their speedy fall into desuetude, and the time of their final abandonment. The fact is indisputable, and is fully brought out in Mr. Lecky's clear and forcible narrative, that with every new year of increasing confidence in the stability of the Protestant Dynasty in Great Britain and Ireland, the enforcement of the penal laws steadily relaxed, and the whole spirit of the Government became more and more tolerant towards the Catholics. So early as 1715 —only six years after the enactments of the penal code had reached their maximum development, the hunt after Catholic bishops and priests had sensibly abated.* That was the year, it will be recollected, when the first Jacobite rebellion was defeated in Scotland, and the political prospect began to be more secure. Mr. Lecky has well summed up the general result in a single sentence: "The policy of extinguishing Catholicism by suppressing its services (?) and banishing its bishops was silently abandoned; before the middle of the eighteenth century the laws against Catholic worship were virtually obsolete, and before

* Lecky, vol. i. p. 168, note.

the close of the eighteenth century the Parliament, which in the beginning of the century had been one of the most intolerant, had become one of the most tolerant in Europe." *

I have dwelt upon the political origin and spirit of the Irish penal laws for one reason mainly—namely, this—that it stands in close connection with a distinction which is of the very highest interest to society, not merely as regards the fair and just interpretation of the past, but as regards our guidance for the future. I know that there are some minds to which the spirit of purely religious intolerance and persecution seems greatly better, and not worse, than the intolerance and persecution which is purely political and purely secular. There is a flavour, perhaps unconscious, of this sentiment in Mr. Lecky's language. It is founded on the feeling that, whereas purely religious fanaticism has the excuse sometimes of a zeal for truth, persecution from political motives alone is comparatively sordid. I understand the feeling, but I hold the very opposite opinion. I look upon the right of every individual mind to an exclusive property in its own spiritual operations and convictions to be the most absolute and the most sacred of all human rights; and I consequently regard the tyranny involved in pure religious persecution as the most wicked of human tempers, and the most atrocious of human crimes. It has done more than anything else to damage and

* Lecky, vol. i. pp. 168, 169.

discredit Christianity, and to throw upon it a false discredit which is to this day a powerful influence in the minds of men. On the other hand, I regard the right of all political communities to defend themselves, their dominion and their laws, as a right which is not only supreme, considered as a mere right, but supreme also as a duty. If in the exercise of this right, and in the discharge of this duty, they have to encounter a system and a power which, in the name of a religion, and under the pretence of a zeal in spiritual truth, is in reality a vast political organisation using the "secular arm" to attack kings, and Governments, and nations—then such political societies have an absolute right, and lie under a supreme obligation, to take the extremest measures in self-defence. And whilst all needless cruelty is criminal, in this as in all other cases, yet assuredly in this particular case there is the largest possible excuse for the excesses of passion. But this was exactly the case of England and of the Irish Protestants during the first twenty-five years of the eighteenth century. They were standing at bay against a Power pretending to be a Christian Church, which was animated with the most cruel spirit of intolerance and persecution,—which inspired the atrocities of Alva in the Low Countries,—which dictated the Massacre of St. Bartholomew in France, and which consecrated that act of supreme atrocity by the issue of a medal by the Pope himself in commemoration of the "Strages Huguenotorum."

CHAPTER VIII.

THE EIGHTEENTH CENTURY—ECONOMIC CAUSES.

THE calm philosophy of Mr. Lecky's narrative is not only delightful in itself, but representing as it does, nearly in perfection, the temper and other highest qualities of the genuine historian, it is invaluable in the confidence with which it inspires us that all facts are truly stated—and no facts, so far as known to the historian, are omitted,—that nothing is sacrificed to the temptations of epigram or antithesis, as is often done in the case of Macaulay, or to the onesidedness of strong convictions, as sometimes in the case of Mr. Froude. But in judging of the character and conduct of the chief actors in such events as the passing of the penal laws in Ireland, the tone of perfect impartiality, even when it is consistently maintained, is apt to fail in its practical application. And when we have to contradict and expose such passionate misrepresentations as the inflated fables of Mr. Gladstone's speeches, it is absolutely necessary to dwell on aspects of the facts which lie in the region of suppressed or neglected elements. Mr. Lecky makes a much more important observation when he points out that the power of mere religious dogma, pure and simple, was itself gradually losing ground during the course of the eighteenth century—with the subdivision of sects, and with the progress of a speculative scepticism. Rapidly among Protestants,—much more slowly among Catholics,—but still on the whole steadily and surely, the spirit of toleration was gaining ground, and the fierce passions of mere religious antipathy were becoming less and less possible as the animating springs of action. The perfect quiescence of the Irish Catholics during the Jacobite rebellions of 1715 and 1745 was partly due no doubt to the hopelessness of any local rebellion in Ireland, but it certainly was also due to the decline of mere religious fanaticism, and the hopes founded on the growing toleration they enjoyed.

Mr. Lecky enters upon a matter in some respects more important, much more difficult to exhaust, and with which his judicial calmness is much more adequate to deal, when he passes from the distribution of the blame attachable to the English Government for the penal laws, to the wholly separate question of the economic effects of those laws considered simply as a cause of the continuous poverty and the later miseries of Ireland. On this question he enumerates facts and considerations which are of great weight. We have all been accustomed to dwell on the economic evils entailed on France by the expulsion of the

Huguenots, and the loss to that country of so many men of energy and resource in all the walks of civil life. We cannot deny or dispute the possibility of parallel effects from the very considerable emigration of Irish Catholics, who could not endure the harassing and often odious disabilities to which they were subject during at least one generation, from the penal laws. Mr. Lecky, however, fully admits that a long-established habit of taking foreign service had grown up among the Catholics of Ireland during previous centuries, and that the emigration of Irishmen of the higher classes during the earlier part of the eighteenth century was by no means a new phenomenon. But he succeeds in showing that it was intensified under the penal laws, and that it took place at a time when every resource of native intelligence and enterprise was specially needed to inaugurate and reinforce the resurrection of Ireland from a condition of the greatest ignorance and impoverishment. Nevertheless, when we consider how small was the number of native Irishmen of the educated classes who were men of any capital or of any previous disposition towards industrial pursuits—when we consider how almost exclusively military their habits had always been, and how almost universally, when they did go abroad, they addicted themselves to military service in France and elsewhere; considering, too, the equally obvious fact that it was the new settlers in Ireland who alone had the resources of knowledge, of agricultural enterprise, and of at least some capital,—it is impossible to doubt that the mere economic evils due to the emigration of Irishmen under the pressure of the penal laws, was quite a minor element among the causes which delayed the improvement of Ireland, and tended to prolong the poverty of its people.

We enter upon a much more important matter when we turn to that other of the two great charges against the conduct of England towards Ireland in the eighteenth century, which rests upon the laws she passed to suppress the freedom of Irish trade and the success of Irish industry. There is only one thing to be said about those laws—but that one thing cannot be too strongly insisted upon, or too absolutely asserted. It is that the doctrines of commercial restriction—the doctrines which now we know as Protection,—were the doctrines universally held and universally practised at that time, not only by every Government, but by every petty municipality in Europe. Mr. Lecky refers to the policy as "selfish," but England was not one whit more selfish than all other nations at the same time; and she acted on precisely the same policy, not only towards Scotland, but towards her own Colonies and Plantations. Most of us are now convinced that the whole of these doctrines were not so much selfish—for nations are, and must be always, self-regarding—as intensely stupid. But it is a stupidity by no means extinct in our own day,—rather, on the contrary, as alive as ever, and ready to be quite as "selfish" and exclusive in action as England was in her dealings with Ireland and Scotland in the early years of the eighteenth century. Moreover, the Irish themselves were as much under the influence of these stupid doctrines as any other people, and acted upon them in their own domestic legislation to a degree which had the worst effect on their own prosperity. It is, therefore, not only an injustice but almost an hypocrisy to dwell on this part of England's conduct towards Ireland in all those matters which come under the general head of what Mr. Gladstone has called "Exclusive Dealing," and of which commercial restrictions are harmless examples indeed, when compared with other applications of the same doctrines which he has done his best to excuse and palliate.

But this is not all we have to say about the conduct of England towards Ireland during the comparatively very short period of her history when she was, at last, responsible for the Government of the country. It is much more important to observe that, exactly as with the penal laws, so also with the laws in restraint of industry and commerce, a steady and even a rapid progress was made during the years of English rule towards the relaxation of those laws, ending in the complete abandonment of them all. There had been no restraints at all on trade with Ireland until about the time of the Restoration,—the first statute dating from 1665 and shutting out Irish cattle from England.

One relaxation very important to Ireland, opening the trade in bacon, took place so early as 1693, whilst practically the whole Provision trade with England was opened so early as 1758. But, as we all know, the spirit of commercial monopoly died hard. It has only been in our own time that it has ceased to be largely represented, in the fiscal legislation of England. It is even now as widespread as ever on the Continent of Europe. It is rife among our own Colonies at the present moment; and there are unmistakable symptoms that the doctrines of Protection are at the present time liable to burst forth in the most short-sighted, selfish, and violent forms amongst our own wage-earning classes at home. But more than this:—the absurdity and injustice of throwing any special blame on England for her conduct towards Ireland in this matter, during the earlier part of last century, is still farther illustrated by the fact that the Irish Parliament and people were themselves saturated with the doctrines of Protection and of commercial restriction, and applied them inside their own country in forms which were almost incredibly ignorant and perverse. In the long catalogue of cases in which, first the French Economists, and afterwards Adam Smith, analysed, exhibited, and exposed the follies and the suicidal consequences of the Protectionist system of fiscal legislation, I know of no case, and no example, more astonishing than that in which Arthur Young has narrated and examined the results of certain acts of fiscal legislation resorted to by the Irish Parliament at the time of which we are now speaking. In the light of Arthur Young's narrative and exposure those acts may well seem to us as if the Irish Parliament had been insane. And yet its acts are nothing more than an extreme example of the ideas at that time dominant all over the world; and our only wonder must be that the very extremeness of the consequences to which they led did not produce the effect of a *reductio ad absurdum* even in Irish eyes. The whole circumstances are so curious and so instructive that it is well worth while to recall them to the mind of English politicians, and of Irish politicians who are inclined to heap up reproaches against the English government of Ireland on the ground of the laws in restraint of trade which were resorted to in the end of the seventeenth and at the beginning of the last century.

A very few years after England had begun to relax her "selfish" policy of excluding Irish produce from her markets, the Irish began to open their eyes to the fact that their own capital, Dublin, was largely fed by wheat imported from England, just as also, in the article of coals, they were enjoying the benefit of a supply which they could not get so cheaply, or even at all, from their own country. According to the doctrines of the "Commercial system" this was a great misfortune. Those doctrines always taught that imports into any country were to be reckoned as a loss to it, and that its exports alone were to be counted as a gain. They had long been anxious to be allowed to export their cattle, sheep, butter, cheese, hides, and other produce of the richest pastures in the world. But what they could not bear was that England should send any of its own produce in return. So a clever Irishman, who was still in high office in the Irish Government when Arthur Young wrote in the year 1780, suggested that the Irish should do two things—first levy a duty on the import of English wheat and flour; secondly, give a large bounty out of Irish taxes to all who would bring Irish, instead of English, wheat and flour to Dublin; and thirdly, limit this bounty strictly to those who would bring in this Irish wheat and flour by land carriage and not by sea. This wonderful idea was adopted, and a law was passed to carry it into effect in 1761. The details were even more wonderful than the conception. The bounty was enormous in amount, and it was given in the form of a mileage upon the distance of land carriage, but excluding a radius of ten miles round Dublin. The effect, of course, was to offer a great bribe, paid out of the public purse, to all tenants and farmers to break up and plough the finest and richest pastures in Ireland, which were best adapted for other produce. The effect, moreover, was to increase the bribe in proportion to the distance of those pastures from a city which lay at one extremity of the Island, and thus to make it operate most strongly on precisely those parts of Ireland in which both soil and climate were least favourable to the kind of produce which was favoured, and best adapted to the kind of produce which was proportionately discouraged. Another effect, of course, also was to discourage Irish shipping—to direct the whole export of the favoured produce in the southern and western provinces out of its natural lines of transit by sea from the great Irish harbours all along her coasts, and to compel that produce to take the costly and laborious route of the inland roads, which had to be traversed by waggons and horses across the whole length and breadth of Ireland, from Cork and Limerick to Donegal and Antrim.

The examination and exposure of this supreme folly by Arthur Young is one of the most instructive parts of a most instructive book. And yet I have hardly ever seen it referred to, or dwelt upon by Irish, or even by English writers. He took, in the first place, the official records and parliamentary returns which exhibited its more direct and immediate cost in money, and in money's worth. His argument upon this head may be summarised as follows:—"I will admit for the sake of argument your assumption that the import of English wheat and flour into Dublin is a pure loss to Ireland, and that the Irish people have a direct interest in checking it and in reducing it to the lowest point. I will admit your assumption that Ireland can best carry on trade by counting her exports only as gain, and her imports as only loss. I will, therefore, add together all the actual cost of your bounty on inland transit during a term of seven years since it began. Against this cost, and in diminution of it, I will agree to set off as pure gain all the English wheat and flour that you have succeeded in excluding during the same term of years. But, on the other hand, you must admit as a loss all the diminution in your exports in the various productions of pasture land which has arisen during the same term of years, and which has clearly been due to the same cause. Calculating the balance on this footing, you will find that you have paid out in the direct form of hard cash upwards of £47,000 in the seven years. You have lost another sum of upwards of £53,000 in the decrease of your sales of beef, butter, tallow, hides, and other produce of cattle: whilst on your sales of wool and woollen yarn, you have lost a third sum of more than £106,000—making up the total cost of your system of bounties on the inland carriage of wheat and flour, to be the large amount of £206,244. Now, taking the credit side of the account, or rather that which you assume to be credit, adding together as gain to you the value of the decrease in imported English corn, some increase in the export of your own corn, and some increase in the export of pork, pigs, bread, and other articles, I find that the whole of these items of assumed gain amount only to £62,732—leaving

an adverse balance of direct loss against your bounty system of £143,510 in the course of only seven years." *
Commenting on this result, arrived at upon indisputable data, Arthur Young very truly observes that, had these results arisen naturally, as a mere consequence of unforeseen events and obscure causes, the friends of Ireland would have been well employed in devising means for remedying so great an evil, whereas they had been busily employed in devising highly artificial means of bringing those results about!

But the importance and significance of Arthur Young's demonstration of the direct, visible, and calculable losses in the form of money, are as nothing compared with the much greater significance of the observations he makes on the indirect, comparatively invisible, and less easily calculable evils and losses, which were quite as certain but far more lasting and destructive. Arthur Young opens fire on this second branch of the subject—by far the most important—in the pregnant remark: "It is the intention and effect of this bounty to turn every local advantage and natural supply topsy-turvy." Nothing more graphic could be said. To fly in the face of the facts and laws of nature—this is about the high-water mark of human folly. Arthur Young asks what would be thought in England, where imports of foreign corn were then more than proportionately large, if it were proposed as a remedy that London

---

* Arthur Young's "Tour in Ireland" (original edition), p. 267.

should be fed, if possible, from the corn grown in Devonshire and Northumberland in preference to that grown in Kent or Essex. And then, too, the imperative condition that it must be brought by land carriage in "a country blessed with such ports and such a vast extent of coast"! "The absurdity and folly are so glaring that it is amazing that sophistry could blind the Legislature to such a degree as to permit a second thought of it." And then again the deliberate discouragement of Irish ships and sailors! He had himself seen in Cork Harbour, above one hundred and twenty miles from Dublin, a few cars being loaded for that market in order to secure the bounty, when a ship was lying at the quay waiting for a freight. "Could invention suggest any scheme more preposterous than this to confound at the public expense all the ideas of common practice and common sense?"*

But this is not all—it is not even the most important part of all that Arthur Young brings before us as to the indirect consequences of this system of bounties in the inland carriage of corn to Dublin. It is but the prelude to, and the vestibule of, the great subject which lies in all the powerful economic causes thus set in motion over the whole of Ireland. How ubiquitous it was in its operation was indicated by the inducement it held out to Capitalists to erect enormous flour-mills— some of them costing £20,000—in far distant parts of Ireland. These brought home to the door of every

* Arthur Young's "Tour in Ireland" (original edition), p. 270.

peasant occupier in Ireland the great bribe which was annually offered out of the public taxes. And what was it a bribe to do? To devote his time and labour to a kind of production which could not otherwise have been conducted at any profit;—to plough up, and thus to destroy the finest pastures, affording the richest milk, and butter, and wool, in order to grow a grain which was after all of very inferior quality, and to do this on a system of husbandry which was more than two hundred years behind even that backward age. There was no rotation of crops: there was bad ploughing, slight manuring, and the old mediæval, wasteful, system of land left fallow for three years before it could be scourged again with the grain crops which brought a tempting profit only because it was paid for at an artificial price. And what effect was all this system having on the rapid increase of a very poor population, which was already pressing hard upon the means of subsistence, and was exposed to scarcities and famines whenever a bad season came, in spite of the new and the immense resource opened up in the recently introduced potato? Not even the wise and sharp eyes of Arthur Young could foresee all the disastrous results which, by steps of natural and inevitable consequence, were being steadily and even rapidly brought about by this destructive system adopted by an Irish Parliament. But, although Arthur Young did not or perhaps could not foresee all those results, he at least saw some of them, and these amongst the most significant. "What," he exclaims, "is the tillage gained by this measure? It is that system which formed the agriculture of England two hundred years ago, and forms it yet in the worst of our 'common fields,' but which all our exertions of enclosing and improving are bent to extirpate—the fallow is a dead loss—one year in three yields nothing, and another one only a trifle, whereas the grass yields a full crop every year. Ought you to turn some of the finest pastures in the world, and which in Ireland yielded twenty shillings an acre, into the most execrable tillage that is to be found on the face of the globe?" If now we bear in mind that, when Arthur Young published his "Tour" in 1780, this disastrous system had been not only in full, but in increasing operation for eighteen years—that the area of its operation was the whole of Ireland—that the population on whom it acted was one in the lowest state of education, and unacquainted with the very rudiments of an improved agriculture—that it appealed to their immediate cupidity as against all the motives which are connected with a permanent or even a long-lasting industry,—we may conceive what an immense effect it must have had in exhausting the soil, in stimulating a pauperised population, in causing an excessive competition for land, and in thus preparing the way for the great famine, which came at last to decimate that population in our own time.

But it did not stop in 1780. The insanity of

confining it to land carriage was indeed abandoned. Carriage by canals was first included, and then came carriage coastways. But the bounty itself went on increasing, and Young's calculation was that, even at the time he wrote, it involved a direct money loss to Ireland of £53,000 a year—besides its vast and indirect effect in ruining her agricultural resources for the future. And if any one should now be disposed to say that I am exaggerating the effects of this purely Irish cause of Irish miseries, let him just look for a moment at the sequel of Young's analysis. He supposes himself to be asked the question whether he would advise this ruinous bounty to be totally and immediately repealed;—and he replies that he could not do so, because of the large amount of capital which had been invested in the trade—in the great flour-mills erected at immense cost all over Ireland. In 1792 they were two hundred and twenty-five in number, one of them at a distance of one hundred and thirty miles from Dublin. He specifies also the prodigious number of men and horses that would be thrown out of employment, and was afraid of the sudden diversion of the supply on which the city of Dublin had so long been fed. Considering the very strong opinion he held on the ruinous effects of the whole policy, and the correspondingly strong language which he uses in condemnation of it, there could be no more striking evidence of the extent to which it had become rooted in the political soil of Ireland,—had become identified with popular interests all over the island,—and was exerting its baneful influence on a future which was then unforeseen.

But another most striking lesson is to be learned from these facts—and that is the absurdity and injustice of the charges made against England on the ground of her selfish departure from sound economic laws in her commercial dealings with Ireland. The disastrous economic effects of this purely internal and native legislation upon the future of the Irish people was probably much greater than the English prohibition against Irish industry of which we hear so much. England had indeed most stupidly prohibited the Irish wool trade, but she had also at least fostered the linen trade. Her other prohibitions had already been largely abated, and were on the way to farther limitation. At the very time when this supreme folly was adopted by the Irish Parliament, England had opened the whole provision-trade to the Irish farmers. Nor is there the least ground for supposing that the Irish Parliament in this matter of bounties and taxes on foreign corn represented Protestant feeling or interests alone. Quite the contrary; it was the great mass of the poor Irish tenantry, and of the poor Irish of Dublin, who were directly interested in the system. If the Irish Parliament had been as exclusively Catholic as it was then exclusively Protestant, it is quite certain that the economic follies it committed would have been, if possible, even greatly aggravated. The whole ideas embodied in these bounties were neither Protestant nor Catholic, but simply Irish, and—it must be confessed—in a great measure European at that time.

There is one thing, however, which is purely Irish—and that is the grotesque inconsistency and confusion of thought, in the language of many Irish writers and of English platform orators who now copy them, involved in their bitter reproaches against England for her commercial legislation at this time. We could not have a better illustration of this than in the language of a well-known authority on the growth of Irish population in the eighteenth century. I refer to Mr. Newenham, who also published in 1805 an elaborate and very interesting book on the whole history of Ireland during that century. He rages against England for her Protectionist system against Ireland; yet he not only defends the system of native bounties, but he specially complains that it was comparatively ineffective because they were not accompanied by such heavy duties on the importation of English corn as might have effectually put an end to that injurious interference with the monopoly of Irish farmers. He triumphs over the fact that the moment the Parliament of Ireland acquired a really independent power in 1782, it immediately adopted this doubly Protectionist policy—increased the native bounties, and also did its best wholly to exclude all English grain. As to any knowledge of economic laws, or any even dawning intelligence on the virtues of Free-trade, Newenham's book is a proof that all parties in Ireland lay in the very depth of darkness even in the present century. There was indeed one most illustrious Irishman, whose powerful intellect and generous spirit are among the glories of his age and country, who did see the follies of the restrictive system. That Irishman was the great thinker Bishop Berkeley, who, long before the days of Adam Smith, had seen his solitary way to the doctrines of free exchange. But all Irishmen except himself were then in the depths of ignorance on the subject. Even later, at a time when wakeful minds were beginning to take in the great ideas of Adam Smith, and some real progress had been made in planting them in the apprehension of the British people, Newenham repudiates what he calls the "ingenious arguments of Dr. Smith," and actually has the blindness to argue that his reasoning against the system of bounties was inapplicable to Ireland, because the bulk of the population had then come to feed almost entirely on potatoes, and nothing they could do in the way of corn could do them any harm!* And yet this writer is one who, in other parts of the same book, gives the most emphatic evidence as to the miserable and wasteful character of the tillage which was thus diligently extended, and of the splendid richness of the pastures

* Newenham's "Ireland" (1809), p. 210, and *passim*.

which were thus as diligently destroyed.* Nor is he less emphatic on the ignorance and improvidence of his countrymen. What could be a more dreadful account of any people, as indicating the steady preparation of some terrible natural retribution at the hands of Nature, than, for example, this sentence of Newenham: "The general aim of the Irish farmers is rather to extract a capital from the land than to render a capital previously acquired, productive of extraordinary annual profit by the instrumentality of the land." † It would be easy to heap passages upon passages out of this book, and out of other books written by Irishmen, which prove that none of them had, or have to this day, the slightest notion of the most elementary principles on which the doctrines of Free-trade are founded, or have the slightest power of reasoning in respect to the natural and artificial causes which were determining the domestic condition of the Irish people.

But there was another cause of special aggravation closely connected with the corn bounties which I have not seen alluded to by any Irish historian or politician. It was a cause lying in the conduct of the great mass of the Irish people, and not merely of the Irish Parliament. The mass of the Irish sub-tenants and cottier cultivators had, indeed, learnt by the follies of the Irish Parliament the secret of getting all its

* Newenham's "Ireland" (1806), pp. 66–68.
† Ibid., p. 78.

capital out of the land without returning anything to its fertility. But they improved upon this lesson by an invention which was really infernal. They found out that by peeling off the turf from good land, by stacking this cut turf, and then by setting it on fire, they could reduce it to ashes in which all the virtue of the land was concentrated and made cheaply accessible to farther exhaustion. Rich crops of wheat and abundant crops of potatoes could thus be raised with no expenditure on other manure. Accordingly all over the richest as well as the poorest parts of Ireland, this hideous waste came to be systematically practised. Mr. William Pilkington, himself an Irish farmer, has given a startling account of it as it prevailed for more than one hundred years—from 1728 to 1846, but it seems to have been at its height from fifty to sixty years ago. So long as a Parliament continued in Ireland it tried to prohibit the practice. Numerous Acts were passed for the purpose—but all in vain. In defiance of law and of contract the ignorant and improvident peasantry persisted in it—the larger tenants derived enormous rents from it, whilst their sub-tenants revelled and bred in a temporary and treacherous plenty. "I have known," says Mr. Pilkington, "the banns of marriage published for thirty-seven young couples in one day in a local chapel, one of three in the same parish."* When any Government tried to

* "Help for Ireland," sixth edition, p. 6. (Deansgate and Ridgefield, Manchester, and 11, Paternoster Buildings, London, 1889.)

enforce the law, they were encountered by the usual resources of Irish outrage. There is a cowardly fear now of attributing to "the masses" any blame. "The majesty that doth hedge a king" now hedges the conduct and position of popular majorities. And so the richest lessons of history are missed. In the practice exposed by Mr. Pilkington we have undoubtedly one of the most fruitful causes of Irish over-population, poverty, and subsequent famine. And it was a cause purely native—characteristically Irish.

I turn, however, to another aspect of this great question in respect to which an extraordinary forgetfulness prevails even among writers of the highest rank in literature and in politics. In estimating the causes of Irish poverty and misfortune, not only in the ninety-two years of English rule, but ever since, we must not fail to take into account those facts and influences which had arisen from the purely native conditions which had prevailed during the five hundred and twenty years which had run their course between A.D. 1170 and A.D. 1690, and especially those which had come to the front during the centuries immediately preceding the final suppression of Irish rebellions by William III. The effect of survivals is great in every nation; but it is enormous among Celts especially, and most enormous of all among Irish Celts who had been practically unconquered for so many centuries, and had been so geographically situated as to be cut off from all the reforming and renovating currents of European history. We have seen the estimate which English statesmen formed of the impoverishing effects of the old Irish customs in respect to the inheritance of property, as well as in respect to the dues, services, and exactions attached to the occupation of land. But now we come across a curious proof of the perfect consciousness of the Irish themselves of the truth of this opinion of English Statesmen. I have before alluded to the circumstances in which this new proof appears. It was the object, as we have seen, of the penal laws to prevent the growth of wealth in the hands of Catholics, and in particular of that kind of wealth—landed property—which was most directly contributory to political influence and power. And how did the Protestant Parliament act in devising the means of attaining this end? They acted on the principle that nothing could be more fatal to the prosperity of Catholics in respect to landed property than simply to insist, in this case, on the retention of the old Irish custom and law of succession. Their conduct may be thus translated into words: "You, Catholic landowners, wish to keep your old Irish religion: very well, gentlemen, if you do, you must keep also your old Irish customs of succession to property. If you wish to have the benefit of the English law of succession you must conform to the English Church." This was an ingenious device—considered as a measure of purely religious persecution, it might hardly be too severe to call it a devilish invention. But, at least, do not let us mistake its immense significance as indicating and admitting the impoverishing and damaging effect, of one of the most prominent of all native usages, on the economic condition of the people. So universal was this admission—so instinctive—so undeniable in its truth, that Mr. Lecky tells us that no one of the penal laws was so effective in the way of inducing conversions to Protestantism, or, as they may be rather called, apostatisms from Rome.

We have only to carry this lesson with us into another branch of old Irish customs, to enable us to judge how very little power the Government of England had, or could have, over the causes which were determining the condition of the people during the only century in which she had any effective power at all. The laws and usages of succession to landed property are, as regards short periods of time, of secondary importance as compared with the laws and usages affecting the occupation of land by the mass of the people. Laws and usages of succession, however bad, take some time to come into operation so far as the production of widespread effects are concerned. But laws, usages, and established customs affecting the relations between the owners and occupiers of land, have an immediate, continuous, and a permanent result on the whole condition of an agricultural people. Now, it is an unquestionable fact—admitted by all

Irish historians, and proved by all Irish records—that the old Irish usages of this kind were not less, but infinitely more severe and exhausting to the occupiers than the corresponding laws and usages of the new English landowners in Ireland. The great feature of the old Irish rents, services, and exactions, was that they were absolutely unfixed, indefinite, and unlimited. As Mr. Prendergast says, the occupiers were "eaten out of house and home." Their one cry was, "Spend me, but defend me"—"defend me from having my cattle stolen, my corn burnt, and very likely my own throat cut—and if you do this you may take all I have beyond the bare means of sustenance." That was the Irish system of landlord and tenant,—or of chief and retainer,—if these titles are fancifully preferred. In so far, therefore, as England was powerful enough to substitute her own tenures for the old Celtic tenures, she conferred an immense benefit on the Irish people.

But it was too late. Many centuries of archaic usages surviving,—prolonged and even aggravated—into times when elsewhere they had been gradually giving way, had left the Irish people in a condition of extreme poverty, and of utter helplessness as regarded any power of emerging from that condition. When Irish writers and many English writers heap epithet upon epithet to describe the "degraded" condition as to habitations, as to food, and as to clothing, in which they saw the Irish peasants, when such things were seen and thought of in the earlier part of the eighteenth century, they are — quite unconsciously—not so much exaggerating the facts as wholly misrepresenting them in one point of paramount importance. The word "degraded" implies a fall from a former condition of comparative wealth and comfort to the actual later condition of poverty and barbarism. And this, beyond doubt, is a very common belief as to the condition of Ireland in the eighteenth century. But it has absolutely no foundation in historical fact. The Irish people all through the Middle Ages lived in cabins of mud and wattles. Even the richer classes did so, only in constructions a little more carefully put together. The habitations of the people had always been mere hovels, and these, when seen by civilised men in the eighteenth century, were very naturally regarded as an indication of some great decline. There is, however, no evidence of this, and abundant evidence to the contrary. It was simply a survival of conditions which were immemorially old. But neither the habitations, nor the food, nor the clothing of the people are in the nature of causes, but only of effects. They were the indications of poverty: they did not operate in producing it. But there was another peculiarity of the Celtic people of Ireland at that time which was also a survival of mediæval times, and this was a cause, and not a mere consequence of poverty indeed—a cause of insuperable power on the condition of the people.

This was the system of communal tillage, or township occupation—otherwise called in its detail the "rundale" system of cultivation. Under this system agricultural improvement was impossible. Each man had his dozen or his score of little patches of arable land changed every year, so that he could never be sure of reaping any fruits from any improved practice. The tillage was what Young described as wretched in the extreme—exhaustion of the land, and producing, even for the shortest time, nothing but the most miserable grain. What could England do to remedy such a state of things? Nothing,—unless it had been to veto the fatuous laws, which Irishmen of all parties concurred in passing in the Irish Parliament, whereby these miserable cultivators were bribed all over Ireland still farther to scourge their land, and to produce more bad grain;—all of which, however bad in quality, had the full benefit of the bounty. Newenham himself admits that the indiscriminate payment of the bounty was an error in a system which he otherwise admires; and Young says distinctly that the grain produced in Ireland under the system was of a very inferior quality. All writers are agreed that these bounties did produce a great increase of tillage in Ireland,—that it displaced more than a corresponding amount of much more valuable produce,—that it did terribly scourge and exhaust the ground,—and that it did tend to stimulate artificially that rapidly swelling population living on the lowest possible diet, which had ultimately to be swept off by famine and emigration.

Then, concurrently with this powerful combination of causes, there was another which, so far as I know, is unique in the history of the world—and that was the introduction of the potato and the discovery of its easy cultivation and of its immense feeding properties. No such sudden and enormous addition to the subsistence of any people has ever been made before, or one which made so little demand for either skill or capital. It came, too, in conjunction with many other circumstances tending to rapid increase of population without any corresponding increase in other resources. The consequences were an object lesson in the breeding capacities of the human race, and on the data of Malthus's famous theory, which stands absolutely alone. The broad fact is, that at the beginning of the century the whole population of Ireland is now generally held not to have exceeded two millions; at the end of it, the population is well known to have reached 4,500,000. But these figures do not represent the whole wonder of the facts if Mr. Lecky's account of them—the result of a careful balancing of all the evidence—be correct. All writers seem agreed that the population of Ireland declined to its lowest point after the massacres of 1641 and during the long and bloody civil wars which followed. At the end of that century, in 1695, it was supposed to be little more than one million. But this is impossible—if it had really crept up to two millions in 1700. Newenham's calculation is that it did not reach the two millions till 1731. Mr. Lecky says that it had reached that figure, or nearly so, in the beginning of the century; but that during the first half of it, the population remained almost stationary—the total in 1750 being about 2,370,000.* If this be so, the enormous increase to four millions and a half in the end of the century had arisen in the course of fifty years. Then in the course of forty-six years more, as we all know, this prodigious number had again doubled, so that, in 1846-47, the population of Ireland is computed to have been eight millions and a quarter. Such a prodigious rapidity of increase has probably never been exhibited in any human society, when it is remembered that the whole of it was due to breeding, and none of it, practically speaking, to immigration. Nay, more; it is to be considered that not only was there no immigration, as in the case of the American States, and as in the case of all great cities whether in the Old or in the New World, but, on the contrary, there was always a very considerable and often a very large emigration from Ireland, and even a very considerable loss by famine and by the diseases consequent on scarcity of food.

On this last point there is, at first sight, a discrepancy between the best authorities. Newenham begins his very interesting book on Irish population

* Lecky's "Ireland," vol. i. p. 239.

with the broad statement that it is not until we enter on the opening of the eighteenth century that we can study the problem as it is presented by undisturbed conditions,—there having been, he says, during that century no wars and no famines. Mr. Lecky, on the contrary, tells us that there were some severe famines in the course of that century, and one, in particular, of exceptional destructiveness in the year 1741–42.* In support of this statement he produces the most conclusive evidence. But Newenham's counter-statement is reconcilable with the facts if we understand him to refer only to famines of the same kind as those which had been constant all through the Middle Ages, and down to the end of the times of rebellions and of civil wars. He,—evidently from the context,—had in his mind only famines produced by the ravages and devastations of chronic wars —during which local famines constantly occurred, and there had been some which even prevailed over large provinces, and affected the whole Island in succession. Famines, it is certain in this sense, wholly ceased with the establishment of English sovereignty. But those on which Mr. Lecky dwells are all the more striking and significant as indicating the emergence of those more permanent economic causes, which had their origin in the survival of mediæval customs, and in the aggravated effect of those customs when they operated under new conditions of population. These are pre-

* Lecky's "Ireland," vol. i. pp. 182, 186, 187.

R

cisely the causes which are most apt to be overlooked, and the effects of them are most apt to be confounded with others, which are of quite inferior, or even of trifling power. The enormous increase of population in Ireland during the eighteenth century is, of course, all the more striking and instructive that it was effected in spite of large emigration, of frequent dearth, and of some severe famines. It is, in an immense degree, the predominant factor in all the results which followed, combined as it was with the low level of poverty in which it began, the low level of agricultural knowledge which prevailed throughout, the insuperable difficulties in the way of improvement presented by communal tenures, and the wide-spreading effects of the most ignorant economic legislation. In this last item England had a share, not only as regards Ireland, but as regards herself also. But the largest and most effective share in this cause was undoubtedly that taken by the Irish Parliament in its ruinous system of corn bounties, and other fiscal follies of a kindred nature. These follies had nothing to do with religion nor with English rule, but were the product of that total ignorance of economic laws which prevailed in both countries and in all parties, whether religious or purely political, at that time.

It is, however, always to be remembered that, as in the case of the individual organism, deleterious ingredients in food, or injurious habits of life, may be almost wholly counteracted and defied by exceptional individual health and strength, but operate with fatal effect on organisms which are less robust, so, in the body politic of human society, causes, tending to deterioration, or to slacken the pace of progress, may be so neutralised by causes of an opposite tendency as to become altogether invisible; whilst in a poorer and feebler community they may operate with fatal effects. This was exactly the case in Ireland, as compared with England and Scotland, during the whole of the eighteenth century, and especially during the earlier half of it. All the three kingdoms had to deal with the same evils in the course of their respective histories; but both in England and in Scotland centuries of gradual progress enabled the constitution of both countries to overcome them. In Ireland they all existed from natural causes in an aggravated degree; and there was no amelioration until it was too late to stop or to check unforeseen developments. "It would be difficult," says Mr. Lecky, with perfect truth, "in the whole compass of history to find another instance in which such various and such powerful agencies concurred to degrade the character and to blast the prosperity of a nation."* And no writer has, I think, on the whole, given so fair an enumeration of those "depressing influences." It is an enumeration which, at least so far as intention and spirit are concerned, is conspicuously conscientious. But it is an enumeration, nevertheless, governed and inspired by

* Lecky's "Ireland," vol. i. p. 240.

this foregone conclusion, that "the greater part of them sprang directly from the corrupt and selfish government of England." This he lays down as incontestable. I hold it, on the contrary, to be in the highest degree contestable, and that the balance lies enormously on the other side. That the adverse influences were, during six out of the proverbial "seven centuries," almost exclusively of native Irish origin, I think, has been clearly shown in the preceding pages. And although the balance may seem to incline against England if we look to the history of the eighteenth century alone, I am convinced that a closer investigation will show that the deeper-seated and most powerful causes were all such as lay entirely outside the conduct, or even the influence, of the English Government.

CHAPTER IX.

CONCLUSIONS.

For the purpose of bringing the conclusion intimated at the close of the last chapter within the reach of some definite process of analysis, I shall now enumerate the causes of Irish misfortune which are specified by Mr. Lecky himself in his sincere desire to omit none. He expresses regret that his narrative has assumed "so polemical a character." But he need not do so. It has undoubtedly been polemical on the other side; and perhaps he is even justified in his opinion that the anti-Irish accounts have assumed "a very unusual amount and malignity of misrepresentation." For my own part, I am disposed to look at all the causes as quite separate from either praise or blame—to consider only what it was but natural and even justifiable for men to do under given conditions of mind and circumstances, and above all to look to the effects of those ancient traditionary customs out of which no men can ever be lifted, except by some external agency or power. I look, therefore, to Mr. Lecky's list of causes operating adversely on the condition of the Irish people, with the greatest interest and curiosity—to see how far he has duly appreciated the comparative power of each.

The first and most fundamental of all Irish disadvantages is its geographical position. It was a condition involving a long train of consequences. It segregated Ireland from the great stream of European history. It precluded her from the unspeakable benefits of Roman conquest. It kept her away from the civilisation of the Latin Church. It effectually prevented her later subjugation by any superior race. It stereotyped barbarous customs, and prolonged them even to our own day. All happier influences seemed to stop when they landed on the shores of England. There they remained, and nobody cared to push across that narrow sea, into a land covered with dense forests and bogs, inhabited by fierce tribes with no possessions tempting to a comparatively civilised invader. In later days, England seemed to intercept geographically even the benefits of commerce. I have heard the feeling on this matter strikingly expressed by a very clever woman of Irish blood, and of Irish marriage, the late Lady Clanricarde—the daughter of George Canning, and the sister of Lord Canning, Governor-General of India. "You," she said, addressing an Englishman, "have always been like a high garden wall standing between us and the sun." But the geographical position of Ireland had a more positive effect than this. It made that island the back door of England, through which every enemy tried to steal or to force his way. It made it impossible for England to give up the policy of ultimate conquest. On the other hand, it was a perpetual incitement to the Irish to invite the foreign enemies of England when they desired to throw off her dominion or her suzerainty. In short, it has been a dominant factor in the whole history of the two countries.

But, dominant and insuperable as have been the effects of geography, the closely related facts of geology have been not less powerful in the case of Ireland. Almost wholly wanting in the great mineral resources of England and of Scotland, Ireland was destitute of the most fruitful of all the causes which broke the strain of a growing population in both those countries—just at the time when it was causing distress, scarcities, and even famines, closely resembling those of Ireland. All over the Celtic area of Scotland, which was much larger than it is now, and even in the low country where township-cultivation prevailed, there were scarcities and seasons of distress, which have been testified to and recorded by a great cloud of witnesses. The incorporating Union with England, in 1707, opened to the population of Scotland the immense resources of free commerce. And all through that century the rising industry of the towns, largely founded on the development of coal-fields, was a resource of enormous value. Ireland had no such resource; so that continual breeding on a potato diet went on unchecked, and with no native outlet for the population. England was certainly not the cause of these two great determinating conditions of Ireland—her geographical position, and her geological structure. Yet no other causes were even comparable with these as acting on the economic condition of the people.

Next comes an Irish condition closely connected with the two last, namely, the tenacious survival of the mediæval custom of communal tillage and pasturing in Townships, or as they were called in Ireland, "Townland" holdings. This indeed was of native origin all over Europe. But in England and Scotland it gradually gave way, in the latter end of the seventeenth and in the first half of the eighteenth centuries, to enclosed and divided farms. In Ireland it survived all through the century, and survives still in the most impoverished districts of the country. Few inquirers have had their eyes fully opened to the deep-seated effects of this system in perpetuating poverty, in wasting the soil, and in making the processes of improvement impossible. Professor Marshall of Cambridge is the only man—so far as I know—who has seen and expressed it as a universal truth.

Next comes the injurious fiscal legislation of the Irish Parliament under the received doctrines of that time; but applying them, as we have seen, with even exceptional blindness, and with exceptionally disastrous effects. Mr. Lecky does mention this policy of corn bounties, and calls it "a very strange tillage law;" but he mentions it in connection with quite another subject, namely, the desire of the Irish Parliament to spend all its revenue so as to leave no surplus that could go to England. Of course, in the abstract, the objection to the bounties depends on whether we do or do not really believe in the doctrines of Freetrade,—as founded on natural laws,—whether, in this last decade of the nineteenth century, we are as unconvinced as our grandfathers were in the beginning of the eighteenth century, that direct money bribes to a very poor and ignorant people, inducing them to spend their labour on a kind of production which would not otherwise be remunerative, is, or is not, a ruinous policy. But even this abstract doctrine is not the only decisive question to be considered in this particular case. I am ready to admit that there may possibly be cases in which industry may be thus turned into some new channel, such as the suggestions of voluntary enterprise would not have discovered. But in the case of the Irish corn bounties we have not only a typical case of violence done to all the teaching of Adam Smith, but a case also in which we have the direct evidence of a most competent witness that the policy was actually and visibly doing enormous harm to the soil of Ireland. We have, moreover, our own later knowledge and experience of the effect it had in producing a terrible evil which not even Arthur Young foresaw—and that is the power it had in stimulating the increase of a population living mainly on potatoes. The evidence is, I think, conclusive that this violation of all economic laws was one which had an immense effect in all the causes which have led to agrarian poverty in Ireland; and although Englishmen at this time were only just beginning to awake to any knowledge of economic laws, it must be at least acknowledged that England had no responsibility whatever in this matter.

Now let us pass to another great source of poverty in Ireland—a cause fully and repeatedly admitted by Mr. Lecky—and that is the universal custom of sub-letting land, and of sub-sub-letting it over and over again, until there often came to be four or five occupiers between the lowest of them and the head landlord. This was essentially and wholly Irish in its origin. England had nothing whatever to do with it. It prevailed all over the Island in defiance of every attempt of the landowners to prohibit it. Even the Irish courts of law took their share in it by discouraging the enforcement of any clause in leases which prohibited sub-letting. Such clauses were supposed to involve a prohibition which was at variance with public policy. There could not possibly be a stronger evidence of the ignorance prevalent in the native atmosphere of Irish opinion. At one time Protestant Ulster was as bad in this way as Catholic Connaught. "It is certain," says Mr. Lecky, " that the competition for land, aggravated by the inveterate habit of sub-letting, had reduced a great part of Ulster to intolerable misery." * The truth is that without it probably the swelling population could not have been fed at all, and the mere increase of numbers without any reference to the condition or standard of life was then regarded as a decisive test of prosperity. The breeding and the subdivision thus acted and reacted upon each other in an inseparable tangle of reciprocal causes and effects. English Protectionist legislation had, of course, its share in limiting employment. But Irish bounties of all kinds had a much more direct and more powerful effect in at once stimulating the breeding of the people, and in impoverishing the land out of which alone they could be fed.

Then, upon another closely related point,—the rents paid in Ireland,—Mr. Lecky is almost the only historian who represents the facts with any tolerable fairness. He does, indeed, quote numerous authors who talk about cottars "ground down to the very dust" by middlemen; and neither he, nor almost anybody else, can ever keep steadily in mind the obvious economic truth that rents are determined, not by those who let the land, but by those who hire it. If Irishmen were "ground down" at all they were ground down by the jostling of each other. High rents are nothing but an index of the great fact of a population pressing hard on the means of subsistence.

* "Ireland," vol. ii. p. 49.

They are not the cause of that fact, but its consequences. Of this pressure, high rents, offered and accepted, are simply the external indication. The fact would not be altered by one hair's-breadth if the index could be artificially kept from working. If the price of land, or the price of any other article, could possibly be kept down at a low point in spite of multitudes of men competing to get it, then the only result would be more speedy famine, because there would be a still more rapid increase of population. But besides all this, Mr. Lecky fairly recognises the fact that, to begin with, land in Ireland was not let either at high rents, or for short and uncertain tenures; but, on the contrary, at very low rents, and for long periods of time. And—contrary to a very widespread popular impression—to this very fact was due in a great degree the excessive breeding. He quotes from Arthur Young the pregnant observation that "if long leases at low rents, and profit incomes given, would have improved it, Ireland had long ago been a garden." The ignorance on this subject among writers and politicians, is profound, but natural. It is true, no doubt, that long tenures at low rents given to men of skill and capital, and of a high standard of life, may lead to great improvement. But it is equally true that the same advantages given to a very poor and ignorant people, with no capital, and with a very low standard of desire, are, on the contrary, the most powerful of all means for ensuring the rapid growth of a pauperised population. In the one case, they are a stimulus to industry: in the other case, they mean nothing but idleness made easy, and improvidence encouraged. All this, again, was purely Irish—England had nothing to do with it. The Irish corn bounty system had much to do with it—in aggravating other natural and inevitable results.

I pass to Education—and here again the blame, if blame there be in any proper sense of the word, lay with the native Irish. Through long centuries the Irish had neglected what we now call popular education. They had indeed, at one ancient time, some celebrated seminaries, and for the higher education men are said to have once come from all parts of Europe. But this had long passed away—and as regards the mass of the people there had never been anything like a general system of education. The Reformation was too closely and too obviously connected with the revival of secular learning in Europe, to give Catholic priests in general, after that event, any great enthusiasm for education. Mr. Lecky justly refers by way of contrast to the admirable system of parochial education which sprang up in Scotland, and which had a large share in arming the people to contend with all the same economic changes which operated at the same time in that country. But the system of Scotch education was purely the product of the Reformation. It did not exist before: it was no part of the Catholic system,—and there were no materials out of which to construct any such system in Ireland. It is absurd to blame the English Government for this defect.

It is not my intention to dwell here on the last scene of all—the great Irish Rebellion of 1798. Mr. Gladstone and others who write and speak in the same spirit of reckless partisanship in order to buttress and vindicate their new policy of surrender to the forces of anarchy, have dwelt on the cruelties perpetrated by the Government troops in the suppression of that rebellion. But they never allude to the earlier horrors perpetrated by the rebels. In this as in all other cases of civil war,—of rebellions, and of suppressions of rebellion—we must look first at the broader aspect of the cause which was fought for by either side, and then at the comparative conduct of the two parties in the strife. Looking at the rebellion of 1798 in the first of these two points of view, one thing to be noted above all others is this—that it was not a Catholic rebellion—it was not a national rebellion—it was not even an agrarian rebellion. It was essentially a Jacobin rebellion. Sympathy with the French Revolution in its wildest excesses, and in its fiercest passions, was the heart and soul of that rebellion. Of course it took advantage of, and allied itself with, every element of discontent and disaffection which had survived from the said history we have here shortly traced. But the Catholics of Ireland held aloof from it, and the genuine old Irish Catholics, who swarmed in the armies of the Continental

Kingdoms, never lent it their aid. Its whole spirit was incarnated in Wolfe Tone, whose autobiographic memoirs present to my mind the most striking picture in our language of a villainous and destructive temper directed against all that can hold human society together. I have no horror of political rebellions merely as such. I am the direct descendant of men who staked all, and lost all, in the armed defence of their country's liberties. But this has little to do with the spirit which animated Wolfe Tone and his "United Irishmen." He had twice offered to sell himself to Mr. Pitt if he were allowed to organise a filibustering expedition for the plunder of the rich Catholic churches on the coast of the Spanish Main. When this piratical offer was contemptuously refused, he conceived a mortal hatred of England. He then tried to sell his country to the French Directory—bargaining with them for his own share in the results of an invasion. He suggested the fiercest measures. He approved of a proclamation warning Irish loyalists that every man taken as prisoner of war would be put to death. He gloated over the prospect of seeing the cities of England and of Scotland at the mercy of the fiends who had murdered the people of La Vendée, and had burnt and devastated that fair province of France. He was, in short, the prey of passions which made him an incarnate fiend. Mr. Lecky treats this man, in my opinion, far too philosophically. It is quite right to be judicial. But there are occasions when the coolest of judges has a public duty to charge the jury strongly against a prisoner. There are occasions when the black cap is inseparable from the ermined robe. And so there are occasions when History, in order to be true, must be severe in the judgments it pronounces. Mr. Lecky says that Wolfe Tone's patriotism was largely compounded of hatreds—that he hated the Parliament of Ireland—that he hated the Irish country gentry, and contemplated their massacre—that he hated the Whig Club—that he hated England, above all things, and looked forward with passionate eagerness to her downfall.* Yes—he did indeed hate all those things and persons. But it ought to be added that he hated and despised religion, and all the restraints it could impose on conduct. He was willing to use it as one of his tools whenever it was convenient for his purpose. He could go to Mass in a Catholic church—profaning the holiest rite of Christianity—in order to deceive a genuine Catholic people. He was a villain, in short, of the deepest dye—caring for nothing except the gratification of his own fierce hatreds, and willing to wade through oceans of blood to some share in the rule of his own country under the Jacobin Chiefs of Paris. Yet this is the man to whom Mr. Gladstone seems to have referred in a letter when he said that unfortunately many of the rebels in 1798 were among the noblest characters in Ireland.

* "History," vol. iii. pp. 507, 508.

But what is the light which this revelation of character and purpose throws on the conduct of the Irish Government and of the Irish loyalists? The Government was in the secret of every movement through an informer of whose character Mr. Lecky draws a picture of the most striking and subtle discrimination. They knew all that the country and the English nation were threatened with. Half-measures would have been a crime in such a case. Then, what was the ocular demonstration set before their eyes, of the true character of the rebellion, in the very first acts of the insurgents? We must remember that we are now looking to causes rather than to reason, as dominating the conduct of men in times of imminent danger, and of great excitement. The opening scenes of any contest—the first acts in any tragedy—are always those which largely determine the temper and the conduct of men. What, in this respect, were the facts as recorded by history? The outbreak began on the 23rd of May, and on the 24th numerous armed bodies were in motion in the counties next to Dublin. On that very first day of action, a small body of forty or fifty militia soldiers were surrounded and burnt to death, or piked, in a small town called Prosperous. A number of civilians were murdered in cold blood. Almost at the same time, an officer of the militia force itself, of a high Catholic family, was discovered to be a traitor. On the 26th of May—only three days after the outbreak—some nineteen Protestants, including a

magistrate, were butchered with the utmost deliberation, and often "with circumstances of aggravated brutality."* On the 27th of May a serious defeat of a picked body of militia still more alarmed the whole country. Enniscorthy was taken by the rebels on the 28th. The important town of Wexford fell on the 30th. A savage mob of armed men was in complete possession of a town full of Protestant and panic-stricken prisoners. The whole jargon of French Jacobin phraseology was in full play. Revolutionary tribunals were sitting. Then came, on the 20th of June, the horrible massacre of Wexford Bridge. The unfortunate Protestant prisoners were brought out to be murdered in batches of ten, fifteen, and twenty at a time. "They were placed in rows of eighteen or twenty, and the pikemen pierced them one by one, lifted them writhing into the air, held them up for a few moments before the yelling multitude, and then flung their bodies into the river. Ninety-seven prisoners are said to have been so murdered, and the tragedy was prolonged for more than three hours." †
I have read the account given by more than an eye-witness—by one of the intended victims, who was waiting his turn to be so tortured and butchered, and was only saved by an alarm among the rebels, which stopped the massacre. His account makes one's blood run cold—and boil—by turns.

* "History," vol. iii. p. 337.
† Ibid., vol. iv. pp. 455, 456.

Now let us remember that all these horrors and events took place—some of them within a week of the first outbreak—all of them within twenty-four days. We may try to imagine, if we can, what a colour they must have given to the whole rebel cause, in the eyes of the vast majority of the people of Ireland,—both Catholic and Protestant,—and what furious but natural passions they must have roused. It is all very well to say, as Mr. Lecky philosophically does, that we may find some "difficulty in striking the balance between the crimes of the rebels, and the outrages of the soldiers." But we are bound to remember which of the two parties set the first example, as well as which of the two parties was representative of the highest interest of Society. Happily the great mass of the people were loyal to the Government. The Rebellion was suppressed largely by the aid of the native yeomanry and militia corps. Many of the Catholic priests and bishops risked their lives in the cause of humanity to both parties. Twice, as is well known, Wolfe Tone brought a French fleet to the west coast to effect the subjugation of his native country by the French. The people did not respond to his infamous invitations. And yet almost all parties are agreed that, if a large French force had succeeded in effecting a landing, and had met with even one temporary success, no human being could have been confident that a very poor, a very ignorant, and a very excitable population might not have joined them, in spite of every effort on the part of their own clergy, and of all by whom, in times of peace, they had been accustomed to be influenced.

Mr. Gladstone's Essay, No. IX. in his "Special Aspects," called "Plain Speaking on the Irish Union," is passionately one-sided and unfair; and he does not scruple to endorse the absurd allegation that "there was a plot of the Government against Ireland to make her condition intolerable, as the only possible means of contriving the surrender of her nationality."* I could easily fill as many pages as he has filled, on the other side, with details of rebel atrocities, and of still more atrocious rebel hopes and aspirations, and with words of passionate invective. But it would be only stupid as well as wicked work to do so. What we want now is a disposition to condemn, as equally horrible, all excesses on both sides, whilst yet keeping a clear hold on the principles and prospects of everlasting right which lay on the Imperial side. The spirit of candour and fairness with which Mr. Gladstone handles this sad epoch in history may be judged by the single fact that in one of his speeches he quoted a passage from a pamphlet published by Mr. Lecky when he was a very young man, which passage Mr. Lecky himself had cancelled in a subsequent edition. Yet Mr. Gladstone quoted it, with no intimation to his hearers of this significant retractation. Nobody could possibly suspect what lay hid under such a quotation. The pleasure of quoting

* "Special Aspects," p. 321.

the past and in the experience of our own time. Still, it was not bad advice. Every hour spent in the study of Irish history has only confirmed me in the opinions which we had held before,—and of which Mr. Gladstone was a foremost exponent until he was confronted by a large addition to the number of Irish members. Surrender to a supposed political necessity is always conceivable. But the passionate espousal of a whole code of doctrines, and opinions, uniformly before rejected, is inconceivable to any man who respects his own intellectual integrity. Submission to the inevitable is one thing: acceptance of the untrue is quite another thing.

We cannot throw on former generations the burdens of our own day. We must judge and think for ourselves on the tendencies of human nature, and on the inevitable effects of certain political experiments. Still, it is no small satisfaction to read the following lines, penned by the greatest Irishman who has ever lived, except perhaps two others—Bishop Berkeley and the Duke of Wellington—lines written by Burke very near his death. Setting aside the "Catholic Question," which has long ago been settled even more liberally and completely than to Burke seemed possible, he says—

"For, in the name of God, what grievance has Ireland, as Ireland, to complain of with regard to Great Britain; unless the protection of the most powerful country upon earth—giving all her privileges, without exception, in common to Ireland, and reserving to herself only the painful pre-eminence of tenfold burdens, be a matter of complaint. The subject, as a subject, is as free in Ireland, as he is in England. As a member of the empire, an Irishman has every privilege of a natural-born Englishman, in every part of it, in every occupation, and in every branch of commerce. No monopoly is established against him anywhere; and the great staple manufacture of Ireland is not only not prohibited, not only not discouraged, but it is privileged in a manner that has no example. I say nothing of the immense advantage she derives from the use of the English capital. In what country upon earth is it that a quantity of linens, the moment they are lodged in the warehouse, and before the sale, would entitle the Irish merchant or manufacturer to draw bills on the terms, and at the time, in which this is done by the warehouseman on London? Ireland, therefore, as Ireland, whether it be taken civilly, constitutionally, or commercially, suffers no grievance." If this was true in the last days of Burke, how much more true must it be now—when so much has been done which he could never contemplate as even possible. I conclude in the words of the same great Irishman—this being indeed the sum and substance of the preceding pages: "I MUST SPEAK THE TRUTH. I MUST SAY THAT ALL THE EVILS OF IRELAND ORIGINATE WITHIN ITSELF: BUT IT IS THE BOUNDLESS CREDIT WHICH IS GIVEN

TO AN IRISH CABAL THAT PRODUCES WHATEVER MISCHIEFS BOTH COUNTRIES MAY FIND IN THEIR RELATION." The particular faction which English parties may be tempted to patronise, may vary from time to time. But the principle of giving what Burke called "boundless credit" to any one of them, is equally vicious. Never, assuredly, was a worse selection made of those who are to have supreme power over their fellow-subjects, than the selection made by the Cabinet of Mr. Gladstone. Every member of that Cabinet of any note is steeped to the lips in former denunciations of their doctrines and of their doings. Not a fraction of evidence has been produced of any change. On the contrary, the unanimous vote for condoning the most horrible form of indiscriminate murder which they lately gave, shows them to be unchanged. We have the rare evidence of a judicial investigation held under circumstances which compelled the judges to limit their finding within the strictest rules of evidence. The giving of a "boundless credit" to them will renew the old desolations of Ireland due to similar causes. What Ireland wants above all things is the rule of a Government which is above all her factions, and which will maintain the authority of just and equal laws. The minority of the Irish people do not now seek any ascendancy. But they have a right to protection—and that, too, as a condition of their allegiance.

LONDON:
PRINTED BY WILLIAM CLOWES AND SONS, LIMITED,
STAMFORD STREET AND CHARING CROSS.

Albemarle Street, London,
March, 1893.

MR. MURRAY'S
GENERAL LIST OF WORKS.

ALBERT MEMORIAL. A Descriptive and Illustrated Account of the National Monument at Kensington. Illustrated by numerous Engravings. By DOYNE C. BELL. With 24 Plates. Folio. 12*l*. 12*s*.

——————————— HANDBOOK. 16mo. 1*s*.; Illustrated, 2*s*. 6*d*.

ABBOTT (REV. J.). Memoirs of a Church of England Missionary in the North American Colonies. Post 8vo. 2*s*.

ABERCROMBIE (JOHN). Enquiries concerning the Intellectual Powers and the Investigation of Truth. Fcap. 8vo. 3*s*. 6*d*.

ACLAND (REV. C.). Manners and Customs of India. Post 8vo. 2*s*.

ACWORTH (W. M.) The Railways of England. With 56 Illustrations. 8vo. 14*s*.

——————— The Railways of Scotland. Map. Crown 8vo. 5*s*.

——————— The Railways and the Traders. The Railway Rates Question in Theory and Practice. Crown 8vo. 6*s*., or *Popular Edit*. 1*s*.

ÆSOP'S FABLES. A New Version. By REV. THOMAS JAMES. With 100 Woodcuts, by TENNIEL and WOLFE. Post 8vo 2*s*. 6*d*.

AGRICULTURAL (ROYAL) JOURNAL. 8vo. Quarterly. 2*s*. 6*d*.

AINGER (A. C.). Latin Grammar. [See ETON.]

————————— An English-Latin Gradus, or Verse Dictionary. On a New Plan, with carefully Selected Epithets and Synonyms. Crown 8vo. (450 pp.) 9*s*.

ALICE (PRINCESS); GRAND DUCHESS OF HESSE. Letters to H.M. THE QUEEN. With a Memoir by H.R.H. Princess Christian. Portrait. Crown 8vo. 7*s*. 6*d*.

AMBER-WITCH (THE). A most interesting Trial for Witchcraft. Translated by LADY DUFF GORDON. Post 8vo. 2*s*.

AMERICA (THE RAILWAYS OF). Their Construction, Development, Management, and Appliances. By Various Writers. With an Introduction by T. M. COOLEY. With 200 Illustrations. Large 8vo. 31*s*. 6*d*.

——— [See BATES, NADAILLAC, RUMBOLD, VILLIERS STUART.]

APOCRYPHA: With a Commentary Explanatory and Critical. By Dr. Salmon, Prof. Fuller, Archdeacon Farrar, Archdeacon Gifford, Canon Rawlinson, Dr. Edersheim, Rev. J. H. Lupton, Rev. C. J. Ball. Edited by HENRY WACE, D.D. 2 vols. Medium 8vo. 50*s*.

ARCHITECTURE: A Profession or an Art. Thirteen short Essays on the qualifications and training of Architects. Edited by R. NORMAN SHAW, R.A., and T. G. JACKSON, A.R.A. 8vo. 9*s*.

ARGYLL (DUKE OF). THE UNSEEN FOUNDATIONS OF SOCIETY: An Examination of the Fallacies and Failures of Economic Science due to Neglected Elements. 8vo. 18*s*.

——————— Unity of Nature. 8vo. 12*s*.

——————— Reign of Law. Crown 8vo. 5*s*.

ARISTOTLE. [See GROTE.]

ARTHUR'S (LITTLE) History of England. By LADY CALLCOTT. *New Edition, continued to* 1878. With Woodcuts. Fcap. 8vo. 1*s*. 6*d*.

——————————— HISTORY OF FRANCE, from the Earliest Times to the Fall of the Second Empire. With Woodcuts. Fcp. 8vo. 2*s*. 6*d*.

AUSTIN (JOHN). GENERAL JURISPRUDENCE; or, The Philosophy of Positive Law. Edited by ROBERT CAMPBELL. 2 Vols. 8vo. 32*s*.

B

AUSTIN (JOHN). STUDENT'S EDITION, compiled from the above work, by ROBERT CAMPBELL. Post 8vo. 12s.

———— Analysis of. By GORDON CAMPBELL. Post 8vo. 6s.

AUSTRALIA. [See LUMHOLTZ.]

BAINES (THOMAS). Greenhouse and Stove Plants, Flowering and Fine-Leaved. Palms, Ferns, and Lycopodiums. With full details of the Propagation and Cultivation. 8vo. 8s. 6d.

BALDWIN BROWN (PROF. G.). The Fine Arts. With Illustrations. Crown 8vo. 3s. 6d. (University Extension Series.)

BARKLEY (H. C.). Bulgaria Before the War. Post 8vo. 10s. 6d.

———— Studies in the Art of Rat-catching. 3s. 6d.

———— Ride through Asia Minor and Armenia. Crown 8vo. 10s. 6d.

BARROW (JOHN). Life of Sir Francis Drake. Post 8vo. 2s.

BATES (H. W.). Records of a Naturalist on the Amazons during Eleven Years' Adventure and Travel. A new Edition of the unabridged work. With a Memoir of the Author by EDWARD CLODD. With Portrait, Coloured Plates, Illustrations, and Map. Medium 8vo. 18s. or Abridged Edition without Memoir, crown 8vo. 7s. 6d.

BATTLE ABBEY ROLL. [See CLEVELAND.]

BEACONSFIELD'S (LORD) Letters, and "Correspondence with his Sister," 1830—1852. Portrait. Crown 8vo. 2s.

BEATRICE, H.R.H. PRINCESS. Adventures in the Life of Count George Albert of Erbach. A True Story. Translated from the German. Portraits and Woodcuts. Crown 8vo. 10s. 6d.

BECKETT (SIR EDMUND), (LORD GRIMTHORPE). "Should the Revised New Testament be Authorised?" Post 8vo. 6s.

BELL (DOYNE C.). Notices of the Historic Persons buried in the Chapel of the Tower of London. Illustrations. Crown 8vo. 14s.

BENJAMIN'S Persia & the Persians. Illustrations. 8vo. 24s.

BENSON (ARCHBISHOP). The Cathedral; its necessary place in the Life and Work of the Church. Post 8vo. 6s.

BERKELEY (HASTINGS). Wealth and Welfare: Crown 8vo. 6s.

———— Japanese Letters; Eastern Impressions of Western Men and Manners. Post 8vo. 6s.

BERTHELOT (M.). Explosives and their Powers. Translated and condensed from the French by C. NAPIER HAKE and WILLIAM MACNAB, F.I.C.E. With Preface by Lt.-Colonel J. P. CUNDILL, R.A., H.M. Inspector of Explosives. With Illustrations. 8vo. 24s.

BERTRAM (JAS. G.). Harvest of the Sea: an Account of British Food Fishes, Fisheries and Fisher Folk. Illustrations. Post 8vo. 9s.

BIBLE COMMENTARY. EXPLANATORY AND CRITICAL. With a REVISION of the TRANSLATION. By BISHOPS and CLERGY of the ANGLICAN CHURCH. Edited by Canon F. C. COOK, M.A.

THE OLD TESTAMENT. 6 VOLS. Medium 8vo. 6l. 15s.

Vol. I. GENESIS—DEUTERONOMY. 30s.
Vol. II. JOSHUA—KINGS. 20s.
Vol. III. KINGS ii.—ESTHER. 16s.
Vol. IV. JOB—SONG OF SOLOMON. 24s.
Vol. V. ISAIAH—JEREMIAH. 20s.
Vol. VI. EZEKIEL—MALACHI. 25s.

THE NEW TESTAMENT. 4 VOLS. Medium 8vo. 4l. 14s.

Vol. I. ST. MATTHEW—ST. LUKE. 18s.
Vol. II. ST. JOHN.—ACTS OF THE APOSTLES. 20s.
Vol. III. ROMANS—PHILEMON. 28s.
Vol. IV. HEBREWS — REVELATION. 28s.

BIBLE COMMENTARY. THE APOCRYPHA. By Various Writers. Edited by HENRY WACE, D.D. 2 vols. Medium 8vo. 50s.
———————— THE STUDENT'S EDITION. Abridged and Edited by REV. J. M. FULLER, M.A. 6 Vols. Crown 8vo. 7s. 6d. each. OLD TESTAMENT. 4 Vols. NEW TESTAMENT. 2 Vols.

BIRD (ISABELLA). Hawaiian Archipelago; or Six Months among the Palm Groves, Coral Reefs, and Volcanoes of the Sandwich Islands. Illustrations. Crown 8vo. 7s. 6d.
——— A Lady's Life in the Rocky Mountains. Illustrations. Post 8vo. 7s. 6d.
——— The Golden Chersonese and the Way Thither. Illustrations. Post 8vo. 14s.
——— Unbeaten Tracks in Japan: Including Visits to the Aborigines of Yezo and the Shrines of Nikko and Isé. Illustrations. Crown 8vo. 7s. 6d.
——— Journeys in Persia and Kurdistan: with a Summer in the Upper Karun Region, and a Visit to the Nestorian Rayahs. Maps and 36 Illustrations. 2 vols. Crown 8vo. 24s.

BISHOP (MRS.). [See BIRD (ISABELLA).]

BLACKIE (C.). Geographical Etymology; or, Dictionary of Place Names. Third Edition. Crown 8vo. 7s.

BLUNT (REV. J. J.). Undesigned Coincidences in the Writings of the Old and New Testaments, an Argument of their Veracity. Post 8vo. 6s.
——— History of the Christian Church in the First Three Centuries. Post 8vo. 6s.
——— The Parish Priest; His Duties, Acquirements, and Obligations. Post 8vo. 6s.

BOOK OF COMMON PRAYER. Illustrated with Coloured Borders, Initial Letters, and Woodcuts. 8vo. 18s.

BORROW (GEORGE). The Bible in Spain; or, the Journeys and Imprisonments of an Englishman in an attempt to circulate the Scriptures in the Peninsula. Portrait. Post 8vo. 2s. 6d.
——— The Zincali. An Account of the Gypsies of Spain; Their Manners, Customs, Religion, and Language. 2s. 6d.
——— Lavengro; Scholar—Gypsy—and Priest. 2s. 6d.
——— Romany Rye. A Sequel to Lavengro. Post 8vo. 2s. 6d.
——— WILD WALES: its People, Language, and Scenery. Post 8vo. 2s. 6d.
——— Romano Lavo-Lil. With Illustrations of the English Gypsies; their Poetry and Habitations. Post 8vo. 5s.

BOSWELL'S Life of Samuel Johnson, LL.D. Including the Tour to the Hebrides. Edited by Mr. CROKER. *Seventh Edition*. Portraits. 1 vol. Medium 8vo. 12s.

BOWEN (LORD JUSTICE). Virgil in English Verse, Eclogues and Æneid, Books I.—VI. Map and Frontispiece. 8vo. 12s.

BRADLEY (DEAN). Arthur Penrhyn Stanley; Biographical Lectures. Crown 8vo. 3s. 6d.

BREWER (REV. J. S.). The Endowments and Establishment of the Church of England. Edited by L. T. DIBDIN, M.A. Post 8vo. 6s.

BRIDGES (MRS. F. D.). A Lady's Travels in Japan, Thibet, Yarkand, Kashmir, Java, the Straits of Malacca, Vancouver's Island, &c. With Map and Illustrations from Sketches by the Author. Crown 8vo. 15s.

B 2

BRITISH ASSOCIATION REPORTS. 8vo.

⁎ The Reports for the years 1831 to 1875 may be obtained at the Offices of the British Association.

Glasgow, 1876, 25s.
Plymouth, 1877, 24s.
Dublin, 1878, 24s.
Sheffield, 1879, 24s.
Swansea, 1880, 24s.
York, 1881, 24s.
Southampton, 1882, 24s.
Southport, 1883, 24s.
Canada, 1884, 24s.
Aberdeen, 1885, 24s.
Birmingham, 1886, 24s.
Manchester, 1887, 24s.
Bath, 1888, 24s.
Newcastle-upon-Tyne, 1889, 24s.
Leeds, 1890, 24s.
Cardiff, 1891, 24s.
Edinburgh, 1892, 24s.

BROADFOOT (Major W., R.E.) Services in Afghanistan, the Punjab, and on the N. W. Frontier of India. Compiled from his papers and those of Lords Ellenborough and Hardinge. Maps. 8vo. 15s.

BROCKLEHURST (T. U.). Mexico To-day: A Country with a Great Future. With a Glance at the Prehistoric Remains and Antiquities of the Montezumas. Plates and Woodcuts. Medium 8vo. 21s.

BRODRICK (Miss). Outlines of Egyptian History: Based on the Work of Mariette Bey. Translated and Edited by MARY BRODRICK. A new and Revised Edition. With Maps. Crown 8vo. 5s.

BRUCE (Hon. W. N.). Life of Sir Charles Napier. [See NAPIER.

BRUGSCH (PROFESSOR). A History of Egypt under the Pharaohs. Derived entirely from Monuments. A New and thoroughly Revised Edition. Edited by M. BRODRICK. Maps. 1 Vol. 8vo. 18s.

BULGARIA. [See BARKLEY, MINCHIN.]

BUNBURY (SIR E. H.). A History of Ancient Geography, among the Greeks and Romans, from the Earliest Ages till the Fall of the Roman Empire. Maps. 2 Vols. 8vo. 21s.

BURBIDGE (F. W.). The Gardens of the Sun: or A Naturalist's Journal in Borneo and the Sulu Archipelago. Illustrations. Cr. 8vo. 14s.

BURGON (DEAN). A Biography. Illustrated by Extracts from his Letters and Early Journals. By E. MEYRICK GOULBURN, D.D. Portraits. 2 Vols. 8vo. 24s.

———— The Revision Revised: (1.) The New Greek Text; (2.) The New English Version; (3.) Westcott and Hort's Textual Theory. Second Edition. 8vo. 14s.

———— Lives of Twelve Good Men. Martin J. Routh, R. J. Rose, Chas. Marriott, Edward Hawkins, Saml. Wilberforce, R. L. Cotton, Richard Gresswell, H. O. Coxe, H. L. Mansel, Wm. Jacobson, C. P. Eden, C. L. Higgins. New Edition. With Portraits. 1 Vol. 8vo. 16s.

BURN (COL.). Dictionary of Naval and Military Technical Terms, English and French—French and English. Crown 8vo. 15s.

BUTTMANN'S LEXILOGUS; a Critical Examination of the Meaning of numerous Greek Words, chiefly in Homer and Hesiod. By Rev. J. R. FISHLAKE. 8vo. 12s.

BUXTON (CHARLES). Memoirs of Sir Thomas Fowell Buxton, Bart. Portrait. 8vo. 16s. *Popular Edition.* Fcap. 8vo. 5s.

———— Notes of Thought. With a Biographical Notice. *Second Edition.* Post 8vo. 5s.

———— (SYDNEY C.). A Handbook to the Political Questions of the Day; with the Arguments on Either Side. 8vo. 10s. 6d.

———— Finance and Politics, an Historical Study. 1783–1885. 2 Vols. 26s.

———— Handbook to the Death Duties. Post 8vo. 3s. 6d.

BYRON'S (LORD) LIFE AND WORKS :—
    LIFE, LETTERS, AND JOURNALS. By THOMAS MOORE. One Volume, Portraits. Royal 8vo. 7s. 6d.
    LIFE AND POETICAL WORKS. *Popular Edition.* Portraits. 2 Vols. Royal 8vo. 15s.
    POETICAL WORKS. *Library Edition.* Portrait. 6 Vols. 8vo. 45s.
    POETICAL WORKS. *Cabinet Edition.* Plates. 10 Vols. 12mo. 30s.
    POETICAL WORKS. *Pocket Ed.* 8 Vols. 16mo. In a case. 21s.
    POETICAL WORKS. *Popular Edition.* Plates. Royal 8vo. 7s. 6d.
    POETICAL WORKS. *Pearl Edition.* 2s. 6d. Cloth, 3s. 6d.
    CHILDE HAROLD. With 80 Engravings. Crown 8vo. 12s.
    CHILDE HAROLD. 16mo. 2s. 6d.
    CHILDE HAROLD. Vignettes. 16mo. 1s.
    CHILDE HAROLD. Portrait. 16mo. 6d.
    TALES AND POEMS. 16mo. 2s. 6d.
    MISCELLANEOUS. 2 Vols. 16mo. 5s.
    DRAMAS AND PLAYS. 2 Vols. 16mo. 5s.
    DON JUAN AND BEPPO. 2 Vols. 16mo. 5s.

CAILLARD (E. M.). Electricity. A Sketch for General Readers. With Illustrations. Crown 8vo. 7s. 6d.

———— The Invisible Powers of Nature. Some Elementary Lessons in Physical Science for Beginners. Post 8vo. 6s.

CALDECOTT (ALFRED). English Colonization and Empire. Coloured Maps and Plans. Crown 8vo. 3s. 6d. (Univ. Extension Series.)

CAMPBELL (LORD). Autobiography, Journals and Correspondence. By Mrs. Hardcastle. Portrait. 2 Vols. 8vo. 30s.

———— Lord Chancellors and Keepers of the Great Seal of England. From the Earliest Times to the Death of Lord Eldon in 1838. 10 Vols. Crown 8vo. 6s. each.

———— Chief Justices of England. From the Norman Conquest to the Death of Lord Tenterden. 4 Vols. Crown 8vo. 6s. each.

———— (THOS.) Essay on English Poetry. With Short Lives of the British Poets. Post 8vo. 3s. 6d.

CAREY (Life of). [See GEORGE SMITH.]

CARLISLE (BISHOP OF). The Foundations of the Creed. Being a Discussion of the Grounds upon which the Articles of the Apostles' Creed may be held by Earnest and Thoughtful Minds in the 19th Century. 8vo. 14s.

CARNARVON (LORD). Portugal, Gallicia, and the Basque Provinces. Post 8vo. 3s. 6d.

———— (Fourth Earl of). Prometheus Bound, translated into English Verse. Crown 8vo. 6s.

CAVALCASELLE'S WORKS. [See CROWE.]

CESNOLA (GEN.). Cyprus; its Ancient Cities, Tombs, and Temples. With 400 Illustrations. Medium 8vo. 50s.

CHAMBERS (G. F.). A Practical and Conversational Pocket Dictionary of the English, French, and German Languages. Designed for Travellers and Students generally. Small 8vo. 6s.

CHILD-CHAPLIN (Dr.). Benedicite; or, Song of the Three Children; being Illustrations of the Power, Beneficence, and Design manifested by the Creator in his Works. Post 8vo. 6s.

CHISHOLM (Mrs.). Perils of the Polar Seas; True Stories of Arctic Discovery and Adventure. Illustrations. Post 8vo. 6s.

CHURTON (Archdeacon). Poetical Remains. Post 8vo. 7s. 6d.

CLARKE (Major G. Sydenham), Royal Engineers. Fortification; Its Past Achievements, Recent Development, and Future Progress. With Illustrations. Medium 8vo. 21s.

CLASSIC PREACHERS OF THE ENGLISH CHURCH. Lectures delivered at St. James'. 2 Vols. Post 8vo. 7s. 6d. each.

CLEVELAND (Duchess of). The Battle Abbey Roll. With some account of the Norman Lineages. 3 Vols. Sm. 4to. 48s.

CLIVE'S (Lord) Life. By Rev. G. R. Gleig. Post 8vo. 3s. 6d.

CLODE (C. M.). Military Forces of the Crown; their Administration and Government. 2 Vols. 8vo. 21s. each.

—————— Administration of Justice under Military and Martial Law, as applicable to the Army, Navy, and Auxiliary Forces. 8vo. 12s.

COLEBROOKE (Sir Edward, Bart.). Life of the Hon. Mountstuart Elphinstone. With Portrait and Plans. 2 Vols. 8vo. 26s.

COLERIDGE (Samuel Taylor), and the English Romantic School. By Prof. Brandl. With Portrait, Crown 8vo. 12s.

—————— Table-Talk. Portrait. 12mo. 3s. 6d.

COLES (John). Summer Travelling in Iceland. With a Chapter on Askja. By E. D. Morgan. Map and Illustrations. 18s.

COLLINS (J. Churton). Bolingbroke: an Historical Study. With an Essay on Voltaire in England. Crown 8vo. 7s. 6d.

COLONIAL LIBRARY. [See Home and Colonial Library.]

COOK (Canon F. C.). The Revised Version of the Three First Gospels, considered in its Bearings upon the Record of Our Lord's Words and Incidents in His Life. 8vo. 9s.

—————— The Origins of Language and Religion. 8vo. 15s.

COOKE (E. W.). Leaves from my Sketch-Book. With Descriptive Text. 50 Plates. 2 Vols. Small folio. 31s. 6d. each.

—————— (W. H.). History and Antiquities of the County of Hereford. Vol. III. In continuation of Duncumb's History. 4to. £2 12s. 6d.

—————— Additions to Duncumb's History. Vol. II. 4to. 15s.

—————— The Hundred of Grimsworth. Part I., 17s. 6d., Pt. II., 25s. 4to.

COOKERY (Modern Domestic). Adapted for Private Families. By a Lady. Woodcuts. Fcap. 8vo. 5s.

COOLEY (Thomas M.). [See America, Railways of.]

CORNEY GRAIN. By Himself. Post 8vo. 1s.

COURTHOPE (W. J.). Life and Works of Alexander Pope. With Portraits. 10 Vols. 8vo. 10s. 6d. each.

CRABBE (Rev. G.). Life & Works. Illustrations. Royal 8vo. 7s.

CRAIK (Henry). Life of Jonathan Swift. Portrait. 8vo. 18s.

CRIPPS (Wilfred). Old English Plate: Ecclesiastical, Decorative, and Domestic, its Makers and Marks. Fourth Edition. Revised and enlarged. With 70 Illustrations and 2010 facsimile Plate Marks. Medium 8vo. 21s.

*** Tables of the Date Letters and Marks sold separately. 5s.

—————— Old French Plate: Its Makers and Marks. A New and Revised Edition. With Tables of Makers' Marks, in addition to the Plate Marks. 8vo. 10s. 6d.

CROKER (Rt. Hon. J. W.). Correspondence and Journals. Edited by the late Louis J. Jennings. Portrait. 3 Vols. 8vo. 45s.

—————— Progressive Geography for Children. 18mo. 1s. 6d.

CROKER (Rt. Hon. J.W.). Boswell's Life of Johnson. [*See* Boswell.]
———— Historical Essay on the Guillotine. Fcap. 8vo. 1s.
CROWE and CAVALCASELLE. Lives of the Early Flemish Painters. Woodcuts. 8vo, 15s.
———— Life and Times of Titian, with some Account of his Family. Illustrations. 2 Vols. 8vo. 21s.
———— Raphael; His Life and Works. 2 Vols. 8vo. 33s.
CUMMING (R. Gordon). Five Years of a Hunter's Life in the Far Interior of South Africa. Woodcuts. Post 8vo. 6s.
CUNNINGHAM (Prof. W.), D.D. The Use and Abuse of Money. Crown 8vo. 3s. (University Extension Series.)
CURTIUS' (Professor) Student's Greek Grammar, for the Upper Forms. Edited by Dr. Wm. Smith. Post 8vo. 6s.
———— Elucidations of the above Grammar. Translated by Evelyn Abbot. Post 8vo. 7s. 6d.
———— Smaller Greek Grammar for the Middle and Lower Forms. Abridged from the larger work. 12mo. 3s. 6d.
———— Accidence of the Greek Language. Extracted from the above work. 12mo. 2s. 6d.
———— Principles of Greek Etymology. Translated by A. S. Wilkins and E. B. England. New Edition. 2 Vols. 8vo. 28s.
———— The Greek Verb, its Structure and Development. Translated by A. S. Wilkins, and E. B. England. 8vo. 12s.
CURZON (Hon. Robert). Visits to the Monasteries of the Levant. Illustrations. Post 8vo. 7s. 6d.
CUST (General). Warriors of the 17th Century—Civil Wars of France and England. 2 Vols. 16s. Commanders of Fleets and Armies. 2 Vols. 18s.
———— Annals of the Wars—18th & 19th Century. With Maps. 9 Vols. Post 8vo. 5s. each.
DAVY (Sir Humphry). Consolations in Travel; or, Last Days of a Philosopher. Woodcuts. Fcap. 8vo. 3s. 6d.
———— Salmonia; or, Days of Fly Fishing. Woodcuts. Fcap. 8vo. 3s. 6d.
DE COSSON (Major E. A.). The Cradle of the Blue Nile; a Journey through Abyssinia and Soudan. Map and Illustrations. 2 Vols. Post 8vo. 21s.
———— Days and Nights of Service with Sir Gerald Graham's Field Force at Suakim. Plan and Illustrations. Crown 8vo. 14s.
DENNIS (George). The Cities and Cemeteries of Etruria. 20 Plans and 200 Illustrations. 2 Vols. Medium 8vo. 21s.
———— (Robert). Industrial Ireland. Suggestions for a Practical Policy of "Ireland for the Irish." Crown 8vo. 6s.
DARWIN'S (Charles) Life and Letters, with an autobiographical Chapter. Edited by his Son, Francis Darwin, F.R.S. Portraits. 3 Vols. 8vo. 36s.
Or popular Edition, condensed in 1 Vol., crown 8vo. 7s. 6d.
———— An Illustrated Edition of the Voyage of a Naturalist Round the World in H.M.S. Beagle. With Views of Places Visited and Described. By R. T. Pritchett. 100 Illustrations. Medium 8vo. 21s.
Journal of a Naturalist during a Voyage round the World. Popular Edition. With Portrait. 3s. 6d.
Origin of Species by Means of Natural Selection. Library Edition. 2 vols. 12s.; or popular Edition. 6s.
Descent of Man, and Selection in Relation to Sex. Woodcuts. Library Ed. 2 vols. 15s.; or popular Ed. 7s. 6d.

DARWIN (CHARLES) *continued*.
    VARIATION OF ANIMALS AND PLANTS UNDER DOMESTICATION. Woodcuts. 2 Vols. 15s.
    EXPRESSIONS OF THE EMOTIONS IN MAN AND ANIMALS. With Illustrations. 12s.
    VARIOUS CONTRIVANCES BY WHICH ORCHIDS ARE FERTILIZED BY INSECTS. Woodcuts. 7s. 6d.
    MOVEMENTS AND HABITS OF CLIMBING PLANTS. Woodcuts. 6s.
    INSECTIVOROUS PLANTS. Woodcuts. 9s.
    CROSS AND SELF-FERTILIZATION IN THE VEGETABLE KINGDOM. 9s.
    DIFFERENT FORMS OF FLOWERS ON PLANTS OF THE SAME SPECIES. 7s. 6d.
    POWER OF MOVEMENT IN PLANTS. Woodcuts.
    THE FORMATION OF VEGETABLE MOULD THROUGH THE ACTION OF WORMS. Illustrations. Post 8vo. 6s.

DERBY (EARL OF). Iliad of Homer rendered into English Blank Verse. With Portrait. 2 Vols. Post 8vo. 10s.

DE ROS (GEORGIANA LADY). A Sketch of the Life of: With some Reminiscences of her Family and Friends, including the Duke of Wellington, by her Daughter, the Hon. Mrs. SWINTON. With Portrait and Illustrations. Crown 8vo.

DERRY (BISHOP OF). Witness of the Psalms to Christ and Christianity. Crown 8vo. 9s.

DICEY (PROF. A. V.). Why England Maintains the Union. Fcap. 8vo. 1s.

DOG-BREAKING. [See HUTCHINSON.]

DÖLLINGER (DR.). Studies in European History, being Academical Addresses. Translated by MARGARET WARRE. Portrait. 8vo. 14s.

———— Essays on Historical and Literary Subjects, translated by MARGARET WARRE. 8vo.

DRAKE'S (SIR FRANCIS) Life, Voyages, and Exploits, by Sea and Land. By JOHN BARROW. Post 8vo. 2s.

DRINKWATER (JOHN). History of the Siege of Gibraltar, 1779-1783. With a Description of that Garrison. Post 8vo. 2s.

DU CHAILLU (PAUL B.). Land of the Midnight Sun; Illustrations. 2 Vols. 8vo. 36s.

———— The Viking Age. The Early History, Manners, and Customs of the Ancestors of the English-speaking Nations. With 1,300 Illustrations. 2 Vols. 8vo. 42s.

———— Equatorial Africa and Ashango Land. Adventures in the Great Forest of Equatorial Africa, and the Country of the Dwarfs. Popular Edition. With Illustrations. Post 8vo. 7s. 6d.

DUFFERIN (LORD). Letters from High Latitudes; a Yacht Voyage to Iceland. Woodcuts. Post 8vo. 7s. 6d.

———— Speeches in India, 1884—8. 8vo. 9s.

———— (LADY). Our Viceregal Life in India, 1884—1888. Portrait. Post 8vo. 7s. 6d.

———— My Canadian Journal, 1872—78. Extracts from Home Letters written while Ld. Dufferin was Gov.-Gen. Portraits, Map, and Illustrations. Crown 8vo. 12s.

DUNCAN (COL.). English in Spain; or, The Story of the War of Succession, 1834-1840. 8vo. 16s.

DÜRER (ALBERT); his Life and Work. By DR. THAUSING. Edited by F. A. EATON. Illustrations. 2 Vols. Medium 8vo. 42s.

EARLE (Professor JOHN). The Psalter of 1539: A Landmark of English Literature. Comprising the Text, in Black Letter Type With Notes. Square 8vo.

EASTLAKE (SIR C.). Contributions to the Literature of the Fine Arts. With Memoir by LADY EASTLAKE. 2 Vols. 8vo. 24s.

EDWARDS (W. H.). Voyage up the River Amazon, including a Visit to Para. Post 8vo. 2s.

ELLESMERE (LORD). Two Sieges of Vienna by the Turks. Post 8vo. 2s.

ELLIOT (MRS. MINTO). The Diary of an Idle Woman in Constantinople. With Plan and Illustrations. Crown 8vo. 14s.

ELLIS (W.). Madagascar Revisited. 8vo. 16s.

———— Memoir. By His Son. Portrait. 8vo. 10s. 6d.

———— (ROBINSON). Poems and Fragments of Catullus. 16mo. 5s.

ELPHINSTONE (HON. M.). History of India—the Hindoo and Mahommedan Periods. Edited by PROFESSOR COWELL. Map. 8vo. 18s.

———————— Rise of the British Power in the East. A Continuation of his History of India in the Hindoo and Mahommedan Periods. Maps. 8vo. 16s.

———————— Life of. [See COLEBROOKE.]

———————— (H. W.). Patterns for Ornamental Turning. Illustrations. Small 4to. 15s.

ELTON (CAPT.). Adventures among the Lakes and Mountains of Eastern and Central Africa. Illustrations. 8vo. 21s.

ELWIN (Rev. WARWICK). The Minister of Baptism. A History of Church Opinion from the time of the Apostles, especially with reference to Heretical and Lay Administration. 8vo. 17s.

ENGLAND. [See ARTHUR—CROKER—HUME—MARKHAM—SMITH —and STANHOPE.]

ESSAYS ON CATHEDRALS. Edited by DEAN HOWSON. 8vo. 12s.

ETON LATIN GRAMMAR. For use in the Upper Forms. By F. H. RAWLINS, M.A., and W. R. INGE, M.A. Crown 8vo. 6s.

———— ELEMENTARY LATIN GRAMMAR. For use in the Lower Forms. Compiled by A. C. AINGER, M.A., and H. G. WINTLE, M.A. Crown 8vo. 3s. 6d.

———— PREPARATORY ETON GRAMMAR. Abridged from the above Work. By the same Editors. Crown 8vo. 2s.

———— FIRST LATIN EXERCISE BOOK, adapted to the Elementary and Preparatory Grammars. By the same Editors. Crown 8vo. 2s. 6d.

———— FOURTH FORM OVID. Selections from Ovid and Tibullus. With Notes by H. G. WINTLE. Post 8vo. 2s. 6d.

ETON HORACE. The Odes, Epodes, and Carmen Sæculare. With Notes. By F. W. CORNISH, M.A. Maps. Crown 8vo. 6s.

———— EXERCISES IN ALGEBRA, by E. P. ROUSE, M.A., and ARTHUR COCKSHOTT, M.A. Crown 8vo. 3s.

———— ARITHMETIC. By REV. T. DALTON, M.A. Crown 8vo. 3s.

EXPLOSIVES. [See BERTHELOT.]

FERGUSSON (JAMES). History of Architecture in all Countries from the Earliest Times. A New and thoroughly Revised Edition. With 1,700 Illustrations. 5 Vols. Medium 8vo.
Vols. I. & II. Ancient and Mediæval. Edited by PHENÉ SPIERS.
III. Indian & Eastern. 31s. 6d. IV. Modern. 2 vols. 31s. 6d.

FITZGERALD (Bishop). Lectures on Ecclesiastical History, including the origin and progress of the English Reformation, from Wicliffe to the Great Rebellion. With a Memoir. 2 Vols. 8vo. 21s.

FITZPATRICK (WILLIAM J.). The Correspondence of Daniel O'Connell, the Liberator. With Portrait. 2 Vols. 8vo. 36s.

FLEMING (Professor). Student's Manual of Moral Philosophy.
With Quotations and References. Post 8vo. 7s. 6d.
FLOWER GARDEN. By Rev. Thos. James. Fcap. 8vo. 1s.
FORD (Isabella O.). Miss Blake of Monkshalton. A Novel.
Crown 8vo. 5s.
FORD (Richard). Gatherings from Spain. Post 8vo. 3s. 6d.
FORSYTH (William). Hortensius; an Historical Essay on the
Office and Duties of an Advocate. Illustrations. 8vo. 7s. 6d.
FORTIFICATION. [See Clarke.]
FRANCE (History of). [See Arthur — Markham — Smith — Students'—Tocqueville.]
FREAM (W.), LL.D. Elements of Agriculture; a text-book prepared under the authority of the Royal Agricultural Society of England. Enlarged Edition. With 256 Illustrations. Crown 8vo. 3s. 6d.
FRENCH IN ALGIERS; The Soldier of the Foreign Legion—
and the Prisoners of Abd-el-Kadir. Post 8vo. 2s.
FRERE (Mary). Old Deccan Days, or Hindoo Fairy Legends
current in Southern India, with Introduction by Sir Bartle Frere.
With Illustrations. Post 8vo. 5s.
GALTON (F.). Art of Travel; or, Hints on the Shifts and Contrivances available in Wild Countries. Woodcuts. Post 8vo. 7s. 6d.
GAMBIER PARRY (T.). The Ministry of Fine Art to the
Happiness of Life. Revised Edition, with an Index. 8vo. 14s.
—————— (Major). The Combat with Suffering. Fcap. 8vo. 3s. 6d.
GARDNER (Prof. Percy). New Chapters in Greek History.
Historical results of recent excavations in Greece and Asia Minor.
With Illustrations. 8vo. 15s.
GEDDES (Prof. P.). Outlines of Modern Botany. With Illustrations. (Univ. Extension Series.)
GEOGRAPHY. [See Bunbury—Croker—Ramsay—Richardson
—Smith—Students'.]
GEOGRAPHICAL SOCIETY'S JOURNAL. (1846 to 1881.)
SUPPLEMENTARY PAPERS. Royal 8vo.
Vol. I., Part i. Travels and Researches in Western China. By E.
Colborne Baber. Maps. 5s.
Part ii.—1. Recent Geography of Central Asia; from Russian
Sources. By E. Delmar Morgan. 2. Progress of Discovery on the Coasts of New Guinea. By C. B. Markham.
Bibliographical Appendix, by E. C. Rye. Maps. 5s.
Part iii.—1. Report on Part of the Ghilzi Country, &c. By
Lieut. J. S. Broadfoot. 2. Journey from Shiraz to Jashk.
By J. R. Preece. 2s. 6d.
Part iv.—Geographical Education. By J. S. Keltie. 2s. 6d.
Vol. II., Part i.—1. Exploration in S. and S.W. China. By A. R.
Colquhoun. 2. Bibliography and Cartography of Hispaniola. By H. Ling Roth. 3. Explorations in Zanzibar
Dominions by Lieut. C. Stewart Smith, R.N. 2s. 6d.
Part ii.—A Bibliography of Algeria, from the Expedition of
Charles V. in 1541 to 1887. By Sir R. L. Playfair. 4s.
Part iii.—1. On the Measurement of Heights by the Barometer.
By John Ball, F.R.S. 2. River Entrances. By H. Robert Mill.
3. Mr. Needham's Journey in South Eastern Tibet. 2s. 6d.
Part iv.—1. The Bibliography of the Barbary States. Part i.
By Sir R. L. Playfair. 2. Hudson's Bay and Strait. By
Commodore A. H. Markham, R.N. 3s.
Vol. III., Part i.—Journey of Carey and Dalgleish in Chinese Turkestan
and Northern Tibet; and General Prejevalsky on the Orography of Northern Tibet. 4s.
Part ii.—Vaughan's Persia, &c. 4s.
Part iii.—Playfair's Bibliography of Morocco. 5s.
Vol. IV.—Ramsay's Asia Minor. 18s.

GEORGE (ERNEST). Loire and South of France; 20 Etchings. Folio. 42s.

GERMANY (HISTORY OF). [See MARKHAM.]

GIBBON'S History of the Decline and Fall of the Roman Empire. Edited with notes by MILMAN, GUIZOT, and Dr. WM. SMITH. Maps. 8 Vols. 8vo. 60s. Student's Edition. 7s. 6d. (See STUDENT'S.)

GIFFARD (EDWARD). Deeds of Naval Daring; or, Anecdotes of the British Navy. Fcap. 8vo. 3s. 6d.

GILBERT (JOSIAH). Landscape in Art: before the days of Claude and Salvator. With 150 Illustrations. Medium 8vo. 30s.

GILL (CAPT.). The River of Golden Sand. A Journey through China to Burmah. Edited by E. C. BABER. With Memoir by Col. YULE, C.B. Portrait, Map, and Illustrations. Post 8vo. 7s. 6d.

—— (MRS.). Six Months in Ascension. An Unscientific Account of a Scientific Expedition. Map. Crown 8vo. 9s.

GLADSTONE (W. E.). Rome and the Newest Fashions in Religion. 8vo. 7s. 6d.

—————— Gleanings of Past Years, 1843-78. 7 Vols. Small 8vo. 2s. 6d. each. I. The Throne, the Prince Consort, the Cabinet and Constitution. II. Personal and Literary. III. Historical and Speculative. IV. Foreign. V. and VI. Ecclesiastical. VII. Miscellaneous.

—————— Special Aspects of the Irish Question; A Series of Reflections in and since 1886. Collected from various Sources and Reprinted. Crown 8vo. 3s. 6d.

GLEIG (G. R.). Campaigns of the British Army at Washington and New Orleans. Post 8vo. 2s.

——— Story of the Battle of Waterloo. Post 8vo. 3s. 6d.

——— Narrative of Sale's Brigade in Affghanistan. Post 8vo. 2s.

——— Life of Lord Clive. Post 8vo. 3s. 6d.

——— Sir Thomas Munro. Post 8vo. 3s. 6d.

GOLDSMITH'S (OLIVER) Works. Edited with Notes by PETER CUNNINGHAM. Vignettes. 4 Vols. 8vo. 30s.

GOMM (F.M. SIR WM.). His Letters and Journals. 1799 to 1815. Edited by F. C. Carr Gomm. With Portrait. 8vo. 12s.

GORDON (SIR ALEX.). Sketches of German Life, and Scenes from the War of Liberation. Post 8vo. 3s. 6d.

——— (LADY DUFF). The Amber-Witch. Post 8vo. 2s. See also Ross.

——— The French in Algiers. Post 8vo. 2s.

GORE, Rev. CHARLES (Edited by). Lux Mundi. A Series of Studies in the Religion of the Incarnation. By various Writers. Popular Edition, Crown 8vo. 6s.

—————— The Bampton Lectures, 1891; The Incarnation of the Son of God. 8vo. 7s. 6d.

—————— The Mission of the Church. Four Lectures delivered in the Cathedral Church of St. Asaph. Crown 8vo. 2s. 6d.

GOULBURN (DEAN). Three Counsels of the Divine Master for the conduct of the Spiritual Life:—The Commencement; The Virtues; The Conflict. Crown 8vo. 9s. (See also BURGON.)

GRAMMARS. [See CURTIUS — ETON — HALL — HUTTON — KING EDWARD — LEATHES — MATTHIÆ — SMITH.]

GRANT (A. J.). Greece in the Age of Pericles. Crown 8vo. (University Extension Series.)

GREECE (HISTORY OF). [See GROTE — SMITH — STUDENTS'.]

GRIFFITH (REV. CHARLES). A History of Strathfieldsaye. With Illustrations. 4to. 10s. 6d.

GROTE'S (George) WORKS :—
  History of Greece. From the Earliest Times to the Death of Alexander the Great. *New Edition.* Portrait, Map, and Plans. 10 Vols. Post 8vo. 5s. each. (*The Volumes may be had Separately.*)
  Plato, and other Companions of Socrates. 3 Vols. 8vo. 45s.; or, New Edition, Edited by Alex. Bain. 4 Vols. Crown 8vo. 5s. each.
  Aristotle. 8vo. 12s.
  Personal Life. Portrait. 8vo. 12s.
  Minor Works. Portrait. 8vo. 14s.
  ——— (Mrs.). A Sketch. By Lady Eastlake. Crown 8vo. 6s.

GUILLEMARD (F. H.), M.D. The Voyage of the Marchesa to Kamschatka and New Guinea. With Notices of Formosa and the Islands of the Malay Archipelago. New Edition. With Maps and 150 Illustrations. One volume. Medium 8vo. 21s.

HAKE (G. Napier) on Explosives. [See Berthelot.]

HALL'S (T. D.) School Manual of English Grammar. With Illustrations and Practical Exercises. 12mo. 3s. 6d.
  ——— Primary English Grammar for Elementary Schools. With numerous Exercises, and graduated Parsing Lessons. 16mo. 1s.
  ——— Manual of English Composition. With Copious Illustrations and Practical Exercises. 12mo. 3s. 6d.
  ——— Child's First Latin Book, comprising a full Practice of Nouns, Pronouns, and Adjectives, with the Verbs. 16mo. 2s.

HALLAM'S (Henry) WORKS :—
  The Constitutional History of England. *Library Edition*, 3 Vols. 8vo. 30s. *Cabinet Edition*, 3 Vols. Post 8vo. 12s. *Student's Edition*, Post 8vo. 7s. 6d.
  History of Europe during the Middle Ages. *Cabinet Edition*, 3 Vols. Post 8vo. 12s. *Student's Edition*, Post 8vo. 7s. 6d.
  Literary History of Europe during the 15th, 16th, and 17th Centuries. *Library Edition*, 3 Vols. 8vo. 36s. *Cabinet Edition*, 4 Vols. Post 8vo. 16s. [Portrait. Fcap. 8vo. 3s. 6d.

HART'S ARMY LIST. (*Published Quarterly and Annually.*)

HAY (Sir J. H. Drummond). Western Barbary, its Wild Tribes and Savage Animals. Post 8vo. 2s.

HAYWARD (A.). Sketches of Eminent Statesmen and Writers, 2 Vols. 8vo. 28s.
  ——— The Art of Dining. Post 8vo. 2s.
  ——— A Selection from his Correspondence. Edited with an Introductory account of Mr. Hayward's Early Life. By H. E. Carlisle. 2 vols. Crown 8vo. 24s.

HEAD'S (Sir Francis) WORKS :—
  The Royal Engineer. Illustrations. 8vo. 12s.
  Life of Sir John Burgoyne. Post 8vo. 1s.
  Rapid Journeys across the Pampas. Post 8vo. 2s.
  Stokers and Pokers; or, the L. and N. W. R. Post 8vo. 2s.

HEBER'S (Bishop) Journals in India. 2 Vols. Post 8vo. 7s.
  ——— Poetical Works. Portrait. Fcap. 8vo. 3s. 6d.

HERODOTUS. A New English Version. Edited, with Notes and Essays by Canon Rawlinson, Sir H. Rawlinson and Sir J. G. Wilkinson. Maps and Woodcuts. 4 Vols. 8vo. 48s.

HERRIES (Rt. Hon. John). Memoir of his Public Life. By his Son, Edward Herries, C.B. 2 Vols. 8vo. 24s.

FOREIGN HAND-BOOKS.

HAND-BOOK—TRAVEL-TALK. English, French, German, and Italian. New and Revised Edition. 18mo. 3s. 6d.

——————— DICTIONARY : English, French, and German. Containing all the words and idiomatic phrases likely to be required by a traveller. Bound in leather. 16mo. 6s.

——————— HOLLAND AND BELGIUM. Map and Plans. 6s.

——————— NORTH GERMANY and THE RHINE,— The Black Forest, the Hartz, Thüringerwald, Saxon Switzerland Rügen, the Giant Mountains, Taunus, Odenwald, Elsass, and Lothringen. Map and Plans. Post 8vo. 10s.

——————— SOUTH GERMANY AND AUSTRIA,—Wurtemberg, Bavaria, Austria, Tyrol, Styria, Salzburg, the Dolomites, Hungary, and the Danube, from Ulm to the Black Sea. Maps and Plans. Two Parts. Post 8vo. 12s.

——————— SWITZERLAND, Alps of Savoy, and Piedmont. Edited by W. A. B. COOLIDGE, M.A. In Two Parts. Maps and Plans. Post 8vo. 10s.

——————— FRANCE, Part I. Normandy, Brittany, the French Alps, the Loire, Seine, Garonne, and Pyrenees. Maps and Plans. 7s. 6d.

——————— FRANCE, Part II. Central France, Auvergne, the Cevennes, Burgundy, the Rhone and Saone, Provence, Nimes, Arles, Marseilles, the French Alps, Alsace, Lorraine, Champagne, &c. Maps and Plans. Post 8vo. 7s. 6d.

——————— THE RIVIERA. From Marseilles to Pisa, and the Routes thither. A new Edition, thoroughly revised, and in a great measure re-written on the spot. With numerous Maps engraved expressly on a large scale. 6s.

——————— MEDITERRANEAN — its Principal Islands, Cities, Seaports, Harbours, and Border Lands. For Travellers and Yachtsmen, with nearly 50 Maps and Plans. Two Parts. Post 8vo. 21s.

——————— ALGERIA AND TUNIS. Algiers, Constantine, Oran, Tlemcen, Bougie, Tebessa, Biskra, the Atlas Range. Edited by Sir R. LAMBERT PLAYFAIR. Maps and Plans. Post 8vo. 12s.

——————— SPAIN, Madrid, The Castiles, The Basque Provinces, Leon, The Asturias, Galicia, Estremadura, Andalusia, Ronda, Granada, Murcia, Valencia, Catalonia, Aragon, Navarre, The Balearic Islands, &c. &c. Maps and Plans. Two Parts. Post 8vo. 20s.

——————— PORTUGAL, LISBON, Oporto, Cintra, Mafra, Madeira, the Azores, Canary Islands, &c. Map and Plan. 12s.

——————— NORTH ITALY, Turin, Milan, Cremona, the Italian Lakes, Bergamo, Brescia, Verona, Mantua, Vicenza, Padua, Ferrara, Bologna, Ravenna, Rimini, Piacenza, Genoa, the Riviera, Venice, Parma, Modena, and Romagna. Maps and Plans. Post 8vo. 10s.

——————— CENTRAL ITALY, Florence, Lucca, Tuscany, The Marshes, Umbria, &c. Maps and Plans. Post 8vo. 6s.

——————— ROME AND ITS ENVIRONS. 50 Maps and Plans. 10s.

——————— SOUTH ITALY AND SICILY, including Naples and its Environs, Pompeii, Herculaneum, Vesuvius; Sorrento; Capri; Amalfi, Prestum, Pozzuoli, Capua, Taranto, Bari; Brindisi and the Roads from Rome to Naples; Palermo, Messina, Syracuse, Catania, &c. Two Parts. Maps. Post 8vo. 12s.

——————— NORWAY, Christiania, Bergen, Trondhjem. The Fjelds and Fjords. An entirely new Edition. Edited by THOS. MICHELL, C.B. Maps and Plans. 7s. 6d.

——————— SWEDEN, Stockholm, Upsala, Gothenburg, the Shores of the Baltic, &c. Maps and Plan. Post 8vo. 6s.

HAND-BOOK—DENMARK, Sleswig, Holstein, Copenhagen, Jutland, Iceland. Maps and Plans. Post 8vo. 6s.

―――――― RUSSIA, St. Petersburg, Moscow, Poland, and Finland. Maps and Plans. Post 8vo. 18s.

―――――― GREECE, the Ionian Islands, Athens, the Peloponnesus, the Islands of the Ægean Sea, Albania, Thessaly, Macedonia, &c. In Two Parts. Maps, Plans, and Views. Post 8vo. 24s.

―――――― CONSTANTINOPLE, BRÚSA, AND THE TROAD. Edited by Colonel Sir Charles Wilson, R.E., G.C.B. Numerous Maps and Plans. Post 8vo. 7s. 6d.

―――――― EGYPT, The Course of the Nile through Egypt and Nubia, Alexandria, Cairo, Thebes, Suez Canal, the Pyramids, Sinai, the Fyoom, &c. Maps and Plans. Post 8vo. 15s.

―――――― HOLY LAND—Syria, Palestine, Moab, Hauran, Syrian Deserts, Jerusalem, Damascus; and Palmyra. Maps and Plans. Post 8vo. 18s. *** Map of Palestine. In a case. 12s.

―――――― BOMBAY — Poonah, Beejapoor, Kolapoor, Goa, Jubulpoor, Indore, Surat, Baroda, Ahmedabad, Somnauth, Kurrachee, &c. Map and Plans. Post 8vo. 15s.

―――――― MADRAS—Trichinopoli, Madura, Tinnevelly, Tuticorin, Bangalore, Mysore, The Nilgiris, Wynaad, Ootacamund, Calicut, Hyderabad, Ajanta, Elura Caves, &c. Maps and Plans. Post 8vo. 15s.

―――――― BENGAL — Calcutta, Orissa, British Burmah, Rangoon, Moulmein, Mandalay, Darjiling, Dacca, Patna, Benares, N.-W. Provinces, Allahabad, Cawnpore, Lucknow, Agra, Gwalior, Naini Tal, Delhi, &c. Maps and Plans. Post 8vo. 20s.

―――――― THE PANJAB—Amraoti, Indore, Ajmir, Jaypur, Rohtak, Saharanpur, Ambala, Lodiana, Lahore, Kulu, Simla, Sialkot, Peshawar, Rawul Pindi, Attock, Karachi, Sibi, &c. Maps. 15s.

―――――― INDIA AND CEYLON, including the Provinces of Bengal, Bombay, and Madras (the Punjab, North-west Provinces, Rajputana, the Central Provinces, Mysore, &c.), the Native States and Assam. With 55 Maps and Plans of Towns and Buildings. Post 8vo. 15s

―――――― JAPAN. Revised and for the most part Rewritten. With 15 Maps. Post 8vo. 15s. net.

ENGLISH HAND-BOOKS.

HAND-BOOK—ENGLAND AND WALES. An Alphabetical Hand-Book. In One Volume. With Map. Post 8vo. 12s.

―――――― LONDON. Maps and Plans. 16mo. 3s. 6d.

―――――― ENVIRONS OF LONDON within a circuit of 20 miles. 2 Vols. Crown 8vo. 21s.

―――――― ST. PAUL'S CATHEDRAL. 20 Woodcuts. 10s. 6d.

―――――― EASTERN COUNTIES, Chelmsford, Harwich, Colchester, Maldon, Cambridge, Ely, Newmarket, Bury St. Edmunds, Ipswich, Woodbridge, Felixstowe, Lowestoft, Norwich, Yarmouth, Cromer, &c. Maps and Plans. Post 8vo. 12s.

―――――― CATHEDRALS of Oxford, Peterborough, Norwich, Ely, and Lincoln. With 90 Illustrations. Crown 8vo. 21s.

―――――― KENT, Canterbury, Dover, Ramsgate, Sheerness, Rochester, Chatham, Woolwich. Maps and Plans. Post 8vo. 7s. 6d.

―――――― SUSSEX, Brighton, Chichester, Worthing, Hastings, Lewes, Arundel, &c. Maps and Plans. Post 8vo. 6s.

HAND-BOOK—SURREY AND HANTS, Kingston, Croydon, Reigate, Guildford, Dorking, Winchester, Southampton, New Forest, Portsmouth, ISLE OF WIGHT, &c. Maps and Plans. Post 8vo. 10s.

———————— BERKS, BUCKS, AND OXON, Windsor, Eton, Reading, Aylesbury, Uxbridge, Wycombe, Henley, Oxford, Blenheim, the Thames, &c. Maps and Plans. Post 8vo. 9s.

———————— WILTS, DORSET, AND SOMERSET, Salisbury, Chippenham, Weymouth, Sherborne, Wells, Bath, Bristol, Taunton, &c. Map. Post 8vo. 12s.

———————— DEVON, Exeter, Ilfracombe, Linton, Sidmouth, Dawlish, Teignmouth, Plymouth, Devonport, Torquay. Maps and Plans. Post 8vo. 7s. 6d.

———————— CORNWALL, Launceston, Penzance; Falmouth, the Lizard, Land's End, &c. Maps. Post 8vo. 6s.

———————— CATHEDRALS of Winchester, Salisbury, Exeter, Wells, Chichester, Rochester, Canterbury, and St. Albans. With 130 Illustrations. 2 Vols. Crown 8vo. 36s. St. Albans separately. 6s.

———————— GLOUCESTER, HEREFORD, AND WORCESTER, Cirencester, Cheltenham, Stroud, Tewkesbury, Leominster, Ross, Malvern, Kidderminster, Dudley, Evesham, &c. Map. Post 8vo. 9s.

———————— CATHEDRALS of Bristol, Gloucester, Hereford, Worcester, and Lichfield. With 50 Illustrations. Crown 8vo. 16s.

———————— NORTH WALES, Bangor, Carnarvon, Beaumaris, Snowdon, Llanberis, Dolgelly, Conway, &c. Maps. Post 8vo. 7s.

———————— SOUTH WALES, Monmouth, Llandaff, Merthyr, Vale of Neath, Pembroke, Carmarthen, Tenby, Swansea, The Wye, &c. Map. Post 8vo. 7s.

———————— CATHEDRALS OF BANGOR, ST. ASAPH, Llandaff, and St. David's. With Illustrations. Post 8vo. 15s.

———————— NORTHAMPTONSHIRE AND RUTLAND— Northampton, Peterborough, Towcester, Daventry, Market Harborough, Kettering, Wellingborough, Thrapston, Stamford, Uppingham, Oakham. Maps. Post 8vo. 7s. 6d.

———————— DERBY, NOTTS, LEICESTER, STAFFORD, Matlock, Bakewell, Chatsworth, The Peak, Buxton, Hardwick, Dove Dale, Ashborne, Southwell, Mansfield, Retford, Burton, Belvoir, Melton Mowbray, Wolverhampton, Lichfield, Walsall, Tamworth. Map. Post 8vo. 9s.

———————— SHROPSHIRE AND CHESHIRE, Shrewsbury, Ludlow, Bridgnorth, Oswestry, Chester, Crewe, Alderley, Stockport, Birkenhead. Maps and Plans. Post 8vo. 6s.

———————— LANCASHIRE, Warrington, Bury, Manchester, Liverpool, Burnley, Clitheroe, Bolton, Blackburne, Wigan, Preston, Rochdale, Lancaster, Southport, Blackpool, &c. Maps & Plans. Post 8vo. 7s. 6d.

———————— THE ENGLISH LAKES, in Cumberland, Westmoreland, and Lancashire; Lancaster, Furness Abbey, Ambleside, Kendal, Windermere, Coniston, Keswick, Grasmere, Ulswater, Carlisle, Cockermouth, Penrith, Appleby, &c. Maps. Post 8vo. 7s. 6d.

———————— YORKSHIRE, Doncaster, Hull, Selby, Beverley, Scarborough, Whitby, Harrogate, Ripon, Leeds, Wakefield, Bradford, Halifax, Huddersfield, Sheffield. Map and Plans. Post 8vo. 12s.

———————— CATHEDRALS of York, Ripon, Durham, Carlisle, Chester, and Manchester. With 60 Illustrations. 2 Vols. Cr. 8vo. 21s.

———————— DURHAM AND NORTHUMBERLAND, Newcastle, Darlington, Stockton, Hartlepool, Shields, Berwick-on-Tweed, Morpeth, Tynemouth, Coldstream, Alnwick, &c. Map. Post 8vo. 10s.

———————— LINCOLNSHIRE, Grantham, Lincoln, Stamford, Sleaford, Spalding, Gainsborough, Grimsby, Boston. Maps and Plans. Post 8vo. 7s. 6d.

———————— WARWICKSHIRE. Map. Post 8vo.

———————— HERTS, BEDS AND HUNTS.

HAND-BOOK—SCOTLAND, Edinburgh, Melrose, Kelso, Glasgow, Dumfries, Ayr, Stirling, Arran, The Clyde, Oban, Inverary, Loch Lomond, Loch Katrine and Trossachs, Caledonian Canal, Inverness, Perth, Dundee, Aberdeen, Braemar, Skye, Caithness, Ross, Sutherland, &c. Maps and Plans. Post 8vo. 9s.

———— IRELAND, Dublin, Belfast, the Giant's Causeway, Donegal, Galway, Wexford, Cork, Limerick, Waterford, Killarney, Bantry, Glengariff, &c. Maps and Plans. Post 8vo. 10s.

HICKSON (DR. SYDNEY J.). A Naturalist in North Celebes; a Narrative of Travels in Minahassa, the Sangir and Talaut Islands, with Notices of the Fauna, Flora, and Ethnology of the Districts visited. Map and Illustrations. 8vo. 16s.

HISLOP (STEPHEN). [See SMITH, GEORGE.]

HOBSON (J. A.). [See MUMMERY.]

HOLLWAY (J. G.). A Month in Norway. Fcap. 8vo. 2s.

HONEY BEE. By REV. THOMAS JAMES. Fcap. 8vo. 1s.

HOOK (DEAN). Church Dictionary. A Manual of Reference for Clergymen and Students. New Edition, thoroughly revised. Edited by WALTER HOOK, M.A., and W. R. W. STEPHENS, M.A. Med. 8vo. 21s.

———— (THEODORE) Life. By J. G. LOCKHART. Fcap. 8vo. 1s.

HOPE (A. J. BERESFORD). Worship in the Church of England. 8vo, 9s.; or, Popular Selections from, 8vo, 2s. 6d.

———— WORSHIP AND ORDER. 8vo. 9s.

HOPE-SCOTT (JAMES), Memoir. [See ORNSBY.]

HORACE; a New Edition of the Text. Edited by DEAN MILMAN. With 100 Woodcuts. Crown 8vo. 7s. 6d.

———— [See ETON.]

HOUGHTON'S (LORD) Monographs. Portraits. 10s. 6d.

———— POETICAL WORKS. Portrait. 2 Vols. 12s.

———— (ROBERT LORD) Stray Verses, 1889-90. Crown 8vo. Second Edition, fcap. 8vo. 5s.

HOME AND COLONIAL LIBRARY. A Series of Works adapted for all circles and classes of Readers, having been selected for their acknowledged interest, and ability of the Authors. Post 8vo. Published at 2s. and 3s. 6d. each, and arranged under two distinctive heads as follows:—

CLASS A.
HISTORY, BIOGRAPHY, AND HISTORIC TALES.

SIEGE OF GIBRALTAR. By JOHN DRINKWATER. 2s.

THE AMBER-WITCH. By LADY DUFF GORDON. 2s.

CROMWELL AND BUNYAN. By ROBERT SOUTHEY. 2s.

LIFE OF SIR FRANCIS DRAKE. By JOHN BARROW. 2s.

CAMPAIGNS AT WASHINGTON. By REV. G. R. GLEIG. 2s.

THE FRENCH IN ALGIERS. By LADY DUFF GORDON. 2s.

THE FALL OF THE JESUITS. 2s.

LIVONIAN TALES. 2s.

LIFE OF CONDE. By LORD MAHON. 3s. 6d.

SALE'S BRIGADE. By REV. G. R. GLEIG. 2s.

THE SIEGES OF VIENNA. By LORD ELLESMERE. 2s.

THE WAYSIDE CROSS. By CAPT. MILMAN. 2s.

SKETCHES OF GERMAN LIFE. By SIR A. GORDON. 3s. 6d.

THE BATTLE OF WATERLOO. By REV. G. R. GLEIG. 3s. 6d.

AUTOBIOGRAPHY OF STEFFENS. 2s.

THE BRITISH POETS. By THOMAS CAMPBELL. 3s. 6d.

HISTORICAL ESSAYS. By LORD MAHON. 3s. 6d.

LIFE OF LORD CLIVE. REV. G. R. GLEIG. 3s. 6d.

NORTH WESTERN RAILWAY. By SIR F. B. HEAD. 2s.

LIFE OF MUNRO. By REV. G. R. GLEIG. 3s. 6d.

CLASS B.
VOYAGES, TRAVELS, AND ADVENTURES.

JOURNALS IN INDIA. By Bishop Heber. 2 Vols. 7s.
TRAVELS IN THE HOLY LAND. By Irby and Mangles. 2s.
MOROCCO AND THE MOORS. By J. Drummond Hay. 2s.
LETTERS FROM THE BALTIC. By A Lady. 2.
NEW SOUTH WALES. By Mrs. Meredith. 2s.
THE WEST INDIES. By M. G. Lewis. 2s.
SKETCHES OF PERSIA. By Sir John Malcolm. 3s. 6d.
MEMOIRS OF FATHER RIPA. 2s.
TYPEE AND OMOO. By Hermann Melville. 2 Vols. 7s.
MISSIONARY LIFE IN CANADA. By Rev. J. Abbott. 2s.
LETTERS FROM MADRAS. By A Lady. 2s.

HIGHLAND SPORTS. By Charles St. John. 3s. 6d.
PAMPAS JOURNEYS. By F. B. Head. 2s.
GATHERINGS FROM SPAIN. By Richard Ford. 3s. 6d.
THE RIVER AMAZON. By W. H. Edwards. 2s.
MANNERS & CUSTOMS OF INDIA. By Rev. C. Acland. 2s.
ADVENTURES IN MEXICO. By G. F. Ruxton. 3s. 6d.
PORTUGAL AND GALICIA. By Lord Carnarvon. 3s. 6d.
BUSH LIFE IN AUSTRALIA. By Rev. H. W. Haygarth. 2s.
THE LIBYAN DESERT. By Bayle St. John. 2s.
SIERRA LEONE. By A Lady. 3s. 6d.

⁎ Each work may be had separately.

HUME (The Student's). A History of England, from the Invasion of Julius Cæsar to the Revolution of 1688. New Edition, revised, corrected, and continued to the Treaty of Berlin, 1878. By J. S. Brewer, M.A. With 7 Coloured Maps & 70 Woodcn's. Post 8vo. 7s. 6d.
⁎ Sold also in 3 parts. Price 2s. 6d. each.

HUNNEWELL (James F.). England's Chronicle in Stone; Derived from Personal Observations of the Cathedrals, Churches, Abbeys, Monasteries, Castles, and Palaces, made in Journeys through the Imperial Island. With Illustrations. Medium 8vo. 24s.

HUTCHINSON (Gen.). Dog Breaking, with Odds and Ends for those who love the Dog and the Gun. With 40 Illustrations. Crown 8vo. 7s. 6d. *⁎* A Summary of the Rules for Gamekeepers. 1s.

HUTTON (H. E.). Principia Græca; an Introduction to the Study of Greek. Comprehending Grammar, Delectus, and Exercise-book, with Vocabularies. *Sixth Edition.* 12mo. 2s. 6d.

HYMNOLOGY, Dictionary of. [See Julian.]

ICELAND. [See Coles—Dufferin.]

INDIA. [See Broadfoot—Dufferin—Elphinstone—Hand-book—Lyall—Smith—Temple—Monier Williams.]

IRBY AND MANGLES' Travels in Egypt, Nubia, Syria, and the Holy Land. Post 8vo. 2s.

JAMES (F. L.). The Wild Tribes of the Soudan: with an account of the route from Wady Halfa to Dongola and Berber. With Chapter on the Soudan, by Sir S. Baker. Illustrations. Crown 8vo. 7s. 6d.

JAMESON (Mrs.). Lives of the Early Italian Painters—and the Progress of Painting in Italy—Cimabue to Bassano. With 50 Portraits. Post 8vo. 12s.

JANNARIS (Prof. A. N.). A Pocket Dictionary of the Modern Greek and English Languages, as actually Written and Spoken. Being a Copious Vocabulary of all Words and Expressions Current in Ordinary Reading and in Everyday Talk, with Especial Illustration by means Distinctive Signs, of the Colloquial and Popular Greek Language, for the Guidance of Students and Travellers. Fcap. 8vo.

JAPAN. [See BIRD—HANDBOOK.]

JENNINGS (L. J.). Field Paths and Green Lanes: or Walks in Surrey and Sussex. Popular Edition. With Illustrations. Cr. 8vo. 6s. [See also CROKER.]

JERVIS (REV. W. H.). The Gallican Church, from the Concordat of Bologna, 1516, to the Revolution. With an Introduction. Portraits. 2 Vols. 8vo. 28s.

JESSE (EDWARD). Gleanings in Natural History. Fcp. 8vo. 3s. 6d.

JOHNSON'S (DR. SAMUEL) Life. [See BOSWELL.]

JULIAN (REV. JOHN J.). A Dictionary of Hymnology. A Companion to Existing Hymn Books. Setting forth the Origin and History of the Hymns contained in the Principal Hymnals, with Notices of their Authors, &c., &c. Medium 8vo. (1626 pp.) 42s.

JUNIUS' HANDWRITING Professionally investigated. Edited by the Hon. E. TWISLETON. With Facsimiles. Woodcuts, &c. 4to. £3 3s.

KEENE (H. G.). The Literature of France. 220 pp. Crown 8vo. 3s. (University Extension Manuals.)

KENDAL (MRS.) Dramatic Opinions. Post 8vo. 1s.

KERR (ROBT.). The Consulting Architect: Practical Notes on Administrative Difficulties. Crown 8vo. 9s.

KING EDWARD VIth's Latin Grammar. 12mo. 3s. 6d.
—————— First Latin Book. 12mo. 2s. 6d.

KIRKES' Handbook of Physiology. Edited by W. MORRANT BAKER and V. D. HARRIS. With 500 Illustrations. Post 8vo. 14s.

KNIGHT (PROF.). The Philosophy of the Beautiful. Two Parts. Crown 8vo. 3s. 6d. each. (University Extension Series.)

KUGLER'S HANDBOOK OF PAINTING.—The Italian Schools. A New Edition, revised. By Sir HENRY LAYARD. With 200 Illustrations. 2 vols. Crown 8vo. 30s.
—————— The German, Flemish, and Dutch Schools. New Edition revised. By Sir J. A. CROWE. With 60 Illustrations. 2 Vols. Crown 8vo. 24s.

LANDOR (A. H. SAVAGE). Alone with the Hairy Ainu, or 3,800 Miles on a Pack Saddle in Yezo, and a Cruise to the Kurile Islands. With Map, and many Illustrations by the Author. Medium 8vo.

LANE (E. W.). Account of the Manners and Customs of Modern Egyptians. With Illustrations. 2 Vols. Post 8vo. 12s.

LAWLESS (HON. EMILY). Major Lawrence, F.L.S.: a Novel. 3 Vols. Crown 8vo. 31s. 6d. Cheap Edition, 6s.
—————— Plain Frances Mowbray, etc. Crown 8vo. 6s.

LAYARD (Sir A. H.). Nineveh and its Remains. With Illustrations. Post 8vo. 7s. 6d.
—————— Nineveh and Babylon. Illusts. Post 8vo. 7s. 6d.
—————— Early Adventures in Persia, Babylonia, and Susiana, including a residence among the Bakhtiyari and other wild tribes. Portrait, Illustrations and Maps. 2 Vols. Crown 8vo. 24s.

LEATHES (STANLEY). Practical Hebrew Grammar. With the Hebrew Text of Genesis i.—vi., and Psalms i.—vi. Grammatical Analysis and Vocabulary. Post 8vo. 7s. 6d.

LENNEP (REV. H. J. VAN). Travels in Asia Minor. With Illustrations of Biblical History and Archæology. 2 Vols. Post 8vo. 24s.

LESLIE (C. R.). Handbook for Young Painters. Illustrations. Post 8vo. 7s. 6d.

LETTERS FROM THE BALTIC. By LADY EASTLAKE. Post 8vo. 2s.
—————— MADRAS. By MRS. MAITLAND. Post 8vo. 2s.

LEVI (LEONE). History of British Commerce; and Economic Progress of the Nation, from 1763 to 1878. 8vo. 18s.

LEWIS (T. HAYTER). The Holy Places of Jerusalem. Illustrations. 8vo. 10s. 6d.

LEX SALICA; the Ten Texts with the Glosses and the Lex Emendata. Synoptically edited by J. H. HESSELS. With Notes on the Frankish Words in the Lex Salica by H. KERN, of Leyden. 4to. 42s.

LIDDELL (DEAN). Student's History of Rome, from the earliest Times to the establishment of the Empire. Woodcuts. Post 8vo. 7s. 6d.

LILLY (W. S.). The Great Enigma. 1. The Twilight of the Gods. 2. Atheism. 3. Critical Agnosticism. 4. Scientific Agnosticism. 5. Rational Theism. 6. The Inner Light. 7. The Christian Synthesis. 8vo. 14s.

LIND (JENNY), THE ARTIST, 1820—1851. Her early Art-life and Dramatic Career. From Original Documents, Letters, Diaries, &c., in the possession of Mr. GOLDSCHMIDT. By Canon H. SCOTT HOLLAND, M.A., and W. S. ROCKSTRO. With Portraits and Illustrations. Crown 8vo.

LINDSAY (LORD). Sketches of the History of Christian Art. 2 Vols. Crown 8vo. 21s.

LISPINGS from LOW LATITUDES; or, the Journal of the Hon. Impulsia Gushington. Edited by LORD DUFFERIN. With 24 Plates. 4to. 21s.

LIVINGSTONE (DR.). First Expedition to Africa, 1840–56. Illustrations. Post 8vo. 7s. 6d.
——————— Second Expedition to Africa, 1858-64. Illustrations. Post 8vo. 7s. 6d.
——————— Last Journals in Central Africa, to his Death By Rev. HORACE WALLER. Maps and Illustrations. 2 Vols. 8vo. 15s.
——————— Personal Life. By Wm. G. Blaikie, D.D. With Map and Portrait. 8vo. 6s.

LOCKHART (J. G.). Ancient Spanish Ballads. Historical and Romantic. Translated, with Notes. Illustrations. Crown 8vo. 5s.
——————— Life of Theodore Hook. Fcap. 8vo. 1s.

LONDON: Past and Present; its History, Associations, and Traditions. By HENRY B. WHEATLEY, F.S.A. Based on Cunningham's Handbook. Library Edition, on Laid Paper 3 Vols. Medium 8vo. 3l. 3s.

LOUDON (MRS.). Gardening for Ladies. With Directions and Calendar of Operations for Every Month. Woodcuts. Fcap. 8vo. 3s. 6d.

LUMHOLTZ (DR. C.). Among Cannibals; An Account of Four Years' Travels in Australia, and of Camp Life among the Aborigines of Queensland. With Maps and 120 Illustrations. Medium 8vo. 21s.

LUTHER (MARTIN). The First Principles of the Reformation, or the Three Primary Works of Dr. Martin Luther. Portrait. 8vo. 12s.

LYALL (SIR ALFRED C.), K.C.B. Asiatic Studies; Religious and Social. 8vo. 12s.
——————— The Rise of the British Dominion in India. From the Early Days of the East India Company. (University Extension Series). With coloured Maps. Crown 8vo. 4s. 6d.

LYELL (SIR CHARLES). Student's Elements of Geology. A new Edition, entirely revised by PROFESSOR P. M. DUNCAN, F.R.S. With 600 Illustrations. Post 8vo. 9s.
——————— Life, Letters, and Journals. Edited by his sister-in-law, MRS. LYELL. With Portraits. 2 Vols. 8vo. 30s.

LYNDHURST (LORD). [See MARTIN.]

McCLINTOCK (SIR L.). Narrative of the Discovery of the Fate of Sir John Franklin and his Companions in the Arctic Seas. With Illustrations. Post 8vo. 7s. 6d.

McKENDRICK (PROF.) and DR. SNODGRASS. The Physiology of the Senses. With Illustrations. (Univ Extension Series).

MACDONALD (A.). Too Late for Gordon and Khartoum. With Maps and Plans. 8vo. 12s.

MACGREGOR (J.). Rob Roy on the Jordan, Nile, Red Sea, Gennesareth, &c. A Canoe Cruise in Palestine and Egypt and the Waters of Damascus. With 70 Illustrations. Crown 8vo. 7s. 6d.

MACKAY (THOMAS). The English Poor. A Sketch of their Social and Economic History; and an attempt to estimate the influence of private property on character and habit. Crown 8vo. 7s. 6d.

—————— A Plea for Liberty: an Argument against Socialism and Socialistic Legislation. Essays by various Writers. With an Introduction by HERBERT SPENCER. Third and Popular Edition. With a New and Original Essay on Self Help and State Pensions by C. J. RADLEY. Post 8vo. 2s.

MACPHERSON (WM. CHARTERIS). The Baronage and the Senate, or the House of Lords in the Past, the Present, and the Future. 8vo. 16s.

MAHON (LORD). [See STANHOPE.]

MAINE (SIR H. SUMNER). A brief Memoir of his Life. By the Right Hon. Sir M. E. GRANT DUFF, G.C.S.I. With some of his Indian Speeches and Minutes. Selected and Edited by WHITLEY STOKES, D.C.L. With Portrait. 8vo. 14s.

—————— Ancient Law: its Connection with the Early History of Society, and its Relation to Modern Ideas. 8vo. 9s.

—————— Village Communities in the East and West. 8vo. 9s.

—————— Early History of Institutions. 8vo. 9s.

—————— Dissertations on Early Law and Custom. 8vo. 9s.

—————— Popular Government. 8vo. 7s. 6d.

—————— International Law. 8vo. 7s. 6d.

MALCOLM (SIR JOHN). Sketches of Persia. Post 8vo. 3s. 6d.

MALLET (C. E.). The French Revolution. Crown 8vo. 3s. 6d. (Univ. Extension Series.)

MARCO POLO. [See YULE.]

MARKHAM (MRS.). History of England. From the First Invasion by the Romans, continued down to 1880. Woodcuts. 12mo. 3s. 6d.

—————— History of France. From the Conquest of Gaul by Julius Cæsar, continued down to 1878. Woodcuts. 12mo. 3s. 6d.

—————— History of Germany. From its Invasion by Marius to the completion of Cologne Cathedral. Woodcuts. 12mo. 3s. 6d.

MARSH (G. P.). Student's Manual of the English Language. Edited with Additions. By DR. WM. SMITH. Post 8vo. 7s. 6d.

MARTIN (SIR THEODORE). Life of Lord Lyndhurst. With Portraits. 8vo. 16s.

MASTERS in English Theology. Lectures by Eminent Divines. With Introduction by Canon Barry. Post 8vo. 7s. 6d.

MATTHIÆ'S GREEK GRAMMAR. Abridged by BLOMFIELD. Revised by E. S. CROOKE. 12mo. 4s.

MAUREL'S Character, Actions, &c., of Wellington. 1s. 6d.

MELVILLE (HERMANN). Marquesas and South Sea Islands. 2 Vols, with Illustrations. Post 8vo.

MEREDITH (MRS. C.) Notes & Sketches of N. S. Wales. Post 8vo. 2s.

MEXICO. [See BROCKLEHURST—RUXTON.]

MICHAEL ANGELO, Sculptor, Painter, and Architect. His Life and Works. By C. HEATH WILSON. Illustrations. 8vo. 15s.

MILL (DR. H. R.). The Realm of Nature: An Outline of Physiography. With 19 Coloured Maps and 68 Illustrations and Diagrams (380 pp.). Crown 8vo. 5s. (University Extension Manuals.)

MILLER (WM.). A Dictionary of English Names of Plants applied among English-speaking People to Plants, Trees, and Shrubs. In Two Parts. Latin-English and English-Latin. Medium 8vo. 12s.

MILMAN'S (DEAN) WORKS:—

HISTORY OF THE JEWS, from the earliest Period down to Modern Times. 3 Vols. Post 8vo. 12s.

EARLY CHRISTIANITY, from the Birth of Christ to the Abolition of Paganism in the Roman Empire. 3 Vols. Post 8vo. 12s.

LATIN CHRISTIANITY, including that of the Popes to the Pontificate of Nicholas V. 9 Vols. Post 8vo. 36s.

HANDBOOK TO ST. PAUL'S CATHEDRAL. Woodcuts. 10s. 6d.

QUINTI HORATII FLACCI OPERA. Woodcuts. Sm. 8vo. 7s. 6d.

FALL OF JERUSALEM. Fcap. 8vo. 1s.

——— (BISHOP, D.D.) Life. With a Selection from his Correspondence and Journals. By his Sister. Map. 8vo. 12s.

MILNE (DAVID, M.A.). A Readable Dictionary of the English Language. Etymologically arranged. Crown 8vo. 7s. 6d.

MINCHIN (J. G.). The Growth of Freedom in the Balkan Peninsula. With a Map. Crown 8vo. 10s. 6d.

MINTO (WM.). Logic, Inductive and Deductive. With Diagrams. Crown 8vo. (University Extension Series.)

MISS BLAKE OF MONKSHALTON. By ISABELLA FORD. A New Novel. Crown 8vo. 6s.

MIVART (ST. GEORGE). The Cat. An Introduction to the Study of Backboned Animals, especially Mammals. With 200 Illustrations. Medium 8vo. 30s.

MOORE (THOMAS). Life and Letters of Lord Byron. [See BYRON.]

MORELLI (GIOVANNI). Italian Painters. Critical Studies of their Works. Translated from the German by CONSTANCE JOCELYN FFOULKES, with an Introductory Notice by Sir HENRY LAYARD, G.C.B. With numerous Illustrations. 8vo.
  Vol. I.—The Borghese & Doria Pamphili Galleries. 15s.
  Vol. II.—The Galleries of Munich and Dresden.

MOSELEY (PROF. H. N.). Notes by a Naturalist during the voyage of H.M.S. "Challenger" round the World in the years 1872-76. *A New and Cheaper Edit.*, with a Memoir of the Author, Portrait, Map, and numerous Woodcuts. Crown 8vo. 9s.

MOTLEY (JOHN LOTHROP). The Correspondence of. With Portrait. 2 Vols. 8vo. 30s.

——— History of the United Netherlands: from the Death of William the Silent to the Twelve Years' Truce, 1609. Portraits. 4 Vols. Post 8vo. 6s. each.

——— Life and Death of John of Barneveld. Illustrations. 2 Vols. Post 8vo. 12s.

MUIRHEAD (JOHN H.). The Elements of Ethics. Crown 8vo. 3s. (University Extension Series.)

MUMMERY (A. F.) AND J. A. HOBSON. The Physiology of Industry: Being an Exposure of certain Fallacies in existing Theories of Political Economy. Crown 8vo. 6s.

MUNRO'S (GENERAL) Life. By REV. G. R. GLEIG. 3s. 6d.

MUNTHE (Axel). Letters from a Mourning City. Naples during the Autumn of 1884. Translated by MAUDE VALERIE WHITE. With a Frontispiece. Crown 8vo. 6s.

MURRAY (JOHN). A Publisher and his Friends: Memoir and Correspondence of the second John Murray, with an Account of the Origin and Progress of the House, 1768—1843. By SAMUEL SMILES, LL.D. With Portraits. 2 Vols. 8vo. 32s.

MURRAY (A. S.). A History of Greek Sculpture from the Earliest Times. With 130 Illustrations. 2 Vols. Medium 8vo. 36s.

———— Handbook of Greek Archæology. Sculpture, Vases, Bronzes, Gems, Terra-cottas, Architecture, Mural Paintings &c. Many Illustrations. Crown 8vo. 18s.

MURRAY'S MAGAZINE. Vols. I. to X. 7s. 6d. each.

NADAILLAC (MARQUIS DE). Prehistoric America. Translated by N. D'ANVERS. With Illustrations. 8vo. 16s.

NAPIER (GENERAL SIR CHARLES). His Life. By the Hon WM. NAPIER BRUCE. With Portrait and Maps. Crown 8vo. 12s.

———— (GENERAL SIR GEORGE T.). Passages in his Early Military Life written by himself. Edited by his Son, GENERAL WM C. E. NAPIER. With Portrait. Crown 8vo. 7s. 6d.

———— (SIR WM.). English Battles and Sieges of the Peninsular War. Portrait. Post 8vo. 5s.

NASMYTH (JAMES). An Autobiography. Edited by Samuel Smiles, LL.D., with Portrait, and 70 Illustrations. Post 8vo, 6s.; or Large Paper, 16s.

———— The Moon: Considered as a Planet, a World, and a Satellite. With 26 Plates and numerous Woodcuts. Medium 8vo. 21s.

NEWMAN (MRS.). Begun in Jest. 3 vols. 31s. 6d.

NEW TESTAMENT. With Short Explanatory Commentary. By ARCHDEACON CHURTON, M.A., and the BISHOP OF ST. DAVID'S. With 110 authentic Views, &c. 2 Vols. Crown 8vo. 21s. bound.

NEWTH (SAMUEL). First Book of Natural Philosophy; an Introduction to the Study of Statics, Dynamics, Hydrostatics, Light, Heat, and Sound, with numerous Examples. Small 8vo. 3s. 6d.

———— Elements of Mechanics, including Hydrostatics, with numerous Examples. Small 8vo. 8s. 6d.

———— Mathematical Examples. A Graduated Series of Elementary Examples in Arithmetic, Algebra, Logarithms, Trigonometry, and Mechanics. Small 8vo. 8s. 6d.

NIMROD, On the Chace—Turf—and Road. With Portrait and Plates. Crown 8vo. 5s. Or with Coloured Plates, 7s. 6d.

NORRIS (W. E.). Marcia. A Novel. Crown 8vo. 6s.

NORTHCOTE'S (SIR JOHN) Notebook in the Long Parliament. Containing Proceedings during its First Session, 1640. Edited, with a Memoir, by A. H. A. Hamilton. Crown 8vo. 9s.

OCEAN STEAMSHIPS: A Popular Account of their Construction, Development, Management, and Appliances. By Various Writers. Beautifully Illustrated, with 96 Woodcuts, Maps, &c. Medium 8vo. 15s.

O'CONNELL (DANIEL). [See FITZPATRICK.]

ORNSBY (PROF. R.). Memoirs of J. Hope Scott, Q.C. (of Abbotsford). 2 vols. 8vo. 24s.

OTTER (R. H.). Winters Abroad: Some Information respecting Places visited by the Author on account of his Health. 7s. 6d.

OVID LESSONS. [See ETON.]

OWEN (LIEUT.-COL.). Principles and Practice of Modern Artillery With Illustrations. 8vo. 15s.

OXENHAM (REV. W.). English Notes for Latin Elegiacs; with Prefatory Rules of Composition in Elegiac Metre. 12mo. 3s. 6d.

PAGET (Lord George). The Light Cavalry Brigade in the Crimea. Map. Crown 8vo. 10s. 6d.

PALGRAVE (R. H. I.). Local Taxation of Great Britain and Ireland. 8vo. 6s.

PALLISER (Mrs.). Mottoes for Monuments, or Epitaphs selected for General Use and Study. With Illustrations. Crown 8vo. 7s. 6d.

PARKER (C. S.), M.P. [See Peel.]

PEEL'S (Sir Robert) Memoirs. 2 Vols. Post 8vo. 15s.

—— Life of: Early years; as Secretary for Ireland, 1812–18, and Secretary of State, 1822–27. Edited by Charles Stuart Parker, M.P. With Portrait. 8vo. 16s.

PENN (Richard). Maxims and Hints for an Angler and Chess-player. Woodcuts. Fcap. 8vo. 1s.

PERCY (John, M.D.). Metallurgy. Fuel, Wood, Peat, Coal, Charcoal, Coke, Fire-Clays. Illustrations. 8vo. 30s.

—— Lead, including part of Silver. Illustrations. 8vo. 30s.

—— Silver and Gold. Part I. Illustrations. 8vo. 30s.

—— Iron and Steel. A New and Revised Edition, with the Author's Latest Corrections, and brought down to the present time. By H. Bauerman, F.G.S. Illustrations. 8vo.

PERRY (J. Tavenor). The Chronology of Mediæval Architecture. A Date Book of Architectural Art, from the Founding of the Basilica of St. Peter, Rome, by Constantine, to the Dedication of the new Building by Pope Urban VIII. Forming a Companion Volume to Fergusson's "History of Architecture." With Illustrations. 8vo.

PERRY (Rev. Canon). History of the English Church. See Students' Manuals.

PHILLIPS (Samuel). Literary Essays from "The Times." With Portrait. 2 Vols. Fcap. 8vo. 7s.

POLLOCK (C. E.). A Book of Family Prayers. Selected from the Liturgy of the Church of England. 16mo. 3s. 6d.

POPE'S (Alexander) Life and Works. With Introductions and Notes, by J. W. Croker, Rev. W. Elwin, and W. J. Courthope. 10 Vols. With Portraits. 8vo. 10s. 6d. each.

PORTER (Rev. J. L.). Damascus, Palmyra, and Lebanon. Map and Woodcuts. Post 8vo. 7s. 6d.

PRAYER-BOOK (Beautifully Illustrated). With Notes, by Rev. Thos. James. Medium 8vo. 18s. cloth.

PRINCESS CHARLOTTE OF WALES. Memoir and Correspondence. By Lady Rose Weigall. With Portrait. 8vo. 8s. 6d.

PRITCHARD (Charles, D.D.). Occasional Thoughts of an Astronomer on Nature and Revelation. 8vo. 7s. 6d.

PSALMS OF DAVID. With Notes Explanatory and Critical by Dean Johnson, Canon Elliott, and Canon Cook. Medium 8vo. 10s. 6d.

PUSS IN BOOTS. With 12 Illustrations. By Otto Speckter. 16mo. 1s. 6d. Or coloured, 2s. 6d.

QUARTERLY REVIEW (The). 8vo. 6s.

QUILL (Albert W.). History of P. Cornelius Tacitus. Books I. and II. Translated into English, with Introduction and Notes Critical and Explanatory. 8vo. 7s. 6d.

RAE (Edward). Country of the Moors. A Journey from Tripoli to the Holy City of Kairwan. Etchings. Crown 8vo. 12s.

—— The White Sea Peninsula. Journey to the White Sea, and the Kola Peninsula. Illustrations. Crown 8vo. 15s.

RAE (GEORGE). The Country Banker; His Clients, Cares, and Work, from the Experience of Forty Years. Crown 8vo. 7s. 6d.

RAMSAY (PROF. W. M.). The Historical Geography of Asia Minor. With 6 Maps, Tables, &c. 8vo. 18s.

RASSAM (HORMUZD). British Mission to Abyssinia. Illustrations. 2 Vols. 8vo. 28s.

RAWLINSON'S (CANON) Five Great Monarchies of Chaldæa, Assyria, Media, Babylonia, and Persia. With Maps and Illustrations. 3 Vols. 8vo. 42s.

——————— Herodotus, a new English Version. *See* page 12.

RAWLINSON'S (SIR HENRY) England and Russia in the East; a Series of Papers on the Condition of Central Asia. Map. 8vo. 12s.

REJECTED ADDRESSES (THE). BY JAMES AND HORACE SMITH. Woodcuts. Post 8vo. 3s. 6d.; or *Popular Edition*, Fcap. 8vo. 1s.

RENTON (W.). Outlines of English Literature. With Illustrative Diagrams. Crown 8vo. (Univ. Extension Series.)

RICARDO'S (DAVID) Works. With a Notice of his Life and Writings. By J. R. M'CULLOCH. 8vo. 16s.

RIPA (FATHER). Residence at the Court of Peking. Post 8vo. 2s.

ROBERTS (DR. R. D.). The Earth's History. An Introduction to Modern Geology. With Coloured Maps and Illustrations. Crown 8vo. 5s. (Univ. Extension Series.)

ROBERTSON (CANON). History of the Christian Church, from the Apostolic Age to the Reformation, 1517. 8 Vols. Post 8vo. 6s. each.

ROBINSON (W.). English Flower Garden. An Illustrated Dictionary of all the Plants used, and Directions for their Culture and Arrangement. With numerous Illustrations. Medium 8vo. 15s.

——————— The Vegetable Garden; or, the Edible Vegetables, Salads, and Herbs cultivated in Europe and America. By M. VILMORIN-ANDRIEUX. With 750 Illustrations. 8vo. 15s.

——————— Sub-Tropical Garden. Illustrations. Small 8vo. 5s.

——————— Parks and Gardens of Paris, considered in Relation to other Cities. 350 Illustrations. 8vo. 18s.

——————— God's Acre Beautiful; or, the Cemeteries of the Future. With 8 Illustrations. 8vo. 7s. 6d.

ROMANS, St. Paul's Epistle to the. With Notes and Commentary by E. H. GIFFORD, D.D. Medium 8vo. 7s. 6d.

ROME. [See GIBBON—LIDDELL—SMITH—STUDENTS'.]

ROMILLY (HUGH H.). The Western Pacific and New Guinea. 2nd Edition. With a Map. Crown 8vo. 7s. 6d.

ROSS (MRS.) The Land of Manfred, Prince of Tarentum and King of Sicily. Illustrations. Crown 8vo. 10s. 6d.

RUMBOLD (SIR HORACE). The Great Silver River: Notes of a Residence in the Argentine Republic. Second Edition, with Additional Chapter. With Illustrations. 8vo. 12s.

RUXTON (GEO. F.). Travels in Mexico; with Adventures among Wild Tribes and Animals of the Prairies and Rocky Mountains. Post 8vo. 3s. 6d.

ST. JOHN (CHARLES). St. John's Wild Sports and Natural History of the Highlands of Scotland. A New Edition, thoroughly revised. With hitherto unpublished Notes by the Author. Edited, with a Memoir of the Author, by the Rev. M. G. WATKINS. With Portrait of Mr. St. John and several new Illustrations. Medium 8vo.

——— ———(BAYLE). Adventures in the Libyan Desert. 2s.

ST. MAUR (Mrs. Algernon), Lady Seymour. Impressions of a Tenderfoot, during a Journey in search of Sport in the Far West. With Map and Illustrations. Crown 8vo. 12s.

SALE'S (Sir Robert) Brigade in Affghanistan. With an Account of the Defence of Jellalabad. By Rev. G. R. Gleig. Post 8vo. 2s.

SALMON (Prof. Geo., D.D.). An Introduction to the Study of the New Testament, and an Investigation into Modern Biblical Criticism, based on the most recent Sources of Information. Crown 8vo. 9s.

—————— Lectures on the Infallibility of the Church. Post 8vo. 9s.

SCEPTICISM IN GEOLOGY; and the Reasons for it. An assemblage of facts from Nature combining to refute the theory of Causes now in Action." By Verifier. Woodcuts. Crown 8vo. 6s.

SCHLIEMANN (Dr. Henry). Ilios; the City and Country of the Trojans. With an Autobiography. Illustrations. Imperial 8vo. 50s.

—————— Tiryns: A Prehistoric Palace of the Kings of Tiryns, discovered by excavations in 1884-5. With Illustrations. Medium 8vo. 42s.

SCHREIBER (Lady Charlotte). English Fans and Fan Leaves. Collected and Described. With 160 Plates. Folio. 7l. 7s.

—————————————— Foreign Fans and Fan Leaves. French, Italian, and German, chiefly relating to the French Revolution, Collected and Described. 150 Plates. Folio. 7l. 7s.

—————————————— Playing Cards of Various Ages and Countries. Vol I., English and Scottish; Dutch and Flemish. With 141 Places. Folio. 3l. 13s. 6d.

SCOTT (Sir Gilbert). The Rise and Development of Mediæval Architecture. With 400 Illustrations. 2 Vols. Medium 8vo. 42s.

SHAIRP (Principal) and his Friends. By Professor Wm. Knight, of St. Andrews. With Portrait. 8vo. 15s.

SHAW (T. B.). Manual of English Literature. Post 8vo. 7s. 6d.

—————— Specimens of English Literature. Post 8vo. 5s.

SHAW (R. Norman). [See Architecture.]

SMILES' (Samuel, LL.D.) WORKS:—
British Engineers; from the Earliest Period to the Death of the Stephensons. Illustrations. 5 Vols. Crown 8vo. 7s. 6d. each.
George Stephenson. Post 8vo. 2s. 6d.
James Nasmyth. Portrait and Illustrations. Post 8vo. 6s.
Jasmin: Barber, Poet, Philanthropist. Post 8vo. 6s.
Scotch Naturalist (Thos. Edward). Illustrations. Post 8vo. 6s.
Scotch Geologist (Robert Dick). Illustrations. 8vo. 12s.
Self-Help. With Illustrations of Conduct and Perseverance. Post 8vo. 6s. In French. 5s.
Character. A Book of Noble Characteristics. Post 8vo. 6s.
Thrift. A Book of Domestic Counsel. Post 8vo. 6s.
Duty. With Illustrations of Courage, Patience, and Endurance. Post 8vo. 6s.
Industrial Biography. Iron-Workers and Tool-Makers. 6s.
Men of Invention. Post 8vo. 6s.
Life and Labour; or, Characteristics of Men of Culture and Genius. Post 8vo. 6s.

SMILES' (SAMUEL, LL.D.) WORKS—*continued*.
    THE HUGUENOTS; Their Settlements, Churches, and Industries in England and Ireland. Crown 8vo. 7s. 6d.
    BOY'S VOYAGE ROUND THE WORLD. Illustrations. Post 8vo. 6s.

SIEMENS (SIR WM.), C.E. Life of. By WM. POLE, C.E. Portraits. 8vo. 16s.

—————— The Scientific Works of: a Collection of Papers and Discourses. Edited by E. F. BAMBER, C.E. Vol. i.—Heat and Metallurgy: ii.—Electricity, &c.; iii.—Addresses and Lectures. Plates. 3 Vols. 8vo. 12s. each.

—————— (DR. WERNER VON). Collected Works of. Translated by E. F. BAMBER. Vol. i.—Scientific Papers and Addresses. ii.—Applied Science. With Illustrations. 8vo. 14s.

SIMMONS' Constitution and Practice of Courts-Martial. 15s.

SMEDES (SUSAN DABNEY). A Southern Planter. Memoirs of Thomas Dabney. Preface by MR. GLADSTONE. Post 8vo. 7s. 6d.

SMITH (DR. GEORGE) Student's Manual of the Geography of British India, Physical and Political. Maps. Post 8vo. 7s. 6d.

—————— Life of Wm. Carey, D.D., 1761—1834. Shoemaker and Missionary. Professor of Sanscrit, Bengalee and Marathee at the College of Fort William, Calcutta. Illustrations. Post 8vo. 7s. 6d.

—————— Life of Stephen Hislop, Pioneer, Missionary, and Naturalist in Central India, 1844-1863. Portrait. Post 8vo. 7s. 6d.

—————— (PHILIP). History of the Ancient World, from the Creation to the Fall of the Roman Empire, A.D. 476. 3 Vols. 8vo. 31s. 6d.

—————— (R. BOSWORTH). Mohammed and Mohammedanism. Crown 8vo. 7s. 6d.

SMITH'S (DR. WM.) DICTIONARIES:—
    DICTIONARY OF THE BIBLE; its Antiquities, Biography, Geography, and Natural History. Illustrations. 3 Vols. 8vo. 105s.
    CONCISE BIBLE DICTIONARY. Illustrations. 8vo. 21s.
    SMALLER BIBLE DICTIONARY. Illustrations. Post 8vo. 7s. 6d.
    CHRISTIAN ANTIQUITIES. Comprising the History, Institutions, and Antiquities of the Christian Church. Illustrations. 2 Vols. Medium 8vo. 3l. 13s. 6d.
    CHRISTIAN BIOGRAPHY, LITERATURE, SECTS, AND DOCTRINES; from the Times of the Apostles to the Age of Charlemagne. Medium 8vo. Now complete in 4 Vols. 6l. 16s. 6d.
    GREEK AND ROMAN ANTIQUITIES. Including the Laws, Institutions, Domestic Usages, Painting, Sculpture, Music, the Drama, &c. Third Edition, Revised and Enlarged. 2 Vols. Med. 8vo. 31s. 6d. each.
    GREEK AND ROMAN BIOGRAPHY AND MYTHOLOGY. Illustrations. 3 Vols. Medium 8vo. 4l. 4s.
    GREEK AND ROMAN GEOGRAPHY. 2 Vols. Illustrations. Medium 8vo. 56s.
    ATLAS OF ANCIENT GEOGRAPHY—BIBLICAL AND CLASSICAL. Folio. 6l. 6s.
    CLASSICAL DICTIONARY OF MYTHOLOGY, BIOGRAPHY, AND GEOGRAPHY. 1 Vol. With 750 Woodcuts. 8vo. 18s.
    SMALLER CLASSICAL DICT. Woodcuts. Crown 8vo. 7s. 6d.
    SMALLER DICTIONARY OF GREEK AND ROMAN ANTIQUITIES. Woodcuts. Crown 8vo. 7s. 6d.
    SMALLER LATIN-ENGLISH DICTIONARY. 12mo. 7s. 6d.

SMITH'S (Dr. Wm.) DICTIONARIES—*continued.*
    COMPLETE LATIN-ENGLISH DICTIONARY. With Tables of the Roman Calendar, Measures, Weights, Money, and a Dictionary of Proper Names. 8vo. 16s.
    COPIOUS AND CRITICAL ENGLISH-LATIN DICT. 8vo. 16s.
    SMALLER ENGLISH-LATIN DICTIONARY. 12mo. 7s. 6d.

SMITH'S (Dr. Wm.) ENGLISH COURSE:—
    SCHOOL MANUAL OF ENGLISH GRAMMAR, WITH COPIOUS EXERCISES, Appendices and Index. Post 8vo. 3s. 6d.
    PRIMARY ENGLISH GRAMMAR, for Elementary Schools, with carefully graduated Parsing Lessons. 16mo. 1s.
    MANUAL OF ENGLISH COMPOSITION. With Copious Illustrations and Practical Exercises. 12mo. 3s. 6d.
    PRIMARY HISTORY OF BRITAIN. 12mo. 2s. 6d.
    SCHOOL MANUAL OF MODERN GEOGRAPHY. Post 8vo. 5s.
    A SMALLER MANUAL OF MODERN GEOGRAPHY. 16mo. 2s. 6d.

SMITH'S (Dr. Wm.) FRENCH COURSE:—
    FRENCH PRINCIPIA. Part I. A First Course, containing a Grammar, Delectus, Exercises, and Vocabularies. 12mo. 3s. 6d.
    APPENDIX TO FRENCH PRINCIPIA. Part I. Containing additional Exercises, with Examination Papers. 12mo. 2s. 6d.
    FRENCH PRINCIPIA. Part II. A Reading Book, containin Fables, Stories, and Anecdotes, Natural History, and Scenes from th History of France. With Grammatical Questions, Notes and copio Etymological Dictionary. 12mo. 4s. 6d.
    FRENCH PRINCIPIA. Part III. Prose Composition, containing Hints on Translation of English into French, the Principal Rules the French Syntax compared with the English, and a Systematic Course of Exercises on the Syntax. 12mo. 4s. 6d. [Post 8vo. 6s.
    STUDENT'S FRENCH GRAMMAR. With Introduction by M. Littré.
    SMALLER GRAMMAR OF THE FRENCH LANGUAGE. Abridged from the above. 12mo. 3s. 6d.

SMITH'S (Dr. Wm.) GERMAN COURSE:—
    GERMAN PRINCIPIA. Part I. A First German Course, containing a Grammar, Delectus, Exercise Book, and Vocabularies. 12mo. 3s. 6d.
    GERMAN PRINCIPIA. Part II. A Reading Book; containing Fables, Anecdotes, Natural History, and Scenes from the History of Germany. With Questions, Notes, and Dictionary. 12mo. 3s. 6d.
    PRACTICAL GERMAN GRAMMAR. Post 8vo. 3s. 6d.

SMITH'S (Dr. Wm.) ITALIAN COURSE:—
    ITALIAN PRINCIPIA. Part I. An Italian Course, containing a Grammar, Delectus, Exercise Book, with Vocabularies, and Materials for Italian Conversation. 12mo. 3s. 6d.
    ITALIAN PRINCIPIA. Part II. A First Italian Reading Book, containing Fables, Anecdotes, History, and Passages from the best Italian Authors, with Grammatical Questions, Notes, and a Copious Etymological Dictionary. 12mo. 3s. 6d. [Children).

SMITH'S (Dr. Wm.) YOUNG BEGINNER'S FIRST LATIN COURSE (for
    I. A FIRST LATIN BOOK. The Rudiments of Grammar, Easy Grammatical Questions and Exercises with Vocabularies. 12mo. 2s.
    II. A SECOND LATIN BOOK. An Easy Latin Reading Book, with an Analysis of the Sentences, Notes, and a Dictionary. 12mo. 2s.
    III. A THIRD LATIN BOOK. The Principal Rules of Syntax, with Easy Exercises, Questions, Vocabularies, and an English-Latin Dictionary. 2s.
    IV. A FOURTH LATIN BOOK. A Latin Vocabulary for Beginners. Arranged according to Subjects an Etymologies. 12mo. 2s.

SMITH'S (Dr. Wm.) LATIN COURSE.

PRINCIPIA LATINA. Part I. First Latin Course, containing a Grammar, Delectus, and Exercise Book, with Vocabularies. 12mo. 3s. 6d.

*** In this Edition the Cases of the Nouns, Adjectives, and Pronouns are arranged both as in the ORDINARY GRAMMARS and as in the PUBLIC SCHOOL PRIMER, together with the corresponding Exercises.

APPENDIX TO PRINCIPIA LATINA. Part I.; being Additional Exercises, with Examination Papers. 12mo. 2s. 6d.

PRINCIPIA LATINA. Part II. A Reading-book of Mythology, Geography, Roman Antiquities, and History. With Notes and Dictionary. 12mo. 3s. 6d.

PRINCIPIA LATINA. Part III. A Poetry Book. Hexameters and Pentameters; Eclog. Ovidianæ; Latin Prosody. 12mo. 3s. 6d.

PRINCIPIA LATINA. Part IV. Prose Composition. Rules of Syntax, with Examples, Explanations of Synonyms, and Exercises on the Syntax. 12mo. 3s. 6d.

PRINCIPIA LATINA. Part V. Short Tales and Anecdotes for Translation into Latin. A New and Enlarged Edition. 12mo. 3s. 6d.

LATIN-ENGLISH VOCABULARY AND FIRST LATIN-ENGLISH DICTIONARY FOR PHÆDRUS, CORNELIUS NEPOS, AND CÆSAR. 12mo. 3s. 6d.

STUDENT'S LATIN GRAMMAR. For the Higher Forms. A new and thoroughly revised Edition. Post 8vo. 6s.

SMALLER LATIN GRAMMAR. New Edition. 12mo. 3s. 6d.

SMITH'S (Dr. Wm.) GREEK COURSE:—

INITIA GRÆCA. Part I. A First Greek Course, containing a Grammar, Delectus, and Exercise-book. With Vocabularies. 12mo. 3s. 6d.

APPENDIX TO INITIA GRÆCA. Part I. Containing additional Exercises. With Examination Papers. Post 8vo. 2s. 6d.

INITIA GRÆCA. Part II. A Reading Book. Containing Short Tales, Anecdotes, Fables, Mythology, and Grecian History. 12mo. 3s. 6d.

INITIA GRÆCA. Part III. Prose Composition. Containing the Rules of Syntax, with copious Examples and Exercises. 12mo. 3s. 6d.

STUDENT'S GREEK GRAMMAR. For the Higher Forms. Post 8vo. 6s.

SMALLER GREEK GRAMMAR. 12mo. 3s. 6d.

GREEK ACCIDENCE. 12mo. 2s. 6d.

PLATO, Apology of Socrates, &c. With Notes. 12mo. 3s. 6d.

SMITH'S (Dr. Wm.) SMALLER HISTORIES:—

SCRIPTURE HISTORY. Maps and Woodcuts. 16mo. 3s. 6d.

ANCIENT HISTORY. Woodcuts. 16mo. 3s. 6d.

ANCIENT GEOGRAPHY. Woodcuts. 16mo. 3s. 6d.

MODERN GEOGRAPHY. 16mo. 2s. 6d.

GREECE. With Coloured Map and Woodcuts. 16mo. 3s. 6d.

ROME. With Coloured Maps and Woodcuts. 16mo. 3s. 6d.

CLASSICAL MYTHOLOGY. Woodcuts. 16mo. 3s. 6d.

ENGLAND. With Coloured Maps and Woodcuts. 16mo. 3s. 6d.

ENGLISH LITERATURE. 16mo. 3s. 6d.

SPECIMENS OF ENGLISH LITERATURE. 16mo. 3s. 6d.

SOMERVILLE (MARY). Physical Geography. Post 8vo. 9s.

—————— Connexion of the Physical Sciences. Post 8vo. 9s.

SOUTH (John F.). Household Surgery; or, Hints for Emergencies. With Woodcuts. Fcap. 8vo. 3s. 6d.

SOUTHEY (Robt.). Lives of Bunyan and Cromwell. Post 8vo. 2s.

STANHOPE'S (Earl) WORKS:—
- History of England from the Reign of Queen Anne to the Peace of Versailles, 1701-83. 9 Vols. Post 8vo. 5s. each.
- Life of William Pitt. Portraits. 3 Vols. 8vo. 36s.
- Notes of Conversations with the Duke of Wellington. Crown 8vo. 7s. 6d.
- Miscellanies. 2 Vols. Post 8vo. 13s.
- British India, from its Origin to 1783. Post 8vo. 3s. 6d.
- History of "Forty-Five." Post 8vo. 3s.
- Historical and Critical Essays. Post 8vo. 3s. 6d.
- Retreat from Moscow, and other Essays. Post 8vo. 7s. 6d.
- Life of Condé. Post 8vo. 3s. 6d.
- Story of Joan of Arc. Fcap. 8vo. 1s.
- Addresses on Various Occasions. 16mo. 1s.

[See also Wellington.]

STANLEY'S (Dean) WORKS:—
- Sinai and Palestine. Coloured Maps. 8vo. 12s.
- Bible in the Holy Land; Extracts from the above Work. Woodcuts. Post 8vo. 3s. 6d.
- Eastern Church. Plans. Crown 8vo. 6s.
- Jewish Church. From the Earliest Times to the Christian Era. Portrait and Maps. 3 Vols. Crown 8vo. 18s.
- Church of Scotland. 8vo. 7s. 6d.
- Epistles of St. Paul to the Corinthians. 8vo. 18s.
- Life of Dr. Arnold. Portrait. 2 Vols. Cr. 8vo. 12s.
- Canterbury. Illustrations. Crown 8vo. 6s.
- Westminster Abbey. Illustrations. 8vo. 15s.
- Sermons Preached in Westminster Abbey. 8vo. 12s.
- Memoir of Edward, Catherine, and Mary Stanley. Cr. 8vo. 9s.
- Christian Institutions. Crown 8vo. 6s.
- Essays on Church and State; 1850—1870. Crown 8vo. 6s.
- Sermons to Children, including the Beatitudes, the Faithful Servant. Post 8vo. 3s. 6d.

[See also Bradley.]

STEPHENS (Rev. W. R. W.). Life and Times of St. John Chrysostom. A Sketch of the Church and the Empire in the Fourth Century. Portrait. 8vo. 7s. 6d.

STREET (G. E.), R.A. Gothic Architecture in Brick and Marble. With Notes on North of Italy. Illustrations. Royal 8vo. 26s.

——— Memoir of. By Arthur E. Street. Portrait. 8vo. 15s.

STUART (Villiers). Egypt after the War. With Descriptions of the Homes and Habits of the Natives, &c. Coloured Illustrations and Woodcuts. Royal 8vo. 31s. 6d.

——— Adventures Amidst the Equatorial Forests and Rivers of South America, also in the West Indies and the Wilds of Florida; to which is added "Jamaica Revisited." With Map and Illustrations. Royal 8vo. 21s.

STUDENTS' MANUALS. Post 8vo. 7s. 6d. EACH VOLUME :—

HUME'S HISTORY OF ENGLAND from the Invasion of Julius Cæsar to the Revolution in 1688. Revised, and continued to the Treaty of Berlin, 1878. By J. S. BREWER, M.A. Coloured Maps and Woodcuts. Or in 3 parts, price 2s. 6d. each.
*** Questions on the above Work, 12mo. 2s.

HISTORY OF MODERN EUROPE, from the Fall of Constantinople to the Treaty of Berlin, 1878. By R. LODGE, M.A.

OLD TESTAMENT HISTORY; from the Creation to the Return of the Jews from Captivity. Woodcuts.

NEW TESTAMENT HISTORY. With an Introduction connecting the History of the Old and New Testaments. Woodcuts.

ECCLESIASTICAL HISTORY; a History of the Christian Church. By PHILIP SMITH, B.A. With numerous Woodcuts. 2 Vols. PART I. A.D. 30—1003. PART II., 1003—1614.

ENGLISH CHURCH HISTORY. By CANON PERRY. 3 Vols. First Period, A.D. 596—1509. Second Period, 1509—1717. Third Period, 1717—1884.

ANCIENT HISTORY OF THE EAST; Egypt, Assyria, Babylonia, Media, Persia, Asia Minor, and Phœnicia. By PHILIP SMITH, B.A. Woodcuts.

——— GEOGRAPHY. By CANON BEVAN. Woodcuts.

HISTORY OF GREECE; from the Earliest Times to the Roman Conquest. By WM. SMITH, D.C.L. Woodcuts.
*** Questions on the above Work, 12mo. 2s.

HISTORY OF ROME; from the Earliest Times to the Establishment of the Empire. By DEAN LIDDELL. Woodcuts.

HISTORY OF THE ROMAN EMPIRE; from the Establishment of the Empire to the reign of Commodus. By J. B. BURY. With Coloured Maps and many Illustrations.

GIBBON'S DECLINE AND FALL OF THE ROMAN EMPIRE. Woodcuts.

HALLAM'S HISTORY OF EUROPE during the Middle Ages.

HALLAM'S HISTORY OF ENGLAND; from the Accession of Henry VII. to the Death of George II.

HISTORY OF FRANCE; from the Earliest Times to the Fall of the Second Empire. By H. W. JERVIS. With Coloured Maps and Woodcuts.

ENGLISH LANGUAGE. By GEO. P. MARSH.

ENGLISH LITERATURE. By T. B. SHAW, M.A.

SPECIMENS OF ENGLISH LITERATURE. By T. B. SHAW. 5s.

MODERN GEOGRAPHY; Mathematical, Physical and Descriptive. By CANON BEVAN, M.A. Woodcuts.

GEOGRAPHY OF BRITISH INDIA. Political and Physical. By GEORGE SMITH, LL.D. Maps.

MORAL PHILOSOPHY. By WM. FLEMING.

STURGIS (JULIAN). Comedy of a Country House. 6s.

SWAINSON (CANON). Nicene and Apostles' Creeds; Their Literary History; together with some Account of "The Creed of St Athanasius." 8vo. 16s.

TACITUS. [See QUILL.]

TEMPLE (SIR RICHARD). India in 1880. With Maps. 8vo. 16s.

——— Men and Events of My Time in India. 8vo. 16s.

TEMPLE (Sir Richard). Oriental Experience. Essays and Addresses delivered on Various Occasions. With Maps and Woodcuts. 8vo. 16s.

THOMAS (Sidney Gilchrist), Inventor; Memoir and Letters. Edited by R. W. Burnie. Portraits. Crown 8vo. 9s.

THOMSON (J. Arthur). The Study of Animal Life. With many Illustrations. Crown 8vo. 5s. (University Extension Manuals.)

THORNHILL (Mark). The Personal Adventures and Experiences of a Magistrate during the Indian Mutiny. Crown 8vo. 12s.

TITIAN'S LIFE AND TIMES. By Crowe and Cavalcaselle. Illustrations. 2 Vols. 8vo. 21s.

TOCQUEVILLE'S State of Society in France before the Revolution, 1789, and on the Causes which led to that Event. 8vo. 12s.

TOZER (Rev. H. F.). Highlands of Turkey, with Visits to Mounts Ida, Athos, Olympus, and Pelion. 2 Vols. Crown 8vo. 24s.

——— Lectures on the Geography of Greece. Post 8vo. 9s.

TRISTRAM (Canon). Great Sahara. Illustrations. Crown 8vo. 15s.

——— Land of Moab: Travels and Discoveries on the East Side of the Dead Sea and the Jordan. Illustrations. Crown 8vo. 15s.

TWINING (Louisa). Symbols and Emblems of Early and Mediæval Christian Art. With 500 Illustrations. Crown 8vo. 6s.

TYLOR (E. B.). Researches into the Early History of Mankind, and Development of Civilization. 3rd Edition. 8vo. 12s.

——— Primitive Culture: the Development of Mythology, Philosophy, Religion, Art, and Custom 2 Vols. 8vo. 3rd Edit. 21s.

UNIVERSITY EXTENSION MANUALS. Edited by Professor Wm. Knight (St. Andrew's). A series of Manuals dealing with Literature, Science, Philosophy, History, Art, &c. Crown 8vo. Prospectus with full particulars will be forwarded on application.

WACE (Rev. Henry), D.D. The Principal Facts in the Life of our Lord, and the Authority of the Evangelical Narratives. Post 8vo. 6s.

——— Christianity and Morality. Boyle Lectures for 1874 and 1875. Seventh Edition. Crown 8vo. 6s.

——— The Foundations of Faith, being the Bampton Lectures for 1879. 8vo. 7s. 6d.

WALES (H.R.H. the Prince of). Speeches and Addresses. 1863-1888. Edited by Dr. J. Macaulay. With Portrait. 8vo. 12s.

WELLINGTON (Duke of). Notes of Conversations with the late Earl Stanhope. 1831-1851. Crown 8vo. 7s. 6d.

——— Supplementary Despatches, relating to India, Ireland, Denmark, Spanish America, Spain, Portugal, France, Congress of Vienna, Waterloo and Paris. 15 Vols. 8vo. 20s. each.

——— Civil and Political Correspondence. Vols. I. to VIII. 8vo. 20s.

———Speeches in Parliament. 2 Vols. 8vo. 42s.

WESTCOTT (Canon B. F.) The Gospel according to St. John, with Notes and Dissertations (Reprinted from the Speaker's Commentary.) 8vo. 10s. 6d.

WHARTON (Capt. W. J. L.), R.N. Hydrographical Surveying: being a description of the means and methods employed in constructing Marine Charts. With Illustrations. 8vo. 15s.

WHITE (W. H.). Manual of Naval Architecture, for the use of Naval Officers, Shipbuilders, and Yachtsmen, &c. Illustrations. 8vo.

WHYMPER (EDWARD). Travels amongst the Great Andes of the Equator. With 140 Original Illustrations, drawn by F. BARNARD, A. CORBOULD, F. DADD. W. E. LAPWORTH, W. H. OVEREND, P. SKELTON, E. WAGNER, E. WILSON, JOSEPH WOLF, and others. Engraved by the Author. With Maps and Illustrations. Medium 8vo. 21s. Net. To range with "Scrambles amongst the Alps."

—————— Supplementary Appendix to the above. With 61 Figures of New Genera and Species. Illus. Medium 8vo. 21s. Net.

—————— How to Use the Aneroid Barometer. With numerous Tables. 2s. 6d. Net.

—————— Scrambles amongst the Alps in the Years 1860—69, including the History of the First Ascent of the Matterhorn. An Edition de Luxe (Fourth Edition). With 5 Maps and 130 Illustrations.

WILBERFORCE'S (BISHOP) Life of William Wilberforce. Portrait. Crown 8vo. 6s.

—————— (SAMUEL, D.D.), Lord Bishop of Oxford and Winchester; his Life. By CANON ASHWELL, and R. G. WILBERFORCE. Portraits. 3 Vols. 8vo. 15s. each.

WILKINSON (SIR J. G.). Manners and Customs of the Ancient Egyptians, their Private Life, Laws, Arts, Religion, &c. A new edition. Edited by SAMUEL BIRCH, LL.D. Illustrations. 3 Vols. 8vo. 84s.

—————— Popular Account of the Ancient Egyptians. With 500 Woodcuts. 2 Vols. Post 8vo. 12s.

WILLIAMS (SIR MONIER). Brahmanism and Hinduism, Religious Thought and Life in India as based on the Veda. Enlarged Edit 18s.

—————— Buddhism; its connection with Brahmanism and Hinduism, and in its contrast with Christianity. With Illus. 8vo. 21s.

WINTLE (H. G.). Ovid Lessons. 12mo, 2s. 6d. [See ETON.]

WOLFF (RT. HON. SIR H. D.). Some Notes of the Past. Contents:—Three Visits to the War in 1870—Prince Louis Napoléon—Unwritten History—Madame de Feuchères—The Prince Imperial. Crown 8vo. 5s.

WOOD'S (CAPTAIN) Source of the Oxus. With the Geography of the Valley of the Oxus. By COL. YULE. Map. 8vo. 12s.

WOODS (MRS.). Esther Vanhomrigh. A Novel. Crown 8vo. 6s.

WORDSWORTH (BISHOP). Greece; Pictorial, Descriptive, and Historical. With an Introduction on the Characteristics of Greek Art, by GEO. SCHARF. New Edition revised by the Rev. H. F. TOZER, M.A. With 400 Illustrations. Royal 8vo. 31s. 6d.

YORK-GATE LIBRARY (Catalogue of). Formed by Mr. SILVER. An Index to the Literature of Geography, Maritime and Inland Discovery, Commerce and Colonisation. Compiled by E. A. PETHERICK. 2nd Edition. Royal 8vo. 42s.

YOUNGHUSBAND (CAPT. G. J.). The Queen's Commission: How to Prepare for it; how to Obtain it, and how to Use it. With Practical Information on the Cost and Prospects of a Military Career. Intended for Cadets, Subalterns, and Parents. Crown 8vo. 6s.

YULE (COLONEL). The Book of Ser Marco Polo, the Venetian, concerning the Kingdoms and Marvels of the East. Illustrated by the Light of Oriental Writers and Modern Travels. With Maps and 80 Plates. 2 Vols. Medium 8vo.

—————— and A. C. BURNELL. A Glossary of Anglo-Indian Colloquial Words and Phrases, and of Kindred Terms; Etymological, Historical, Geographical, and Discursive. Medium 8vo. 36s.

www.ingramcontent.com/pod-product-compliance
Lightning Source LLC
Chambersburg PA
CBHW030235240426
43663CB00037B/836